Beginning Google Maps
API 3

Gabriel Svennerberg

Apress®

Beginning Google Maps API 3

ISBN-13 (pbk): 978-1-4302-2802-8

ISBN-13 (electronic): 978-1-4302-2803-5

Printed and bound in the United States of America 9 8 7 6 5 4 3 2 1

President and Publisher: Paul Manning
Lead Editor: Matt Wade
Technical Reviewer: Rob Drimmie
Editorial Board: Clay Andres, Steve Anglin, Mark Beckner, Ewan Buckingham, Gary Cornell,
    Jonathan Gennick, Jonathan Hassell, Michelle Lowman, Matthew Moodie, Duncan Parkes,
    Jeffrey Pepper, Frank Pohlmann, Douglas Pundick, Ben Renow-Clarke,
    Dominic Shakeshaft, Matt Wade, Tom Welsh
Coordinating Editors: Mary Tobin and Jennifer L. Blackwell
Copy Editor: Kim Wimpsett
Compositor: Mary Sudul
Indexer: John Collin
Artist: April Milne
Cover Designer: Anna Ishchenko

Distributed to the book trade worldwide by Springer Science+Business Media, LLC., 233 Spring Street, 6th Floor, New York, NY 10013. Phone 1-800-SPRINGER, fax (201) 348-4505, e-mail orders-ny@springer-sbm.com, or visit www.springeronline.com.

For information on translations, please e-mail rights@apress.com, or visit www.apress.com.

Apress and friends of ED books may be purchased in bulk for academic, corporate, or promotional use. eBook versions and licenses are also available for most titles. For more information, reference our Special Bulk Sales–eBook Licensing web page at www.apress.com/info/bulksales.

The source code for this book is available to readers at www.apress.com.

To my son, Ludvig, who was born during the writing of this book.

Contents at a Glance

Contents

About the Author

Photographer:
Kristin Horn Sellström

■ **Gabriel Svennerberg** is a usability-oriented web developer from Sweden. He's been working in the web industry for more than a decade and is known in the web developer community for evangelizing usability and web standards. He's also known for spreading knowledge about the Google Maps API through his website, *In usability we trust*, which features articles about Google Maps, usability, and other things related to web development. It's found at www.svennerberg.com.

In his current job at Saab Security Solutions (www.saabgroup.com), Gabriel is busy designing and building web applications for situation awareness and crisis management. These applications always incorporate maps in some way, and the Google Maps API is one of the mapping solutions being used.

Gabriel lives in Växjö, Sweden, with his fiancée, Petronella, and their son Ludvig.

About the Technical Reviewer

■ **Rob Drimmie** is a software developer with a bias toward web-based applications. The best things about him are his wife and children. He likes pho and hamburgers but has never eaten both at the same sitting.

Acknowledgments

First of all, I would like to thank my beloved fiancée, *Petronella Frisk*, for putting up with me spending evenings and weekends writing this book. Thank you for your patience and support! I couldn't have done it without you!

Many thanks to *Tom Skinner* for helping me with the initial reviews of the chapters and with testing the examples. Your help has been immensly valuable to me. If not for you, the book would have been a lot poorer. I would also like to thank you for your words of encouragement at the times when I needed it the most. Also thanks to *Charlie Irish*, who helped proofread Chapter 5, before I used it as a beta chapter.

My former college *Chris Jangelöv* has been a source of inspiration over the years. I probably owe it to him that I entered into the world of web standards, usability, and blogging in the first place. Thank you, Chris, for always having new ideas and being encouraging.

I would also like to extend a thanks to my employer, *Saab Security Solutions* in Växjö, for letting me take some time off to work on the book. This was very much needed since a day has only 24 hours—something that I've been acutely aware of since becoming a parent.

The people at *Apress* also deserve thanks for guiding me through the process of writing this, my first book.

Last but not least, I would like to thank the readers of my blog, *In usability we trust*, whose feedback, words of encouragement, and questions have been invaluble for writing this book. They motivated me to undertake this endeavor and encouraged me during times of despair. They also gave me plenty of ideas of what to write about and what problems to address. Thanks a lot!

Introduction

This book started out as an idea in spring 2009. I had written quite a few articles and tutorials about the Google Maps API v2 and thought that I could reuse them to write a book. That shouldn't take too long, I thought. Shortly after, during Google I/O 2009, Google announced that it was releasing version 3 of the API. This release was a total remake of the old one, and I soon realized that I now had to write a book about this version instead. This rendered my intital plan to reuse my old articles completely useless. I also had to learn the new API; it was, after all, a complete remake. In retrospect, I'm glad that I did. The new API has a much cleanear programming interface and is more well structured than the old one. It just feels better to program with. And now that the book is being published, version 2 is deprecated, and version 3 is the recommended alternative for new map applications.

Writing this book became a bigger undertaking than I first anticipated, but it has also been a lot more fun and interesting journey than I expected (even if I've despaired at times). Writing this, my first book, has been a learning experience. When I started the project, I had no clue how to go about it. I didn't now how to get it published or how to structure it. But it all somehow unfolded as the work progressed, and here I am now, with a finished book.

My journey with Google Maps started in 2007, when I created my very first map. It was a map showing the location of a restaurant. It not only let you see the location of the restaurant but also allowed you to enter an address in a text field to get driving directions. Very cool stuff. Since then, I've created a lot of maps using the API, not the least as part of my job as a web developer and interaction designer at Saab Security Solutions.

My hope for this book is that you as a reader will be able to quickly grasp the concepts of the Google Maps API so that you can create your own map solutions. In fact, after reading this book, I hope that you're not only able to create your own maps but that you're also able to deal with many of the common pitfalls most developers encounter when building Google Maps solutions.

Who This Book Is For

This book is primarily for web designers/developers who want to learn how to use the Google Maps API on their own web sites. But even if you're not in the field, you should be able to learn the concepts since they're thoroughly described. It certainly helps if you have a basic understanding of how to create a web page and how the Web works, but other than that, you should be able to learn how to use the API from just this book.

This book is also for those of you who have been using version 2 of the API. I've dedicated a whole chapter for you, Chapter 2, where I explain the differences between the two versions so that you can easily transfer your old maps to the new API.

Downloading the Code

You can download all the code for the examples from the book's web site at
`http://www.svennerberg.com/bgma3`. It's also available on the Apress website at
`http://apress.com/book/view/1430228024`

CHAPTER 1

■■■

Introducing the Google Maps API

On today's Web, mapping solutions are a natural ingredient. We use them to see the location of things, to search for the position of an address, to get driving directions, and to do numerous other things. Most information has a location, and if something has a location, it can be displayed on a map.

There are several mapping solutions including Yahoo! Maps and Bing Maps, but the most popular one is Google Maps. In fact, according to Programmableweb.com, it's the most popular API on the Internet. According to the site's May 2010 statistics, 43 percent of all mashups use the Google Maps API (www.programmableweb.com/apis). In comparison, the second most popular API was Flickr with 11 percent, and the second most popular mapping API was VirtualEarth (Bing Maps) with 3 percent.

Applications and web sites that are combining data or functionality from two or more sources are commonly referred to as *mashups*. Mashups are becoming increasingly popular and have revolutionized the way information is being used and visualized.

Mapping solutions are one important ingredient in a lot of these mashups. The Google Maps API lets you harness the power of Google Maps to use in your own applications to display your own (or others') data in an efficient and usable manner.

An example of a mashup using the Google Maps API is the coverage of the Deepwater Horizon oil spill in the Gulf of Mexico. It combines data of the extent of the oil spill with Google Maps to visualize its massive impact (Figure 1-1); see http://mw1.google.com/mw-earth-vectordb/disaster/gulf_oil_spill/gulf_oil_map.html.

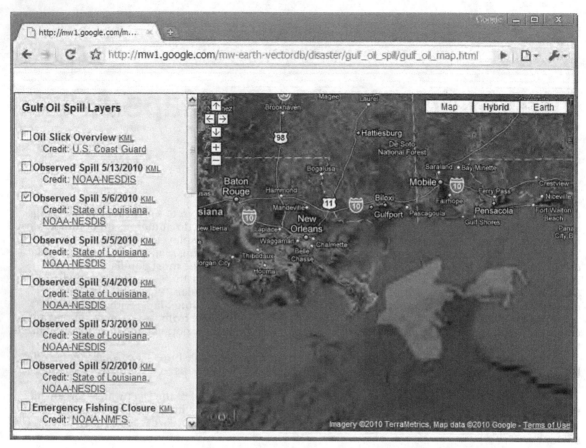

Figure 1-1. The impact of the Deepwater Horizon oil spill visualized in Google Maps

This book is about the Google Maps JavaScript API. Other APIs are available, such as the Maps API for Flash and the Static Maps API. These are both great additions but are not covered in this book.

A Brief History

Google Maps was introduced in a blog post on Google in February 2005. It revolutionized the way maps on web pages work by letting the user drag the map to navigate it. This was new at the time. The map solutions used then were expensive and required special map servers, yet they didn't deliver the same level of interactivity.

Google Maps was originally developed by two Danish brothers, Lars and Jens Rasmussen. They cofounded Where 2 Technologies, a company dedicated to creating mapping solutions. The company was acquired by Google in October 2004, and the two brothers then created Google Maps. (They are also the men behind Google Wave.)

Before there was a public API, some developers figured out how to hack Google Maps to incorporate maps on their own web sites. This led Google to the conclusion that there was a need for a public API, and in June 2005 it was publically released. The first mashup on the Internet is often considered to be

Housingmaps.com, a combination of Google Maps with realty listings from Craiglist.org plotted on it. It was in fact created before the public API was released and was hacked together by developer Paul Rademacher. At the time, this was pretty revolutionary and started a new era of mashing information from different sources.

During the Google I/O conference in May 2009, version 3 of the API, which this book is about, was announced. And in May 2010 (incidentally also during the Google I/O conference and during the making of this book), it was announced as graduated from beta. It's now the recommended choice for new Google Maps applications and the next step in the history of Google Maps.

How It Works

When seeing the dynamic nature of Google Maps, you might think there is something magical going on under the hood. But there's really nothing magical about it. It's just HTML, CSS, and JavaScript working together. The map tiles are images that are loaded in the background with Ajax calls and then inserted into a <div> in the HTML page. As you navigate the map, the API sends information about the new coordinates and zoom levels of the map in Ajax calls that return new images. And that's it! No magic involved whatsoever.

The API itself basically consists of JavaScript files that contain classes with methods and properties that you can use to tell the map how to behave. Exactly what those classes are and how to use them is the subject of this book.

A New API

The new API is a complete remake. It not only features a brand new is also completely rewritten under the hood. Why did the Google Maps team take such a drastic measure?

Slimmed-Down Feature Set

Back when the Google Maps API was first API but built, other JavaScript libraries such as Prototype, MooTools, and jQuery weren't available. That's the reason the Maps API contains methods for making Ajax calls and other things that we now rely on other third-party libraries to do for us.

Nowadays, we also rely on debugging tools such as the Firefox extension Firebug and the built-in tools in IE8 and Chrome/Safari for debugging our code. These haven't been available that long either, so the old Maps API contains classes for writing debug information in a console window.

Apart from that, the old API was originally created for serving Google's own mapping solution found at www.google.com/maps. This service contains a lot of features that most mappers don't need, making the API even more bloated.

Since 2005, an explosion in mobile use of web content has occurred. The old API wasn't intended to be used on these devices and is therefore slower than necessary. Attempts to make the old API faster on these devices have been made, but because of its architecture, developers have been limited in what they've been able to accomplish. For this reason, Google decided to build the new API from scratch.

Focus on Performance

The second item on Google's UX guidelines states that "Every millisecond counts" (www.google.com/corporate/ux.html). This is something the API team has embraced, and therefore a main focus for the new API was to increase performance on both mobile and desktop platforms.

The main legacy pitfall was the architecture of the old API. It was built using a synchronous model. Because of this, the browser had to download and run a lot of scripts sequentially before it could actually display the map. A major goal with the new API was to modularize it so that the necessary code is loaded first, displaying the map, and everything else is loaded later.

The result of the efforts of the API team is an API that is significantly faster on mobile platforms such as iPhone and Android and also a lot faster on desktop platforms.

■ **Tip** If you want to know more about how the new API was built and what led to those decisions, I recommend you watch the first part of the talk, *Performance Tips for Geo API Mashups,* from the 2009 Google I/O developer conference where Marcelo Camelo explains it all. See `http://code.google.com/intl/sv-SE/events/io/2009/sessions/PerformanceTipsGeoApiMashups.html`.

Mapping Fundamentals

In the next chapter, you'll get your hands dirty and start creating your very first map. But before you do that, a basic understanding of how mapping works will make it easier to learn the API. Actually, you don't need to worry that much about how maps work since the Google Maps API takes care of most of it for you. You do, however, need to understand how coordinates work.

Coordinates

Coordinates are used to express locations in the world. There are several different coordinate systems. The one being used in Google Maps is the Word Geodetic System 84 (WGS 84), which is the same system the Global Positioning System (GPS) uses. The coordinates are expressed using *latitude* and *longitude*. You can think of these as the y and x values in a grid.

■ **Note** A source of confusion is the order the values are presented. Although the values in a grid are normally presented with the x value first and the y value second, latitude and longitude do the opposite. They are presented with the latitude value (the equivalent of y) first and the longitude value (the equivalent of x) second.

Latitude measures from south to north, and longitude measures from west to east. At the equator, the latitude is 0. This means that everything below the equator (the south hemisphere) has a negative number, and everything above it (the north hemisphere) has a positive number. Similarly, there's a zero line for the longitude too. It's called the *prime meridian*, and for historical reasons it runs through Greenwich, England. Every position that is located east of this line has a positive number, and everything west has a negative number (Figure 1-2).

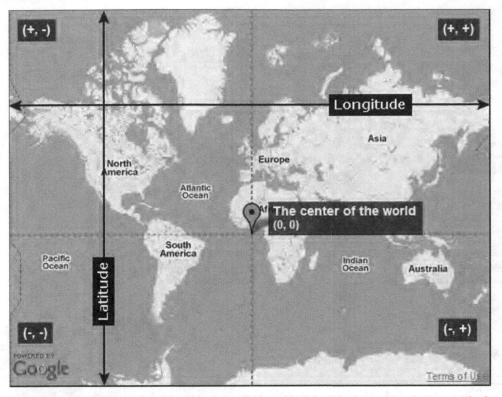

Figure 1-2. The center of the world at latitude 0 and longitude 0 lays somewhere outside the west coast of Africa

The coordinates are expressed using decimal numbers separated with a comma. The latitude always precedes the longitude value (latitude, longitude). The position for New York City, for example, is 40.714, -74.005. The positive value for the latitude is because it resides north of the equator, and the negative value for longitude is because it's positioned west of the prime meridian.

■ **Note** On physical maps, coordinates are expressed in degrees, so the position for New York City would be 40° 42' 50" N, 74° 00' 17" W. This isn't something you need to worry about since the Google Maps API uses the decimal degree form only.

In Figure 1-3, several major cities in the world are marked. Check out their coordinates, and think about why they are positive or negative.

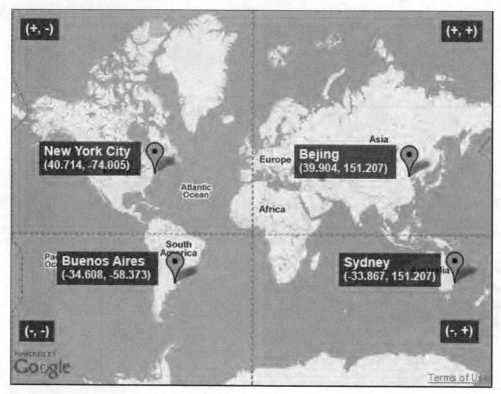

Figure 1-3. The coordinates for some major cities in the world. Notice when the values are negative and when they are positive.

Summary

This chapter gave you a little bit of information about what the Google Maps API is and how it can be used. It also gave you a primer on how coordinates work. This knowledge will come in handy in the next chapter, where you will start to create your very first map.

CHAPTER 2

Transferring from Version 2 to 3

Version 3 of the Google Maps API is a complete remake. This means that in order to transfer your existing code from v2 to v3, you will need to rewrite most of it. This chapter is meant primarily for readers who are already familiar with v2. It will show the main differences between the old and new APIs and how to perform common tasks. It's not a complete reference, but it will provide you with pointers to other parts of the book where you can learn more about how to use specific features. This chapter assumes that you have a pretty good understanding of JavaScript in general and of v2 of the API in particular.

If you haven't used the Google Maps API at all before and plan to only use v3, I recommend that you skip this chapter and go straight to Chapter 3, where I will introduce v3 from scratch.

What's Different?

The new API is a lot different from the old one. In this section, I will outline the most notable differences.

A New Namespace

In v2 of the API, all objects reside in the global namespace and are identified by a naming convention that says that all Google-related objects will start with a capital G.

In v3, a much better approach is used. Instead of cluttering the global namespace with lots and lots of global variables and objects, they now all reside in the namespace google.map. There are lots of reasons why this is a better approach, but the most important one is that it mitigates the potential problem with collisions with other JavaScript code.

What does this mean? Simply put, it means that you will, for example, refer to the Marker object with google.maps.Marker in v3, whereas you referred to it as GMarker in v2.

GLOBAL VARIABLES ARE EVIL

Douglas Crockford, JavaScript guru and author of *JavaScript: The Good Parts*, claims that global variables are evil. In the blog post "Global Domination" at the YAHOO! User Interface Blog, he writes the following:

> "Global variables are a source of unreliability and insecurity.... Reducing our dependency on globals increases the likelihood that collisions are avoided and that the program components work harmoniously."

Read more on his thoughts on this at www.yuiblog.com/blog/2006/06/01/global-domination/.

Extensive Use of Object Literals

Another difference is that in v3 object literals are almost exclusively used to pass parameters. I think that this is brilliant since it makes the API consistent and makes it really easy to extend. Version 2 also used objects and object literals to pass parameters but to a lesser extent and less consistently.

For example, when creating a new marker, all parameters are passed as an object literal, including the position:

```
var marker = new google.maps.Marker({
  position: new google.maps.LatLng(40.756, -73.986),
  map: map,
  title: 'A marker'
});
```

This makes the API both more consistent and more easily extendable. Imagine, for example, that in the future a need arises for a parameter that adds a marker at several locations on the same map. Extending the API with this would then be as simple as adding a `positions` property to the `options` object that would take an array of `google.maps.LatLng` objects as its value. This addition would feel natural and wouldn't break any other functionality.

■ **Warning** When creating an object literal, be sure not to have a comma after the last property since it will make Internet Explorer choke.

Asynchronous by Nature

The v2 API relied heavily on synchronous method calls. This made it hard to modularize the API and was probably the biggest reason for the total remake. The new API is asynchronous by nature, which allows it to be modularized.

What's the point of modularizing the API? The answer is simply performance. The old API had to load big parts of the API before displaying a simple map, even parts of the API that weren't used. The new API being modularized only needs to load the necessary parts before initializing the map. Therefore, the perceived performance is much better; in other words, the map shows up on the web page much faster.

Synchronous vs. Asynchronous

When using the synchronous method, everything happens in a sequence. If you call methodA, it must finish running before methodB is invoked. If the methods instead are asynchronous, you can call methodA and methodB, and they can run parallel to each other.

Consider this example where you invoke two methods after one another:

```
methodA();
methodB();
```

methodA takes longer than methodB to run. Figure 2-1 shows how they would execute using synchronous vs. asynchronous method calls.

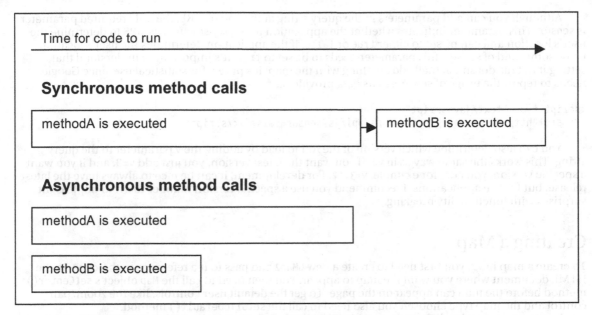

Figure 2-1. The difference between synchronous and asynchronous method calls

In the asynchronous method call, `methodB` doesn't have to wait for `methodA` to finish. This is great because you get better performance, but it also means that you can't rely on a method call to be finished when you invoke another method later in the code. This behavior has consequences in how you use v3. In some cases, you need to check whether an object is properly initialized before you can interact with it, whereas in v2 you didn't have to do this because it all happened sequentially.

One example of this is when you need to access the bounds of the map. You can't just call the `getBounds()` method of the `Map` object after you've initialized the map, because at that point the map isn't ready and it doesn't have any bounds. Instead, you have to listen to the bounds_changed event before trying to grab it. The bounds_changed event fires whenever the bounds of the map have changed. One of those occurrences is when the map has loaded. It also occurs whenever you pan or zoom the map.

```
google.maps.event.addListener(map, 'bounds_changed', function() {
  var bounds = map.getBounds();
});
```

Converting from Version 2 to 3

In this section, you will learn how to perform basic tasks such as creating a map and adding markers and also compare how these tasks are done in v2 vs. v3.

Adding a Reference to the API

The most significant change here is that you no longer need an API key. This is really convenient since you don't have to create a new API key for every domain that you want to use Google Maps on.

Although you can add parameters in the query string at the end of URL, the only required parameter is sensor. This parameter indicates whether the application uses a sensor such as GPS to determine the user's location and can be set to either true or false. If the application determines the user's location using some kind of sensor, this parameter needs to be set to true. It's important to understand that setting it to true doesn't actually do anything with the map; it's purely for statistical use since Google needs to report the usage of sensors to its data providers.

```
<script type="text/javascript"
    src="http://maps.google.com/maps/api/js?sensor=false"></script>
```

You can also determine which version of the API to load by adding the v parameter to the query string. This works the same way as in v2. If you want the latest version, you just add v=3, and if you want a specific version, you add, for example, v=3.12. For development, it can be nice to always have the latest release, but for live applications, I recommend you use a specific version number to avoid unpleasant surprises with functionality breaking.

Creating a Map

To create a map in v2, you first need to create a new GMap2 and pass to it a reference to the <div> in the HTML document where you want the map to appear. You then need to call the Map object's setCenter() method before the map can appear on the page. To get the default user controls, like the zoom/pan control and the map type chooser, you also need to call the setUIToDefault() method.

Version 3 works a bit differently, and it's no longer called GMap2 but google.maps.Map. Its immediate appearance is very similar to v2. It takes a reference to a <div> as its first argument and a MapOptions object as its second argument. The main difference is what you define inside MapOptions (Figure 2-2).

MapOptions has three required properties: zoom, center, and mapTypeId. The zoom property determines the initial zoom level, center determines the initial position, and mapTypeId determines the initial map type. After defining these three properties, the map is fully initialized and instantly visible on the web page.

Another difference is that the default UI is enabled by default, so there's no need to explicitly add it. If, on the other hand, you don't want it to appear, you can disable it by setting the property disableDefaultUI to true in MapOptions.

When it comes to the map type, in v2 the map defaulted to road maps. In v3 you must explicitly tell the map which map type to use in order for it to initialize.

Version 2

```
//Creating a new map
var map = new GMap2(document.getElementById('map'));

// Setting the center of the map which will display it on the web page
map.setCenter(new GLatLng(54, 12));

// Adding navigation and map type controls to the map
map.addControl(new GLargeMapControl());
map.addControl(new GMapTypeControl());
```

Version 3

```
// Create a new map that is immediately displayed on the web page
var map = new google.maps.Map(document.getElementById('map'), {
```

```
  zoom: 6,
  center: new google.maps.LatLng(54, 12);
  mapTypeId: google.maps.MapTypeId.ROADMAP,
});
```

You might have noticed that creating a `LatLng` is a bit different too. It's actually created the same way as in v2 but now uses the `google.maps.LatLng` object instead of `GLatLng`.

Figure 2-2. v2 vs. v3. The biggest difference in appearance is the look of the navigation bar, but it also groups the map type options a bit differently.

In v2 you typically checked to see whether the browser was compatible using the `GBrowserIsCompatible()` method before initializing the map. What it does is to see whether the browser is in the list of supported browsers and then returns `true`. If it can't recognize the browser, it checks to see whether it supports the native DOM method `document.getElementId()`. If it does, it returns `true`. Otherwise, it returns `false`.

There's no equivalent to this method in v2, so you have to check this in some other way, possibly by checking whether the browser supports `getElementById()`.

```
// Check if the browser support document.getElementById
If (document.getElementById) {
  // Init the API
}
```

■ **Tip** An excellent JavaScript library for testing browser capabilities is EnhanceJS, which is an open source library provided by the filament group. With this library, not only can you check which JavaScript function the browser supports, but you can also check how well it handles CSS. You can learn about it and download it at `http://code.google.com/p/enhancejs/`.

Another method that has been dropped in v3 is the GUnload() method. It's run when the user leaves the page, typically when window.onunload triggers. It's used to free up browser resources caused by memory leaks, particularly in Internet Explorer 6 and older. This method has no equivalent in v3, probably because Internet Explorer 6 is not a supported browser in v3.

Further Reading

To learn more about how to create a map, check out Chapter 3. To learn more about the MapOptions object and how all of its properties work, read Chapter 4. That chapter will explain all the options available.

Markers

How markers work in v3 is a bit different from v2. First, the Marker object is called Marker instead of GMarker and resides in the google.maps namespace. Second, instead of several parameters, it takes only one, which is a MarkerOptions object.

Another difference is that in v2 you first had to create a marker and then add it to the map using the addOverlay() method of the Map object. In v3 you can instantly add the marker to the map by passing a reference to the Map object in the MarkerOptions object.

Version 2

```
// Create a marker
var marker = new GMarker(new GLatLng(54, 12));

// and add it to a map
map.addOverlay(marker);
```

Version 3

```
// Create a marker and instantly add it to a map
var marker = new google.maps.Marker({
  position: new google.maps.LatLng(54, 12),
  map: map
});
```

Of course, you don't have to instantly add the marker to the map. By omitting the map property, you just create the marker and can then add it to the map later by using its setMap() method.

```
// Create the marker
var marker = new google.maps.Marker({
  position: new google.maps.LatLng(54, 12)
});

// And add it to a map
marker.setMap(map);
```

Marker Icons

In v2, to change the default icon of a marker, you had to create a GIcon object and assign it to the marker by using the icon property of the GMarkerOptions object. Alternatively, you could use the setImage() method of the Marker object and pass a URL to an image as its parameter.

In v3 you have a few more options. You can set the icon directly using the icon property of the MarkerOptions object, or you can set it later using the setIcon() method of the Marker object. In both cases, you can choose whether to use a full-fledged MarkerImage object or simply to use a URL to an image.

In v2 the GIcon object included everything about the marker icon, such as its shadow, its printImage, and so on. In v3 this is handled differently. For example, the icon shadow is handled as a separate property in the MarkerOptions object. It's called shadow and also takes either a MarkerImage object or a URL to an image as its value.

All the alternative icons you could define in v2, such as printImage, mozPrintImage, and transparent are dropped, so you only need to worry about providing one image for the icon and one for its shadow.

In its simplest form, changing the marker icon requires that you only provide it with a URL for the icon and one for the shadow. Well, you could actually omit the shadow property if you like. When changing the default icon, the default shadow is also removed.

Version 2

```
// Create a custom icon
var myIcon = new GIcon(G_DEFAULT_ICON, 'icon.png');

// Create a marker and add it to the map
var marker = new GMarker(new GLatLng(54, 12), {
  icon: myIcon
});

map.addOverlay(marker);
```

Version 3

```
var marker = new google.maps.Marker({
  position: new google.maps.LatLng(54, 12),
  map: map,
  icon: 'icon.png',
  shadow: 'shadow.png'
});
```

In v2 the GIcon object has a property called imageMap. It's used to define the clickable part of the icon and takes an array of integers as its value. In v3 this is defined by using the shape property of the MarkerOptions object, which takes a MarkerShape *object* as its value. This object has two properties, type and coord. The type property defines the kind of shape you would like to use, such as a polygon, circle, or rectangle. The coord property takes an array of integers defining the points in the shape. It works just like an ordinary HTML ImageMap.

Version 2

```
// Create a custom icon
var myIcon = new GIcon(G_DEFAULT_ICON, 'icon.png');
myIcon.imageMap = [4,4, 29,4, 29,29, 22,29, 17,35, 16,35, 10,29, 4,29, 4,4]
```

```
// Create a marker and add it to the map
var marker = new GMarker(new GLatLng(54, 12), {
  icon: myIcon
});

map.addOverlay(marker);
```

Version 3

```
var marker = new google.maps.Marker({
  position: new google.maps.LatLng(54, 12),
  map: map,
  icon: 'icon.png',
  shape: {
    type: 'poly',
    coord: [4,4, 29,4, 29,29, 22,29, 17,35, 16,35, 10,29, 4,29, 4,4]
  }
});
```

Another new feature in v3 is the ability to use sprites as marker icons. Sprites are an excellent way of speeding up your map (and web page) since it reduces the number of files that need to be downloaded. How to use them are a bit tricky but is covered in detail in Chapter 6.

Further Reading

How to use markers is extensively covered in Chapter 5 and in Chapter 9. How to use the MarkerImage object and sprites is explained in full detail in Chapter 6.

InfoWindows

The handling of InfoWindow objects has changed quite a bit in v3. First, let me just say that InfoWindow objects in v3 do not have all the capabilities of InfoWindow objects in v2. One of the most missed features is probably tabbed windows, but they also lack support for maximizing the InfoWindow. Maybe these features will be introduced in v3 at a later time, but as of the time of writing, that's unknown.

Another big difference from v2 is that you now can have several InfoWindow objects open at the same time. In v2 the InfoWindow wasn't really an overlay object like markers and polygons; it was something that was attached to the map and reused each time it was opened. You didn't have to worry about creating one because the API did that in the background for you.

Now, in v3, InfoWindow objects are essentially an overlay. This means you have to treat them the same way you treat other overlays such as, for example, markers (Figure 2-3). This leads to new problems that you need to take care of. One of those problems is how to restrict the use of InfoWindow objects so that you have only one at a time on the map. The solution to this is to create one InfoWindow object that you reuse each time you need to open one. How to do this is described in detail in Chapter 5.

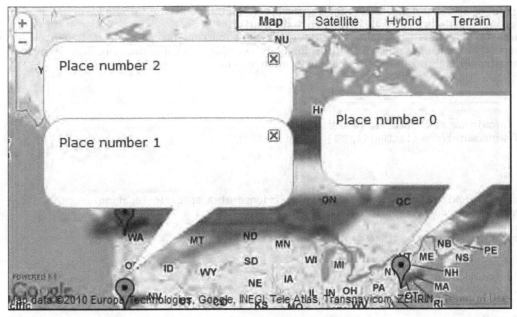

Figure 2-3. *In v3 it's possible to have several* InfoWindow *objects open at the same time, something that was impossible in v2.*

In some ways, InfoWindow objects were easier to use in v2, but in v3 they are more powerful and conform better to how the other overlay objects work.

Here's an example of how to tie an InfoWindow to a marker and open it on the marker's click event. In v2 you can just call the openInfoWindowHtml() method of the Marker object. In v3 you need to first create an InfoWindow object and then open it using its open() method.

Version 2

```
// Add a click event to a marker that will open an InfoWindow
GEvent.addListener(marker, 'click', function() {
  marker.openInfoWindowHtml('Some text');
});
```

Version 3

```
// Create a new InfoWindow object
var infoWindow = new google.maps.InfoWindow({
  content: 'Some text'
});

// Add a click event to a marker
google.maps.addListener(marker, 'click', function() {
  // Add the InfoWindow to the map
  infoWindow.open(map, marker);

});
```

15

Passing the Map object and the Marker object to the open() method adds the InfoWindow to the specified map and positions it correctly in relation to the marker.

Of course, you don't have to associate the InfoWindow with a marker. You can associate it with a polyline or a polygon or just provide it with a position of its own and attach it to the map. Here's how to create an InfoWindow that is positioned at a certain location on a map:

Version 2

```
// Open an InfoWindow at a specific position
map.openInfoWindowHtml(new GLatLng(54, 12), 'Some text');
```

Version 3

```
// Create a new InfoWindow object that will be positioned at a specific location
var infoWindow = new google.maps.InfoWindow({
  content: 'Some text',
  position: new google.maps.LatLng(54, 12)
});

// Add the infoWindow to the map
infoWindow.open(map);
```

Further Reading

To learn more about how InfoWindow objects work in v3 and how to handle several of them, refer to Chapter 5. To learn even more about InfoWindow objects and a few tips and tricks, read Chapter 7.

Polylines

Polylines conform to the same principles as the other objects. They reside in the google.maps namespace, and their constructors take only one argument, a PolylineOptions object. This is in contrast to v2, where you specify the polyline style using arguments to the constructor. These arguments are baked in as properties of the PolylineOptions object.

As with the Marker object, you can instantly add the polyline to the map by providing PolylineOptions with the map property.

Version 2

```
// Create an array with points
var points = [
    new GLatLng(37.7671, -122.4206),
    new GLatLng(36.1131, -115.1763),
    new GLatLng(34.0485, -118.2568)
];

// Create a new polyline
var polyline = new GPolyline(points, '#ff0000', 5, 0.7);

// Add the polyline to the map using map.addOverlay()
map.addOverlay(polyline);
```

Version 3

```
// Create an array with points
var points = [
  new google.maps.LatLng(37.7671, -122.4206),
  new google.maps.LatLng(36.1131, -115.1763),
  new google.maps.LatLng(34.0485, -118.2568),
];

// Create a new polyline and instantly add it to the map
var polyline = new google.maps.Polyline({
  path: points,
  strokeColor: '#ff0000',
  strokeWeight: 5,
  strokeOpacity: 0.7,
  map: map
});
```

Encoded Polylines

Apart from the syntax changes, polylines work just about the same in v3 as in v2 with one major difference. In v2 there's the possibility to encode the polylines to get better performance. This is done with the fromEncoded() method. This reduces the complexity (the number of points) of a polyline at different zoom levels. So if you zoom out, you will see polylines with fewer points, and as you zoom in, the number of displayed points increases. This make sense since while zoomed out, you don't benefit from detailed polylines, and vice versa. But to be honest, using encoded polylines in version 2 is rather awkward.

The possibility to pre-encode a polyline is currently not available in version 3 of the API. That's mostly a good thing because now all that stuff is done internally in the API, so you don't have to worry about it. This is really good since you get all this functionality without having to do anything. On the other hand, it's also potentially bad since you have no control over how it works. If, for example, you pre-encode your polylines on the server, you have to first decode them before you can add them to the map. If you're interested in digging deeper into this matter, there's an interesting discussion on the subject in the Google Maps JavaScript API v3 group. Check it out at http://tinyurl.com/32q7kff.

Further Reading

To learn more about how to use polylines in v3, including how to let the user dynamically add polylines by clicking in the map, check out Chapter 8.

Polygons

The code for creating polygons works very much the same way as for polylines. The differences between v3 and v2 are basically the same as for polylines. Polygons in v3 have a PolygonOptions object that contains all the properties for styling them. In v2 this is done by passing them as individual arguments to the GPolygon object's constructor.

Here's how to add a simple polygon with a red border and red semi-transparent background to a map:

17

Version 2

```
// Create an array with points
var points = [
    new GLatLng(37.7671, -122.4206),
    new GLatLng(36.1131, -115.1763),
    new GLatLng(34.0485, -118.2568)
];

// Create a new polygon
var polygon = new GPolygon(points, '#ff0000', 5, 0.7, '#ff0000', 0.3);

// Add the polygon to the map using map.addOverlay()
map.addOverlay(polygon);
```

Version 3

```
// Create an array with points
var points = [
  new google.maps.LatLng(37.7671, -122.4206),
  new google.maps.LatLng(36.1131, -115.1763),
  new google.maps.LatLng(34.0485, -118.2568),
];

// Create a new polygon and instantly add it to the map
var polyline = new google.maps.Polyline({
  path: points,
  strokeColor: '#ff0000',
  strokeWeight: 5,
  strokeOpacity: 0.7,
  fillColor: '#ff0000',
  fillOpacity: 0.3,
  map: map
});
```

A new feature in v3 is the ability to create *donuts*, which are polygons with holes in them. This provides you with a lot more flexibility when marking out certain areas in a map. In Figure 2-4, the Pentagon is marked using a polygon donut.

Figure 2-4. Polygon donuts used to mark the Pentagon. Screenshot from http://gmaps-samples-v3. googlecode.com/svn/trunk/poly/pentagon.html.

As with polylines, the reduction of polygon detail at different zoom levels is now automatically handled by the API. This also means that it's no longer possible to create encoded polygons using the fromEncoded() method.

Further Reading

To learn more about how to create polygons and use polygons, check out Chapter 8.

Events

Whereas the event methods were found in GEvent in v2, all the event methods in v3 reside in google.maps.event. Other than that, the methods themselves look the same, but there are a few differences.

As an example of the similarities between the old and the new API, here's how to add a click event to a marker in v2 and v3, respectively:

Version 2

```
var handle = GEvent.addListener(marker, 'click', function(e) {
  // Do something
});
```

Version 3

```
var handle = google.maps.event.addListener(marker, 'click', function(e) {
  // Do something
});
```

An interesting difference, though, is what is passed to the event listener, which in this example is the variable e. In v2 this varies widely depending on the object and the kind of event being captured. In v3 the behavior is a bit more coherent. When it comes to events triggered by some kind of mouse event (click, dragstart, and so on), most of the time a MouseEvent object is returned. As of this writing, this object has only one property, latLng, but it's a much more consistent way of handling mouse events.

Version 3

```
var handle = google.maps.event.addListener(polyline, 'click', function(e) {
  var positionClicked = e.latLng;
});
```

All the overlay objects work like this, except for one unfortunate exception, the Marker object. It returns a MouseEvent object for drag, dragend, and dragstart, but not for the other mouse events. These instead return a browser-specific object. Therefore, when you need to grab the LatLng being clicked, you have to get it from the marker itself.

Version 3

```
var handle = google.maps.event.addListener(marker, 'click', function(e) {
  var positionClicked = marker.getPosition();
});
```

A New Method

A nice addition in v3 is the addListenerOnce() method. It removes itself once it has run. This is very useful in cases where you need to check that an object is fully initialized before interacting with it. In the case of checking for the bounds of the map to be available before trying to grab it, you need to listen for the event only once (as the map is loading). In that case, this method is perfect since it will run once and then remove itself.

Version 3

```
google.maps.event.addListenerOnce(map, 'bounds_changed', function() {
  var bounds = map.getBounds();
});
```

Further Reading

To read more about the available methods in google.maps.event, check out the API reference in Appendix A.

Summary

This chapter provided a head start for those readers already familiar with v2 of the API. Ideally it will get you started converting your existing applications to v3, but since this is only an overview of the most important changes, you will probably want to read some of the other chapters for a more in-depth description on how to use different parts of the API. I also encourage you to check out the API reference in Appendix A, which will give you even more tools for solving your immediate problems.

CHAPTER 3

■ ■ ■

Creating Your First Map

A Google map resides in a web page. So, the first thing you need to do is to set up that page. This includes creating an HTML page and a style sheet for it. Once you have everything set up, you can insert the actual map. In this chapter, I will guide you through all the necessary steps to create your very first Google Maps page.

Setting the Scene

Before you start creating a map, you need to set up the web page for it. This includes creating an HTML file and a style sheet.

The HTML Page

The core of every web page is the HTML file. It's important to code it properly since it forms the foundation for everything else. Without a solid foundation, the stuff you build upon it will easily break.

Web browsers are very forgiving and will often render a page correctly even if the HTML is slightly faulty. I do, however, recommend that you make sure the HTML is coded properly, for a number of reasons:

- **Debugging**
  If you don't have the HTML right, strange errors may occur in your CSS or JavaScript that are really hard to find. Both the CSS and a lot of the JavaScript code relies on the HTML being correct, so to make it easier for yourself, make sure that your HTML is correct by validating it frequently. This will save you a lot of time and grief.

- **Performance**
  In addition, correct HTML code renders faster than incorrect HTML. If done properly, the browser will interpret the HTML in *strict mode*, in which it assumes that you know what you are doing. Incorrectly done, and it will switch to *quirks mode*, in which it's a lot more forgiving in its interpretation of the code. This means that you can get away with sloppy code, but since the browser has to guess what you mean, the page takes longer to render.

- **Quality**
  Naturally, you want to look professional, and you just don't look good with HTML that doesn't validate. Invalid code is the sign of a developer who doesn't know what he's doing.

What Flavor of HTML to Use

Several flavors of HTML are in use today. The most common ones are HTML 4.01 and XHTML 1.0, but there are others such as XHTML 1.1 and HTML 5.

I tend to use XHTML 1.0 Strict in my work. I like that it's more structured than regular HTML, so all the examples throughout this book will be in this version. You could, of course, use HTML 4.01, but if you do, I recommend that you use the strict version of it.

Right now there's a lot of buzz around HTML 5. It looks really promising but is still in a draft version, and there will be some time before you can actually start using it in live applications. For test purposes or for personal projects, on the other hand, it's entirely possible to start using it right away. In modern browsers such as Firefox 3.5 and Safari 4, there's already some support for it, and they degrade gracefully for elements not yet supported. Check out these articles for more information on how to start using HTML 5 right now:

- `http://articles.sitepoint.com/article/html-5-snapshot-2009`

- `www.alistapart.com/articles/previewofhtml5`

Validate Your Code

So, how do you know that your HTML is correct? The best way is to check your code with W3C's HTML validator. It validates all flavors of HTML. You validate your file by entering the URL to the web page you want validated. If your HTML file is on your computer or on a closed server, you can either upload the file or paste the code into a text field.

If your code validates, you will get a nice green notification that the document has been successfully checked (Figure 3-1).

Figure 3-1. A successfully checked web page, incidentally being the home page of my blog

If, on the other hand, the page doesn't validate, you will get an angry red message that tells you so (Figure 3-2). Don't be intimidated by the number of errors. Often several errors depend on a single error, so it probably looks worse than it is. The good news is that you will get pointers to where the problems are, so it's easy to find and correct them.

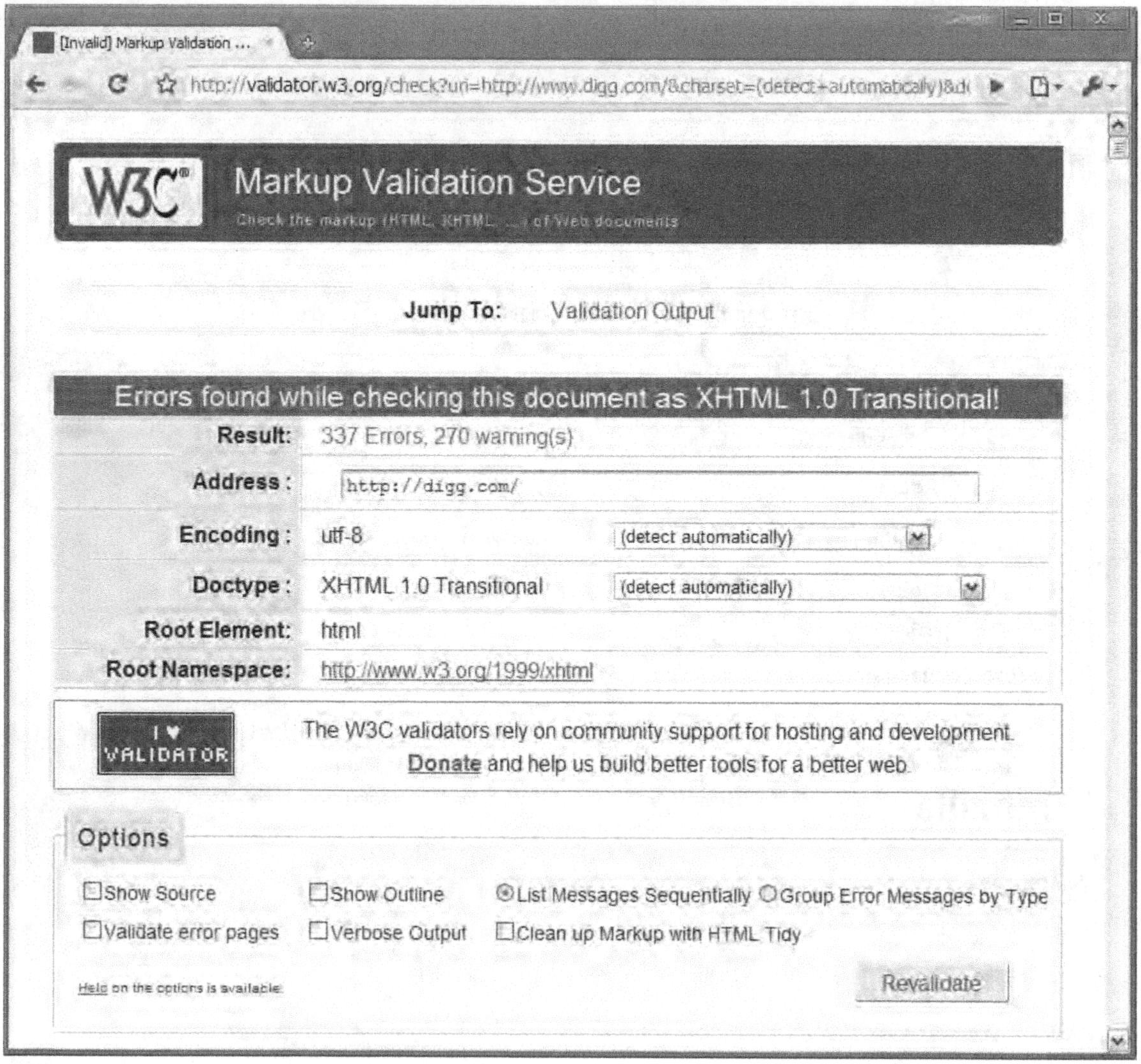

Figure 3-2. It looks like Digg.com has some problems with its XHTML.

Unfortunately, a lot of sites don't validate. It's probably a lot easier to find sites that don't validate than ones that do. I still don't think that this justifies being sloppy about it. Code that validates will always be better than code that doesn't.

You'll find this validator at http://validator.w3.org.

Other Tools

If you're using Firefox, there are several extensions that you can use to validate your code without having to visit W3C's web site. The following are three very useful extensions that I use.

Page Validator

The Page Validator extension was created by Michael Langely. It adds a menu option in your Tools menu. When you select the menu item, it sends the page you're currently on to the W3C validator page.

```
https://addons.mozilla.org/en-US/firefox/addon/2250
```

Html Validator

The Html Validator extension, which was created by Marc Gueury, is specifically used for validating web pages. It puts a small icon in the lower-right part of the browser window, which immediately tells you whether the page validates. When you double-click it, a View Source window opens with a list of errors. I find this feature extremely useful since it enables me to quickly find errors and correct them.

Unfortunately, this extension is not available for Mac OS, but if you're a Windows user, I highly recommend it.

```
https://addons.mozilla.org/en-US/firefox/addon/249
```

Web Developer Toolbar

Validating HTML is just one of the things you can do with the Web Developer Toolbar extension. The Web Developer Toolbar, created by Chris Pederick, is an indispensable tool for all web developers since it's chock-full of useful tools. The validate page function provides you with a shortcut to the W3C validator.

```
https://addons.mozilla.org/en-US/firefox/addon/60
```

With these tools at your disposal, you are more than ready to get started.

Laying the Foundation

OK, so I've decided to use XHTML 1.0 Strict. Now let's start coding. You'll start by creating a file called index.html. Initially it will look like Listing 3-1.

Listing 3-1. The Initial XHTML Code

```
<!DOCTYPE html PUBLIC "-//W3C//DTD XHTML 1.0 Strict//EN"
    "http://www.w3.org/TR/xhtml1/DTD/xhtml1-strict.dtd">

<html xmlns="http://www.w3.org/1999/xhtml">
  <head>
    <title>My first Google Map</title>
    <meta http-equiv="Content-Type" content="text/html; charset=UTF-8" />
  </head>
```

```
<body>
  <h1>My first map</h1>
  <div id="map"></div>
</body>
</html>
```

The Doctype

At the very top of the web page there's a doctype declaration:

```
<!DOCTYPE html PUBLIC "-//W3C//DTD XHTML 1.0 Strict//EN"
    "http://www.w3.org/TR/xhtml1/DTD/xhtml1-strict.dtd">
```

This is used to tell the browser how to interpret the page. If you don't have a correct doctype, the browser will immediately go into quirks mode. Be sure to get this right! I've never been able to learn it by heart, so I usually copy and paste it from existing pages. The good news if you're using HTML 5 is that the doctype is simply as follows:

```
<!DOCTYPE html>
```

I'm pretty sure that I'll be able to completely memorize this one.

The <head>

The <head> section of the page contains a few important elements. First there's the *title*, which sets the title of the page, and then there's a *meta element*, which tells what kind of character encoding you're using. This element is necessary for the document to be valid! I recommend using UTF-8 since it includes special characters for all languages.

```
<head>
  <title>My first Google Map</title>
  <meta http-equiv="Content-Type" content="text/html; charset=UTF-8" />
</head>
```

■ **Tip** To learn more about character encoding, which is a whole science in itself, read the article "The Absolute Minimum Every Software Developer Absolutely, Positively Must Know About Unicode and Character Sets (No Excuses!)" by Joel Spolsky at www.joelonsoftware.com/articles/Unicode.html.

The <body>

Finally, the <body> element contains the elements that will be visible on the web page. In this example case, you're not going to have a lot of stuff here. But you will have a heading (<h1>) and a <div> element. The <div> element will eventually contain the map and will have the attribute id="map". This is important, because it's through this ID that you will target this element, both from your style sheet and from your JavaScript. You'll learn more about this later in the chapter.

```
<body>
  <h1>My first map</h1>
  <div id="map"></div>
</body>
```

■ **Tip** You can get standard compliant HTML templates from the Web Standards Project. These will provide you with a good starting point for your web pages. See www.webstandards.org/learn/reference/templates/.

The Style Sheet

To set the size of the map, you need to style the <div> that will contain the map. The size of this container defines the size of the map.

It's good practice to keep the HTML and CSS separated; therefore, you will put the CSS in a separate file called style.css. To have a neat structure, you will organize the files in a folder structure where the style sheets go in a folder called css.

style.css will contain only a couple of definitions, including some basic styling for the body and more importantly styling for the map container. Since you've set the id attribute on the <div> to map (<div id="map">), you can target it with the selector #map in the CSS.

First you need to define the dimensions of the <div> with the attributes width and height. The width attribute is set to 100% so that it will span the whole page from side to side, and the height is set to 500 pixels. Additionally, you will add a black 1-pixel border to the <div> with the help of the attribute border.

```
#map {
  width: 100%;
  height: 500px;
  border: 1px solid #000;
}
```

When I create CSS files, I normally include a header section that explains what the CSS is for, who made it, and when it was created. Comments in CSS start with /* and end with */ and can span multiple lines.

With the header and some additional styling, the whole CSS file will look like Listing 3-2.

Listing 3-2. The Complete CSS File

```
/*-------------------------------------
  Author:      Gabriel Svennerberg
  Email:       gabriel@svennerberg.com
  Created:     2010-03-17
  Description: Stylesheet for example 1
-------------------------------------*/
body {
  font-family: Verdana, Geneva, Arial, Helvetica, sans-serif;
  font-size: small;
  background: #fff;
}
#map {
  width: 100%;
```

```
  height: 500px;
  border: 1px solid #000;
}
```

You also need to make a reference in the HMTL that points to the CSS file. It's done with the `<link>` element that resides inside the `<head>` section of the page. Since you've put `style.css` in a folder called `css`, the reference to it will look like `href="css/style.css"`. The other attributes of the `<link>` element are `type`, `rel`, and `media`. What they do is basically to let the browser know that the file it's pointing to is a CSS file and that it will be used for all media types.

```
<link type="text/css" href="css/style.css" rel="stylesheet" media="all" />
```

■ **Warning** It's really important to set at least the height of the map container because if you don't, the map will have a height of 0 and will therefore be invisible. This is something a lot of people miss and spend a lot of time trying to figure out.

Inserting a Reference to the Google Maps API

Now that you have a web page set up, you're ready to load the Google Maps API. The API is a JavaScript file that is hosted on Google's servers. It's loaded with a `<script>` element in the `<head>` section of the page. The `<script>` element can be used to add remote scripts into a web page, and that's exactly what you want to do here.

The `<script>` element has two attributes that you need to use. The first one is `type`, which you want to set to `text/javascript`, and the other one is `src`, which you want to set to the URL pointing to the API.

```
<script type="text/javascript"
  src="http://maps.google.com/maps/api/js?sensor=false"></script>
```

The URL points to the location of the API, but you also need to pass a query string with the key *sensor*. It's used to tell whether the device using the map has a device for determining the geolocation, like for example a GPS. It must explicitly be set to either `true` or `false`: `true` if the device has a sensor and `false` if it does not. Devices with a sensor are usually mobile phones or other handheld devices.

As far as I know, the reason you need to tell whether the device has a sensor or not is for licensing reasons. Google needs to give its map data providers statistics for the usage of the maps. It has absolutely nothing to do with enabling a geolocation service, so don't confuse it with that.

```
<script type="text/javascript"
  src="http://maps.google.com/maps/api/js?sensor=false"></script>
```

Determining Whether the Device Has a Sensor

There are ways to determine whether a device has a sensor, but I will not dwell on that at the moment. Your best bet is to set the sensor to `false`, unless you're absolutely certain that the devices that will use your map have some kind of sensor.

Localizing

The Google Maps API will automatically try to determine in which language to display its user interface. If you explicitly want to set a certain language for your map, you can do so by using an optional parameter in the query string. By adding &language=sv at the end of the query string, for example, you force the user interface to use Swedish as its language.

```
<script type="text/javascript"
  src="http://maps.google.com/maps/api/js?sensor=false&language=sv"></script>
```

Initializing the Map

Now that you have the Google Maps API linked in, you need to write some JavaScript code to do something with it. The first thing you need to is to somehow initialize the map. This is done with JavaScript. Like with the style sheet, it's best practice to keep it separated from the HTML. Therefore, create an external JavaScript file called map.js, and for the sake of good structure, you should place it in a folder called js.

You now have a file structure that looks like Figure 3-3.

Figure 3-3. *A nice and tidy file structure*

To include the JavaScript file in the web page, you create a <script> element in the <head> section of the page. It's important that it's inserted after the <script> element that includes the Google Maps API in order to make sure that the API is loaded before trying to use it.

```
<script type="text/javascript" src="js/map.js"></script>
```

■ **Note** The correct way to mark up a <script> tag is to use the attributes src and type. You sometimes see the attribute language="JavaScript" being used, but that's a deprecated attribute that was introduced during the browser wars, and it should be avoided at all costs.

Now the HTML file is complete and looks like Listing 3-3.

Listing 3-3. The Complete XHTML Code

```
<html xmlns="http://www.w3.org/1999/xhtml">
  <head>
    <meta http-equiv="Content-Type"
      content="text/html; charset=UTF-8" />
    <title>My first map</title>
    <link type="text/css" href="css/style.css" rel="stylesheet"
      media="all" />
    <script type="text/javascript"
      src="http://maps.google.com/maps/api/js?sensor=false"></script>
    <script type="text/javascript" src="js/map.js"></script>
  </head>
  <body>
    <h1>My first map</h1>
    <div id="map"></div>
  </body>
</html>
```

Time to Start Coding

You've set the scene, you have your files in an ordered structure, and you've inserted the Google Maps API. This means that you're all good to go. It's time to start coding. But before you do that, I will tell you a little about a few core concepts of the JavaScript language.

Variables in JavaScript

A variable is a container with a specific name. This container can store a lot of things such as strings, numbers, and objects. To create a variable, or *declare* it as it's called in programming, JavaScript uses the keyword var. To create a variable called numberOfApples and assign it the value 3, the code is as follows:

```
var numberOfApples = 3;
```

You can now use this variable to access its value. To bring up an alert that will display the numberOfApples value, you can write this:

```
alert(numberOfApples);
```

We can also change its value.

```
numberOfApples = 5;
```

Some programming languages such as C# and Java have strongly typed variables, which mean that when a variable is declared, its type must also be determined and can never be changed. So, if you decide that a variable can store only numbers, it's impossible to store a string of text in it. In JavaScript, which is a *loosely typed* language, you don't need to think about this. You can store whatever you like in its variables.

There are some rules about how a variable is named. The names can contain both letters and numbers, but they can't start with a number. They can also contain certain characters such as, for example, underscores, but they can't have spaces. So, to make a variable more readable, you can use underscores instead of spaces. Another technique is to use *camelCasing*, which means that each new word (except the first one) in the variable name starts with an uppercase letter.

```
var variable_name;
var variableName;
```

Also note that variable names are case sensitive, so `variableName` and `variablename` will refer to two different variables.

■ **Warning** Always use the `var` keyword when defining variables. It's possible to omit it, but doing so automatically makes the variable global, which means that it will be available everywhere. This might sound convenient but is in fact the source of many errors and problems, so always try to avoid it. To read more about why this is bad, read Douglas Crockford's excellent article "Global Domination" at `www.yuiblog.com/blog/2006/06/01/global-domination/`.

Common Data Types

Even if JavaScript is a loosely typed language, it still has different data types. I will briefly describe the three most basic ones.

Strings

Strings are text. When you define a string, you can use either single or double quote marks around it. I tend to use single quote marks, but that's just a matter of personal preference.

```
var fruit = 'apple';
var fruit = "apple";
```

But what if you need to have a single or double quote in the string? In these cases, you can use something called *escaping*. What this means is that a backslash (\) is inserted before the character being escaped. The JavaScript interpreter will then know that the character that follows it is part of the string and discard any other meaning it might have.

```
var text = 'I\'m hungry';
var myScreen = "I have a 22\" screen";
```

Worth mentioning also is that to escape a backslash, you put a backslash in front of it.

Numbers

Numbers aren't enclosed inside quote marks but are simply assigned. All kinds of numbers can be used.

```
var myAge = 37;
var temperature = -3;
var processorSpeed = 2.66;
```

Booleans

Booleans can have only two values, true or false. This might not seem much, but it's actually the logic on which computers are constructed—you know, ones and zeros. You can actually use 1 instead of true and 0 instead of false since they mean the same thing. Actually, any numbers except 0 will return true, so all you'll need to remember is that 0 is false.

```
var male = true;
var female = 0; // false
```

■ **Tip** You might have noticed that I always include a semicolon at the end of each line of code. This is actually optional in JavaScript, but I strongly suggest that you always use semicolons since omitting them makes the JavaScript interpreter guess where they should be. This leads to slower performance and potentially hard-to-find bugs.

Functions

Functions are one of the core features of a programming language. They are perfect for reusing code. A simple function that will throw an alert with the classic phrase "Hello world" looks like this:

```
function message() {
  alert('Hello world!');
}
```

To execute it, you call it by its name, including its parentheses:

```
message();
```

This will result in the alert shown in Figure 3-4 being thrown.

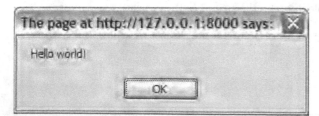

Figure 3-4. Hello world!

All it does right now is to throw the alert "Hello world" each time you call it, but if you want it to be a bit more useful, such as throwing an alert with a phrase of your choice, then you need to provide it with arguments. Arguments are used to pass values to the function.

```
function shout(phrase) {
  alert(phrase);
}
```

```
shout('Hello world again!');
```

Since you now can pass values to the function, you can reuse it for different scenarios. Consider the following example:

```
function add(val1, val2) {
  alert(val1 + val2);
}
```

```
add(4, 6);
```

You now have a function that adds two numbers. Calling it and passing 4 and 6 as its arguments will produce an alert box with "10" (see Figure 3-5).

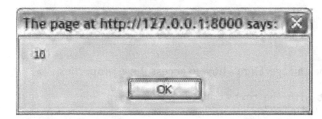

Figure 3-5. 4+6=10

Functions can also be stored inside variables:

```
var add = function(val1, val2) {
  alert(val1 + val2);
}
```

```
add(4, 6);
```

For all practical use, there's actually no difference between this function and the one you created before. It's just another way of constructing it.

■ **Note** Functions in JavaScript are first-class objects. What that means is that functions are a kind of object that can do all the things that other objects can do. This is one of the reasons that JavaScript is so powerful. The article "Functions Are First-Class Objects in JavaScript" by Helen Emerson explains this concept very nicely. See http://helephant.com/2008/08/functions-are-first-class-objects-in-javascript/.

Objects

JavaScript is an object-oriented language, which means that it has objects. In fact, the entire Google Maps API is built around objects. An object can be described as a container of functions and variables. When functions and variables are part of an object, they are called *methods* and *properties*. To use a method or property of an object, *dot notation* is used. This means that first you write the name of the object, then you write a dot (.), and finally you write the name of the method or property you want to use.

```
myObj.calculate(); // Calling the calculate object
myObj.name // Accessing the name property
```

Object Literals

Object literals are a convenient way of creating objects. The syntax for creating an object literal is as follows:

```
var author = {
  name: 'Gabriel Svennerberg',
  age: 37
}
```

This creates an object with the properties name and age. Here's how to access these properties:

```
alert(author.name); // Will bring up an alert with the text "Gabriel Svennerberg"
alert(author.age); // Will bring up an alert with "37"
```

You could provide it with methods by adding functions to it as well:

```
var author = {
  name: 'Gabriel Svennerberg',
  age: 37,
  tellName: function() {
    alert(author.name);
  }
}
```

To invoke the method, you call it by its object and method name:

```
author.tellName() // will display an alert with the text "Gabriel Svennerberg"
```

Debugging Tool: Firebug

An extremely useful tool for debugging your JavaScript code is a Firefox extension called Firebug. It was originally created by Joe Hewitt but is now maintained and being further developed by the people in the Firebug Working Group. I actually don't know how I coped before using Firebug. It has completely revolutionized how you're able to debug your JavaScript code (and HTML/CSS code).

I strongly suggest that you install it and learn how to use it, because it will be of enormous help when you start coding. Read more about it, and install it at http://getfirebug.com/.

Setting Up the Map

OK, so now that you know a bit about variables and functions, you will start doing actual coding against the Google Maps API. You will write your code in the file map.js, which you created earlier.

To create a map and insert it on the web page, you need to initialize it. This is done by creating a new instance of the object google.maps.Map (Table 3-1). It takes two arguments:

- A reference to the HTML element that the map will reside inside. In this case, you need the <div> with the id attribute map.

- An object literal called MapOptions that contains the initial settings for the map like the starting zoom level, where the center of the map should be, and what kind of map should be displayed.

Table 3-1. Definition of the Map Constructor

Constructor	Description
Map(mapDiv:node, opts?MapOptions)	Creates a map object and inserts it inside the mapDiv

THE GOOGLE.MAPS NAMESPACE

As you might have noticed, the classes and methods of the Google Maps API v3 is always prefixed with google.maps. That's something called a *namespace*. It's very convenient since it minimizes the risk of *name collisions*, which is when methods and variables have the same name. This risk increases as the project gets more complex and as the number of external JavaScript libraries being used increases. Therefore, it's good practice to keep code in a namespace.

So, whenever you need to use a class or call a method in the Google Maps API v3, they are always prefixed with google.maps.

The Map Container

Do you remember that you inserted a <div> with the attribute id="map" in the web page? Now it will come to good use since you want to insert the map inside it. To do this, you need to make a reference to it in your script and pass it to the map object. You're going to use the native DOM method getElementById() for this (Table 3-2). This method takes the ID of an HTML element as its argument and returns a reference to the targeted HTML element. Note that the same ID can be used only once in each HTML document. Therefore, getElementById() always return either a reference to a single HTML element or, if it can't find a matching element, the value null. So, what is null? It's essentially nothing! Therefore, when getElementById() can't find a matching element, it will return null; in other words, it returns nothing.

Table 3-2. Definition of document.getElementById

Method	Return value	Description
document.getElementById(id:string)	A reference to an HTML element or null	This method searches the document for an element with the correct ID.

You create a variable called mapDiv and by using the getElementById() method assign it a reference to <div id="map">.

```
var mapDiv = document.getElementById('map');
```

MapOptions

MapOptions resides in an object that is passed to the map. It contains information about how you want your map to look and behave. This object is in the form of an *object literal*. As you've already seen, an object literal is an object that is created on the fly, which means that at the same time you create it, you also provide it with its values.

Using this feature of the JavaScript language, you create a variable called options with the three properties that are required to make the map work:

- **center**
  Defines the center of the map with a coordinate. The coordinate must be of type google.maps.LatLng (Table 3-3).

- **zoom**
  Defines the initial zoom level of the map. It must be a number between 1 and 23, where 1 is zoomed all the way out and 23 is zoomed all the way in. (The deepest zoom level can actually vary depending on the available map data.)

- **mapTypeId**
  Defines what type of map you initially want to display. All map types are found in the google.maps.MapTypeId object. To get a regular map, you need to set this to google.maps.MapTypeId.ROADMAP. If you instead wanted a satellite image, you would set it to google.maps.MapTypeId.SATELLITE.

Before you create the object literal, you will prepare the value for the center property since it must be an object of the type google.maps.LatLng.

Table 3-3. Definition of the LatLng Constructor

Method	Description
LatLng(lat: number, lng:number, noWrap?boolean)	The arguments are passed in the order latitude, longitude. If noWrap is set to true, it will use the numbers as they are passed; otherwise, it will force latitude to lie within the -90 to +90 degrees range and longitude to be in the -180 to +180 degree range.

```
var mapDiv = document.getElementById('map');
var latlng = new google.maps.LatLng(37.09, -95.71);
```

Notice the use of the new keyword. It's used to initialize an object, which means that it creates a new instance of the object LatLng. LatLng must be initialized with two arguments, which are the latitude and the longitude that defines the position. In this case, it's a position at the center of the United States. Without these arguments, LatLng cannot be created, because LatLng must always have a position.

Let's create the object literal options and feed its properties with the proper values:

```
var mapDiv = document.getElementById('map');
var latlng = new google.maps.LatLng(37.09, -95.71);

var options = {
  center: latlng,
  zoom: 4,
  mapTypeId: google.maps.MapTypeId.ROADMAP
};
```

Now you have all the components necessary for creating a map. You have a reference to the <div> (mapDiv), and you have an map options object (options). Let's put them to good use and pass them to the map object:

```
var mapDiv = document.getElementById('map');
var latlng = new google.maps.LatLng(37.09, -95.71);
var options = {
  center: latlng,
  zoom: 4,
  mapTypeId: google.maps.MapTypeId.ROADMAP
};

var map = new google.maps.Map(mapDiv, options);
```

OBJECT LITERALS AND JSON

Maybe you recognize the object literal as similar to JSON? If that's the case, you are absolutely right. JSON is a subset of the object literal with the difference that object literals can contain functions, something that JSON cannot.

To read more about object literals and JSON, check out these articles:

"Show Love to the Object Literal"
www.wait-till-i.com/2006/02/16/show-love-to-the-object-literal/

"JSON in JavaScript"
www.json.org/js.html

"JSON Is a Subset of the Object Literal"
http://snook.ca/archives/javascript/json_is_a_subse/

Making the Code Run on Page Load

You want this code to run once the web page has loaded. If you tried to use your code as it is now, the map won't load, and you will get an error deep inside the Google Maps API. That's because the `<div>` has not yet been loaded in the browser when your JavaScript is loaded. What this means is that `document.getElementById('map')` won't find anything and will return `null`. This happens because when it runs, the `<div>` doesn't exist in the browser. Because you now pass a `null` value to the Google Maps API instead of a container, it will have nowhere to insert the map, and an error will occur.

To get around this, you need to wait for the document to load before you run the script. This is done by utilizing something called *event listeners*. The `window` object, which is the "mother" object of a web page, has an event listener called `onload` that is triggered when the entire web page has finished loading. By using it, you make sure that your map `<div>` exists before running the script.

The basic construction of it looks like this:

```
window.onload = function() {
  // Code we want to run
}
```

What you do is that you assign an anonymous function to the `onload` event of the `window` object. So when the `onload` event is triggered, the code inside the anonymous function is executed. Anonymous functions are functions without names. Since they don't have names, they can't be reused, but they are still very useful for containing code that will be run on situations like these.

```
window.onload = function() {
  alert('This pops ups when the entire web page has finished loading');
}
```

To put this to use in your code, you simply put the code you have written so far inside the anonymous function (see Listing 3-4).

***Listing 3-4.** Almost There*

```
window.onload = function() {
  var mapDiv = document.getElementById('map');
  var latlng = new google.maps.LatLng(37.09, -95.71);
  var options = {
    center: latlng,
    zoom: 4,
    mapTypeId: google.maps.MapTypeId.ROADMAP
  };

  var map = new google.maps.Map(mapDiv, options);
}
```

You finally have something usable! This code will create a map that'll look like Figure 3-6. It will have all the basic functionality of a regular Google map, such as being able to zoom in and out, to pan the map, and to change the map type.

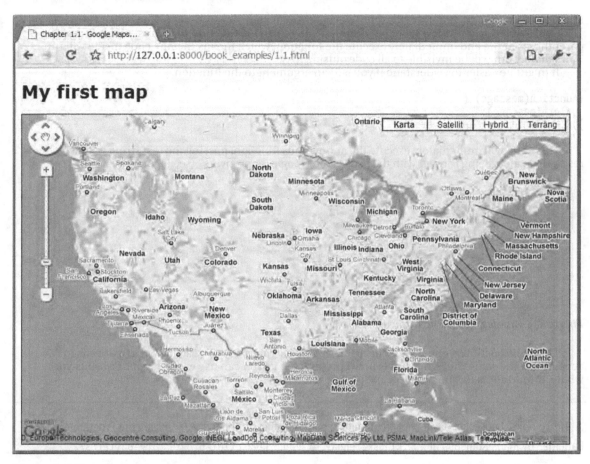

Figure 3-6. Your first map

Encapsulating the Code

Although you now have a functioning map, you're not quite done. You are currently cluttering the global namespace with all your variables. This might not be a big deal in a simple web page like the one you're currently working on. But if you're constructing a map that will be part of a bigger project, using global variables can turn out to be a big problem. The problem that can arise is that naming collisions between conflicting code occur. It's therefore important to contain your code so that you isolate it from the outside world.

To make sure that your code doesn't clutter the global namespace, you will encapsulate it inside a self-executing anonymous function. The pattern looks like this:

```
(function() {
  // The code
})();
```

It might look a bit odd, but it's really quite clever. First, an anonymous function looks like function() { }. By encapsulating it inside a set of parentheses, you return the function to the rest of the code. The parentheses at the end immediately execute the function, which means that the code inside will run immediately but will be invisible to all code outside it.

It might be easier to understand if you add an argument to the function:

```
(function(message) {
  alert(message);
})('Hello Google Maps lovers');
```

This code will immediately execute the anonymous function, passing the text string to it, which will result in an alert being thrown with the text "Hello Google Maps lovers" (see Figure 3-7).

Figure 3-7. An alert box being thrown

This construction is one way of encapsulating code. That said, you can use other patterns to accomplish the same thing, but this is how I prefer to do it. You can use whatever pattern suits you; what's important is to somehow encapsulate the code.

■ **Tip** To read about other JavaScript programming patterns, check out the article "JavaScript Programming Patterns" by Klaus Komenda at www.klauskomenda.com/code/javascript-programming-patterns/.

Applying this pattern to the example, the final code will look like Listing 3-5.

Listing 3-5. The Final JavaScript Code

```
(function() {
  window.onload = function() {
    var mapDiv = document.getElementById('map');
    var latlng = new google.maps.LatLng(37.09, -95.71);
    var options = {
      center: latlng,
      zoom: 4,
      mapTypeId: google.maps.MapTypeId.ROADMAP
    };

    var map = new google.maps.Map(mapDiv, options);
  }
})();
```

The map will look and work the same way, but your variables will no longer be available for outside code, thereby not cluttering the global namespace.

Creating Maps for Mobile Devices

Better support for mobile devices was one of the main goals for Google Maps API v3. It is specifically adapted to work well on advanced mobile devices such as the iPhone and mobile phones using the Android OS. Creating maps for these devices is done the same way as for desktop browsers, but since they have smaller screens and have other ways of interacting with the items on the screen, such as the zoom-to-pinch gesture on the iPhone, there are some considerations that need to be made.

Since the screens are smaller, you probably want the map to fill the entire screen. You do this by setting the height and width of the <div> containing the map to 100 percent.

For the iPhone, there's a special <meta> element that can be used for disabling the zoom-to-pinch behavior for the browser. The <meta> element must be positioned within the <head> section of the web page; it looks like this:

```
<meta name="viewport" content="initial-scale=1.0, user-scalable=no" />
```

You should also be aware that there's no such thing as hover (mouseover) on mobile devices, so you shouldn't build functionality that relies solely on that being available.

You can find more information on how to develop web pages specifically for these devices here:

- **Safari Dev Center (iPhone)**
  http://developer.apple.com/safari/

- **Android Developers**
  http://developer.android.com/index.html

Summary

In this chapter, you learned how to set up a web page and how to insert a fully functional Google map in it. The map has all the basic functionality, which means that you can pan it, zoom in and out of it, and change the map type. You now have a solid map to build from. You also learned about some of the basic features of the JavaScript language.

With the knowledge gained from this chapter, you're ready to examine how you can tweak the map to look and behave the way you want, and that's exactly what you're going to do in the next chapter where you will examine all the properties of the MapOptions object.

■ ■ ■

Taking the Map Further with MapOptions

In the previous chapter, you learned how to create a simple map using a minimum number of settings. You also learned about the MapOptions object, which holds all the settings for the map. You learned that the required MapOptions properties are center, zoom, and mapTypeId. But there are other properties as well that you can use to make the map behave and look the way you want.

In this chapter, you will look at all the properties of the MapOptions object and learn what to do with them.

The properties available can roughly be divided into three categories: properties that control the user interface, properties that control the map container, and properties that control the cursor. You will examine each category and see how you can utilize the available properties.

A Fresh Start

Before diving into the different properties of the MapOptions object, let's start fresh with a new map (see Listing 4-1).

Listing 4-1. The Starting JavaScript Code for This Chapter

```
(function() {

  window.onload = function() {

    // Creating an object literal containing the properties
    // you want to pass to the map
    var options = {
      zoom: 3,
      center: new google.maps.LatLng(37.09, -95.71),
      mapTypeId: google.maps.MapTypeId.ROADMAP
    };

    // Creating the map
    var map = new google.maps.Map(document.getElementById('map'), options);

  };

})();
```

Controlling the User Interface

In this category, you'll find all the properties for controlling the user interface. The user interface consists of several user controls for controlling or monitoring the map, such as the zoom control or the scale. In the following sections, each property is described in detail.

disableDefaultUI

By setting this property to true, you will disable the default user interface. This means the default zoom control and the map type chooser will not be displayed. Even if you disable the default user interface, you can still enable or disable these controls individually. The default value is false.

Listing 4-2 shows an example of how to disable the default user interface. Figure 4-1 shows a map with the default UI turned on, and Figure 4-2 shows a map with the default UI turned off.

Listing 4-2. The disableDefaultUI Property

```
var options = {
  zoom: 3,
  center: new google.maps.LatLng(37.09, -95.71),
  mapTypeId: google.maps.MapTypeId.ROADMAP,
  disableDefaultUI: true
};
```

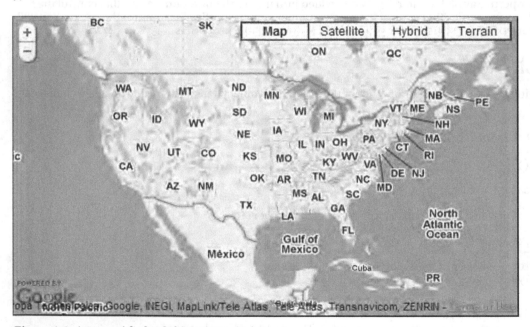

Figure 4-1. A map with the default UI turned on

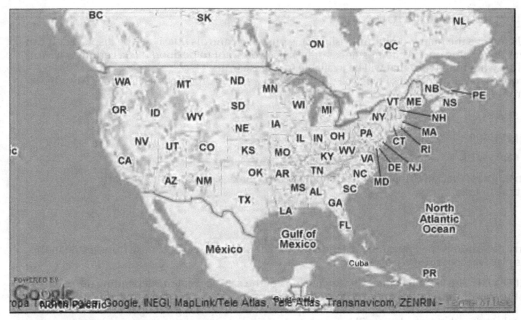

Figure 4-2. *A map with the default UI turned off*

mapTypeControl

With this property, you control whether the `mapTypeControl` will be displayed. The `mapTypeControl` is positioned in the upper-right corner of the map (Figure 4-3). You use it to choose what map type to show. Set it to true to display it and to `false` to hide it. The default value is true.

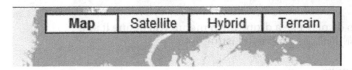

Figure 4-3. *A map with the* `mapTypeControl` *enabled*

To hide the map type, set `mapTypeControl` to `false` (Listing 4-3).

Listing 4-3. *The* `mapTypeControl` *Property*

```
var options = {
  zoom: 3,
  center: new google.maps.LatLng(37.09, -95.71),
  mapTypeId: google.maps.MapTypeId.ROADMAP,
  mapTypeControl: true
};
```

mapTypeControlOption

If you decide to have the map type control visible, this property controls *how* it will be displayed. It can look different depending on the circumstances or because you want to position it in a certain way. You can also define what map types that will be available to choose from.

This property takes an object of type google.maps.MapTypeControlOptions as its value. This object has three properties:

- style
- position
- mapTypeIds

When using mapTypeControlOptions, you should always make sure to set the property mapTypeControl to true.

style

This property determines the appearance of the control. The values you can choose from reside in the google.maps.MapTypeControlStyle object.

- DEFAULT: The DEFAULT value will vary the look of the mapTypeControl depending on the size of the window and possibly other factors. As of the time of writing, this means that the horizontal bar will be displayed if the map is big enough; otherwise, the drop-down will be used.

- HORIZONTAL_BAR: This option will display the standard bar.

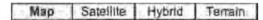

- DROPDOWN_MENU: This option will display the control as a drop-down list. It's great when the map is small or you want it to use up as little space as possible for some other reason.

If, for example, you want this control to display like a drop-down menu, you define it as a google.maps.MapTypeControlStyle.DROPDOWN_MENU, as shown in Listing 4-4.

Listing 4-4. The mapTypeControlOptions Property

```
var options = {
  zoom: 3,
  center: new google.maps.LatLng(37.09, -95.71),
  mapTypeId: google.maps.MapTypeId.ROADMAP,
  mapTypeControl: true,
  mapTypeControlOptions: {
    style: google.maps.MapTypeControlStyle.DROPDOWN_MENU
  }
};
```

■ **Note** The `mapTypeControlOptions` value is an object literal with different properties instead of just a single value. This construction might seem a little cumbersome at first, but it's actually really clever. Having it constructed this way, it's easy to add more properties as the API evolves. Right now, it has three properties: `style`, `position`, and `mapTypeIds`. When I started experimenting with the API, it had only one property, `style`.

position

The default position of this control is in the upper-right corner. But you can actively define it to be positioned somewhere else (Figure 4-4). To do this, you will have to use the `google.maps.ControlPosition` class. This class has several predefined positions:

- BOTTOM
- BOTTOM_LEFT
- BOTTOM_RIGHT
- LEFT
- RIGHT
- TOP
- TOP_LEFT
- TOP_RIGHT

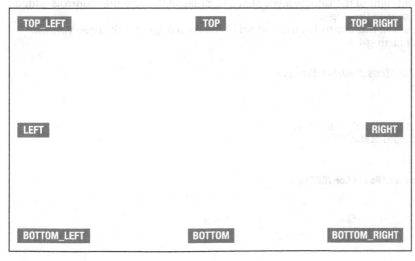

Figure 4-4. All positions for a control

In theory, this is a no-brainer, but in reality all positions don't work quite the way you would expect. Figure 4-5 shows where each position using the `mapControlType` control will end up.

Figure 4-5. All control positions in the map

As you can see, the control doesn't display properly in all positions. The bottom-right corner doesn't work at all, and LEFT and RIGHT will display at the same position as TOP_LEFT and TOP_RIGHT. The control set to BOTTOM_LEFT displays it a bit right of the Google logo. That's because of the rule that controls added first to the map are displayed closer to the edge.

So, let's say you want to position this control at the bottom of the map (Figure 4-6). Then you will need to write the code shown in Listing 4-5.

Listing 4-5. The mapTypeControlOptions *Position Property*

```
var options = {
  zoom: 3,
  center: new google.maps.LatLng(37.09, -95.71),
  mapTypeId: google.maps.MapTypeId.ROADMAP,
  mapTypeControl: true,
  mapTypeControlOptions: {
    position: google.maps.ControlPosition.BOTTOM
  }
};
```

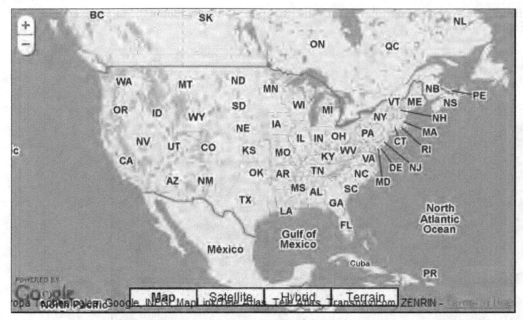

Figure 4-6. The mapTypeControl *positioned at the bottom*

These positions are relative to the other controls in the map. So, if you have two controls at the same position, the one added first will be the one closest to the edge of the map.

mapTypeIds

The map type control displays the different map types available for the user. You can control which map types will appear with the help of the property mapTypeIds. It takes an array containing the different MapType controls you want to use.

Listing 4-6 shows how to add ROADMAP and SATELLITE as possible choices for the mapControlType control. Don't worry if you find the syntax confusing. I will explain how arrays work in more detail in Chapter 5.

Listing 4-6. The mapTypeControlOptions mapTypeIDs *Property*

```
var options = {
  zoom: 3,
  center: new google.maps.LatLng(37.09, -95.71),
  mapTypeId: google.maps.MapTypeId.ROADMAP,
  mapTypeControl: true,
  mapTypeControlOptions: {
    mapTypeIds: [
      google.maps.MapTypeId.ROADMAP,
      google.maps.MapTypeId.SATELLITE
    ]
  }
};
```

This will create a map type control with only the two options that you defined, Map and Satellite, available (Figure 4-7).

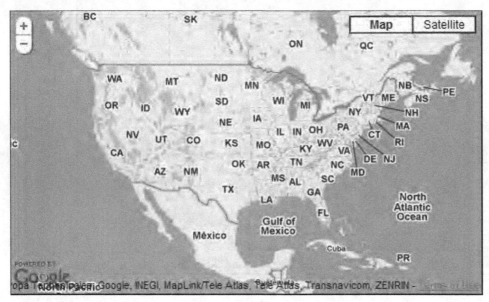

Figure 4-7. *The* mapTypeControl *contains the options Map and Satellite only.*

Using Them All Together

As the examples have shown, you can use any of these properties independent from the others. But let's wrap it all up by trying an example that includes all of them.

For this example, I want the map type control to be displayed in the upper part of the map and be in the form of a drop-down list with only the Map and Satellite map types to choose from (see Listing 4-7 and Figure 4-8).

Listing 4-7. *Using All the Properties of* mapTypeControlOptions

```
var options = {
  zoom: 3,
  center: new google.maps.LatLng(37.09, -95.71),
  mapTypeId: google.maps.MapTypeId.ROADMAP,
  mapTypeControl: true,
  mapTypeControlOptions: {
    style: google.maps.MapTypeControlStyle.DROPDOWN_MENU,
    position: google.maps.ControlPosition.TOP,
    mapTypeIds: [
      google.maps.MapTypeId.ROADMAP,
      google.maps.MapTypeId.SATELLITE
    ]
  }
};
```

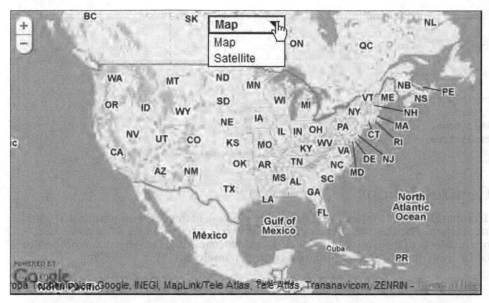

Figure 4-8. *Using all the properties of* `mapTypeControlOptions`*, you get a* `mapTypeControl` *that is positioned at the top as a drop-down list with only two available choices.*

navigationControl

This property displays or hides the navigation control. That is the control that typically resides in the upper-left part of the map with which you can zoom and sometimes pan the map (Figure 4-9). Its appearance has changed a bit since the old version of the API, but it essentially works the same way.

Figure 4-9. *The default appearance of the navigation control. To the left is the big version and to the right the small one.*

Listing 4-8 shows the code for enabling the navigationControl.

Listing 4-8. The navigationControl Property

```
var options = {
  zoom: 3,
  center: new google.maps.LatLng(37.09, -95.71),
  mapTypeId: google.maps.MapTypeId.ROADMAP,
  disableDefaultUI: true,
  navigationControl: true
};
```

navigationControlOptions

With the navigationControlOptions property, you determine the look of the navigation control. It works very much the same as the mapTypeControlOptions property in that it takes an object as its value. The object in question is an object of the type google.maps.NavigationControlOptions. It has two properties that you will recognize from the mapTypeControlOptions object, namely, position and style.

position

This property is of type google.maps.ControlPosition and works exactly the same way as the MapType control. Listing 4-9 shows the code for positioning the navigation control in the upper-left part of the map.

Listing 4-9. navigationControlOptions Position Property

```
var options = {
  zoom: 3,
  center: new google.maps.LatLng(37.09, -95.71),
  mapTypeId: google.maps.MapTypeId.ROADMAP,
  disableDefaultUI: true,
  navigationControl: true,
  navigationControlOptions: {
    position: google.maps.ControlPosition.TOP_RIGHT
  }
};
```

This code will result in Figure 4-10.

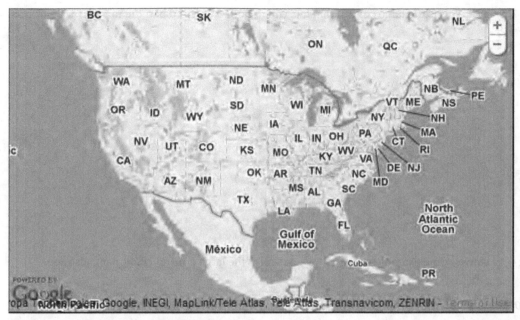

Figure 4-10. Notice the navigation control in the top-right corner. Depending on the size of the map, the API will either render this small version or render the big one.

style

The style of the navgationControl comes in four flavors that all reside in the google.maps.NavigationControlStyle class:

- **DEFAULT:** If set to this value, the control will vary according the map size and other factors. As of now, that means it will display either the small or large control, but that might change in future releases.

- **SMALL:** This is the small control. It only enables you to zoom the map.

- **ANDROID:** This control is specially tailored for Android smart phones. It differs not only in look from the other controls but also in position since its default position is at the bottom center of the map.

- ZOOM_PAN: This is the large control that lets you to both zoom and pan the map.

Listing 4-10 shows some example code on how to display the large control (zoom_pan); also see Figure 4-11.

Listing 4-10. The navigationControl Property

```
var options = {
  zoom: 3,
  center: new google.maps.LatLng(37.09, -95.71),
  mapTypeId: google.maps.MapTypeId.ROADMAP,
  navigationControl: true,
  navigationControlOptions: {
    style: google.maps.NavigationControlStyle.ZOOM_PAN
  }
};
```

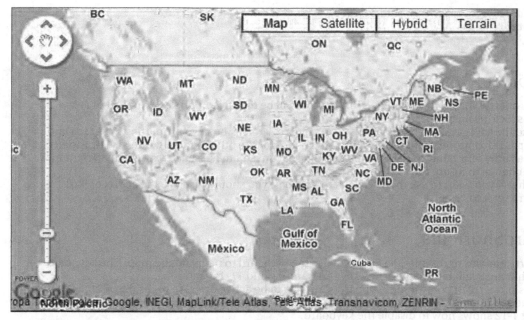

Figure 4-11. You've forced the API to display the large mapNavigationControl even though it would normally display the small control for a map this size.

Note that if you want to use this property, you should also explicitly set the property navigationControl to true.

scaleControl

This property determines whether the scale control will be displayed. Set it to true to display the control and false to hide it. This control is not displayed by default, so if you want it to show, you have to explicitly set this property to true.

The scale control is typically positioned in the lower-left corner of the map and is used to get a sense of the scale of the map. It looks like Figure 4-12.

Figure 4-12. The scale control

Listing 4-11 shows the code to enable the scale control.

Listing 4-11. The scaleControl Property

```
var options = {
  zoom: 3,
  center: new google.maps.LatLng(37.09, -95.71),
```

```
    mapTypeId: google.maps.MapTypeId.ROADMAP,
    scaleControl: true
};
```

scaleControlOptions

With this property, you control how the scale control will be displayed. It takes an object of type `google.maps.ScaleControlOptions` as its value.

Just like the `NavigationControlOptions`, `ScaleControlOptions` has two properties, `position` and `style`. The `position` property works the same way it does for the other controls. The `style` property currently has only one value, and that is the default, so it doesn't make sense to use it at all right now. This might change in future releases, though.

Note that if you want to use the `scaleControlOptions`, you should also use the `scaleControl` property and set it to true.

keyboardShortcuts

This property enables or disables the ability to use the keyboard to navigate the map. The keyboard shortcuts that are available are the arrow keys for panning and +/- for zooming.

Set this property to true for the keyboard shortcuts to be active or false to disable them. The default value is true.

Listing 4-12 shows how to disable the keyboard.

Listing 4-12. The keyboardShortcuts Property

```
var options = {
    zoom: 3,
    center: new google.maps.LatLng(37.09, -95.71),
    mapTypeId: google.maps.MapTypeId.ROADMAP,
    keyboardShortcuts: false
};
```

disableDoubleClickZoom

Normally when you double-click in a map, it zooms in. To disable this behavior, set the `disableDoubleClickZoom` property to true like in Listing 4-13.

Listing 4-13. The disableDoubleClickZoom Property

```
var options = {
    zoom: 3,
    center: new google.maps.LatLng(37.09, -95.71),
    mapTypeId: google.maps.MapTypeId.ROADMAP,
    disableDoubleClickZoom: true
};
```

The default value of this property is false.

draggable

The default behavior is that you can pan the map by dragging it. If you for some reason would like to disable it, you'll have to set the draggable property to false, as shown in Listing 4-14.

Listing 4-14. The draggable Property

```
var options = {
  zoom: 3,
  center: new google.maps.LatLng(37.09, -95.71),
  mapTypeId: google.maps.MapTypeId.ROADMAP,
  draggable: false
};
```

The default value of this property is true.

scrollwheel

Normally you can use the scroll wheel of the mouse to zoom in and out of the map. If you want to disable this, you'll have to set the scrollwheel property to false (Listing 4-15).

Listing 4-15. The scrollwheel Property

```
var options = {
  zoom: 3,
  center: new google.maps.LatLng(37.09, -95.71),
  mapTypeId: google.maps.MapTypeId.ROADMAP,
  scrollwheel: false
};
```

The default value of this property is true.

streetViewControl

This property shows or hides the Street View control, popularly called the *pegman*. The default value of this property is false, which means that Street View is not available. If you set it to true, the map will display an orange pegman right above the zoom control (Listing 4-16).

Listing 4-16. The disableDoubleClickZoom Property

```
var options = {
  zoom: 3,
  center: new google.maps.LatLng(37.09, -95.71),
  mapTypeId: google.maps.MapTypeId.ROADMAP,
  streetViewControl: true
};
```

When you start to drag the pegman, the streets that you can drop it to will be highlighted in blue (Figure 4-13).

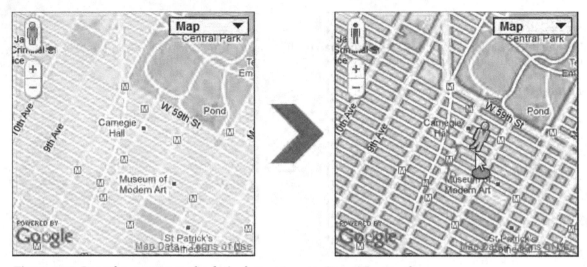

Figure 4-13. Drag the pegman to the desired street to enter Street View mode

Once you drop the pegman on a valid street, you will enter Street View mode (Figure 4-14). To go back to the map, you have to click the *X* in the upper-right corner of the view.

Figure 4-14. Street View mode

■ **Note** Not all places have street view available. To see what regions that are covered, check out www.google.com/intl/en_us/help/maps/streetview/where-is-street-view.html.

streetView

You can create a separate StreetViewPanorama to display the Street View in. You then pass it as the value for the streetView property. If you don't, Street View will use the map's <div> to do this. Exactly how Street View works is not covered in this book, but you can safely skip this property and set streetViewControl to true if you are content with the default Street View.

Controlling the Map Container

The map container is the HTML element that contains the map. Typically it's a <div> with id="map" or something similar. The MapOptions object contains some properties that control the behavior of this container.

noClear

Normally when the map loads, it automatically clears the map container (<div>) of any content, before inserting the map into it. If for some reason you want to override that behavior, you'll find this property useful. If you set noClear to false, it will preserve the content of the map container when adding the map to it.

There could be situations when you want to have your own elements positioned over the map and want them to be in the map container. I would probably put them outside the map container and position them on top of the map anyway, but at least now you know that it's possible to keep them on the inside.

Here's the code for preserving the content of the map container when the map is added to it:

```
var options = {
  zoom: 3,
  center: new google.maps.LatLng(37.09, -95.71),
  mapTypeId: google.maps.MapTypeId.ROADMAP,
  noClear: true
};
```

The default value of noClear is false.

backgroundColor

This property also affects the map container. It sets the color of the container's background. This is typically visible when you pan the map and before the map tiles have been loaded.

Either you can use a hexadecimal value code for setting the color or you can use the standard keywords for color in HTML and CSS like red, blue, and yellow.

Hexadecimal RGB values starts with a # character followed by six hexadecimal digits. The digits are divided in three pairs where the first one represents the color red, the second green, and the last one blue. The values range from 00 to FF, where 00 means nothing of that particular color and FF means maximum. The color red is #FF0000 (R=FF, G=00, B=00). If you convert this into normal numbers, it would be (R=255, G=0, B=0).

Here's how to set the background color to red using hexadecimal values:

```
var options = {
  zoom: 3,
  center: new google.maps.LatLng(37.09, -95.71),
  mapTypeId: google.maps.MapTypeId.ROADMAP,
  backgroundColor: '#ff0000'
};
```

■ **Tip** To learn more about how the color values work and what keywords you can use, check out the Wikipedia article on web colors at http://en.wikipedia.org/wiki/Web_colors.

Controlling the Cursor

This is the final category of properties, and it consists of properties that control how the cursor will look in different situations.

draggableCursor

With this property, you can control what cursor to use when it's hovering over a draggable object in the map. You can set this either by providing it with the name of a cursor such as "pointer" or "move" or by providing it with a URL to an image that you would like to use. The default cursors are the same that you can use using the CSS property cursor. Table 4-1 lists the more useful ones. Note that they can vary in appearance depending on which OS and browser you're running. For a complete list of cursors available, check out http://reference.sitepoint.com/css/cursor.

Table 4-1. Some of the Standard Cursors Available

Cursor	Name	Comment
+	crosshair	Could be good for marking a position with great accuracy.
⬉	default	The default cursor.
⬉?	help	Indicates that help can be found.
✛	move	Could be used for indicating that something is movable.
☝	pointer	Standard cursor for indicating that something is clickable.
I	text	Great for hinting that the user can write here.
⧗	wait	Hinting the user that the system is working. This is often an hourglass.

The move cursor is, in my opinion, the only one of the standard cursors that is suitable for hinting that something is draggable. Here's how to set the map to use the move cursor over draggable objects:

```
var options = {
  zoom: 3,
  center: new google.maps.LatLng(37.09, -95.71),
  mapTypeId: google.maps.MapTypeId.ROADMAP,
  draggableCursor: 'move'
};
```

If you find the standard cursors too limiting for your needs, you can use your own images instead. Be aware, though, that there are benefits of using the standard ones and potential drawbacks with using custom ones. The standard cursors look slightly different in different operating systems but will be familiar to the user. On the contrary, custom cursors, if not carefully selected, can be unfamiliar to the user and become yet another thing that the user needs to learn. If you still decide to go with custom images, this is how it's done.

To use an image, you provide the draggableCursor property with a URL instead of a keyword. Using an image called myCursor.png that resides in a folder on the server called img would will in the following:

```
var options = {
  zoom: 3,
  center: new google.maps.LatLng(37.09, -95.71),
  mapTypeId: google.maps.MapTypeId.ROADMAP,
  draggableCursor: 'img/myCursor.png'
};
```

draggingCursor

This property works the same way as draggableCursor. The only difference is that it controls the cursor being used while dragging an object in the map.

```
var options = {
  zoom: 3,
  center: new google.maps.LatLng(37.09, -95.71),
  mapTypeId: google.maps.MapTypeId.ROADMAP,
  draggingCursor: 'move'
};
```

Controlling the Map Settings with Methods

So far, we've set the maps settings directly on the MapOptions object. This is certainly a good way to do it when you're setting up the map. But what if you want to change one of the properties after the map has been initialized? You can't do it by manipulating the MapOptions object directly, so you have to do it some other way! Fortunately, the map object provides a number of methods to help you.

There are two kinds of methods: the generic setOptions() method and specific methods for each of the properties. Let's start by examining the setOptions() method.

setOptions

This is a method of the map object, and it takes a MapOptions object as its sole attribute. To use it, you create an object literal, just as you did when you were creating a map, and you pass it to this method.

So, to change the zoom level of the map, you could do this:

```
var options = {
  zoom: 12
};
map.setOptions(options);
```

A more compact way of doing it is to create the object literal inside the setOptions() method:

```
map.setOptions({
  zoom: 12
});
```

Now you changed only one value, but it's when you need to change several properties at the same time that this method is especially useful. Say, for example, that you want to change the zoom level and the map type:

```
map.setOptions({
  zoom: 12,
  mapTypeId: google.maps.MapTypeId.SATELLITE
});
```

With this method, you can change almost all the properties of the MapOptions object. But there are a few properties that can't be changed:

- backgroundColor
- disableDefaultUI
- noClear

When it comes to these, you have to be careful to define them right away when initializing the map.

The Specific Methods

Specific methods are available both for setting the value of a property and for getting its current value. These methods are available only for the required properties of the MapOptions object: center, zoom, and mapTypeId.

Getting and Setting the Zoom Level

To get the current zoom level, there's a method called getZoom(). It returns a number that indicates the current zoom level. This means that if the zoom level of the map is 6, this method will return "6." To set the zoom level, use setZoom(). It takes a number, indicating the desired zoom level, as its only argument.

- getZoom(): Returns a number indicating the current zoom level of the map
- setZoom(zoomlevel:number): Sets the zoom level of the map

```
var zoomLevel = map.getZoom();
map.setZoom(12);
```

Changing the Center of the Map

It's important to be able to center the map on a certain point. With these methods, you can both get it and set it:

- getCenter(): Returns a number indicating the current zoom level of the map
- setCenter(latlng:LatLng): Sets the center of the map using a LatLng.

Getting and Setting the mapType

These methods enable you to examine the current map type as well as change it to another type:

- getMapTypeId(): Returns a string indicating the current mapTypeId
- setMapTypeId(mapTypeId:MapTypeId): Sets the mapTypeId using one of the values in google.maps.MapTypeId

Putting the Methods to Use

You're going to build an example where you're going to put these methods to good use. In this example, you'll going to start with a basic map and then add a few buttons that will execute these methods when you push them.

To set a good starting point, you start with the code in Listing 4-17. It will create a basic map with a zoomed-out view of the United States.

Listing 4-17. A Starting Point

```
(function() {
  window.onload = function() {

    // Creating a MapOtions object with the required properties
    var options = {
      zoom: 3,
      center: new google.maps.LatLng(37.09, -95.71),
      mapTypeId: google.maps.MapTypeId.ROADMAP
    };

    // Creating the map
    var map = new google.maps.Map(document.getElementById('map'), options);

    // New code will go here

  };
})();
```

The HTML between <body> and </body> will look like this:

```
<input type="button" value="getValues" id="getValues" />
<input type="button" value="changeValues" id="changeValues" />

<div id="map"></div>
```

This will provide you with a page that looks something like Figure 4-15.

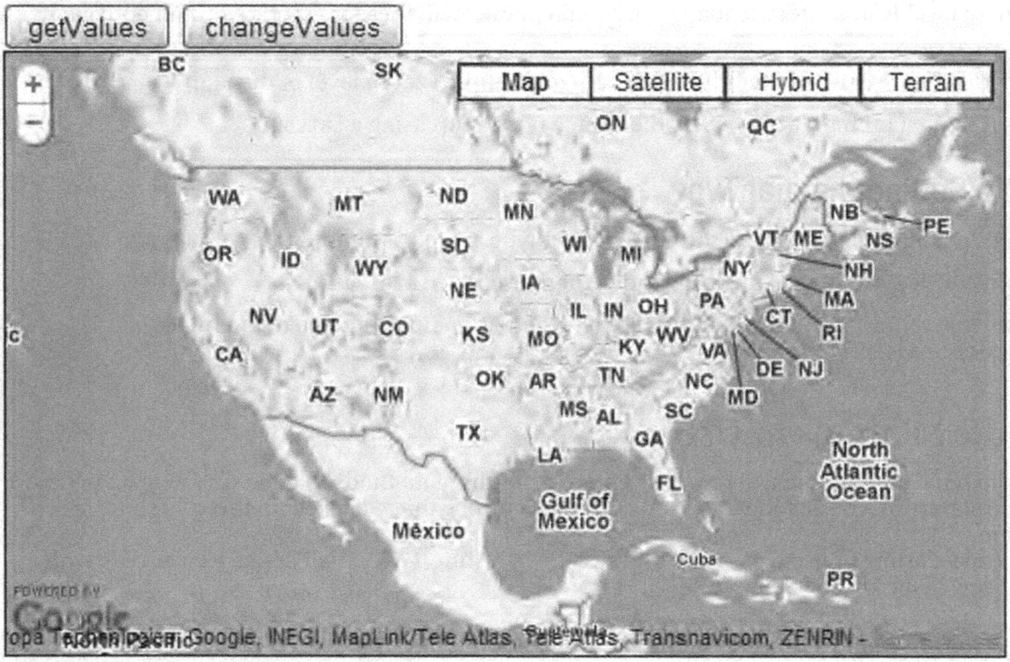

Figure 4-15. The example map

The page has two buttons with the IDs getValues and changeValues. Right now these buttons do absolutely nothing when they're clicked, but you're going to use their IDs to attach click events to them. By using the JavaScript method document.getElementById(), you create a reference to them. After you've pinpointed the buttons, you're going to add a little something extra, a click event with the help of the onclick event listener. Let's start with the getValues button. Insert this code right after the creation of the map:

```
document.getElementById('getValues').onclick = function() {
  // put code here
}
```

An anonymous function is attached to the onclick event, and it's inside this function that you will put the code to retrieve values from the map.

The first value that you will get is the zoom level of the map. To do this, you're going to use the getZoom() method. To display the value that this method returns, you're going to use an alert, and you're also going to add some text that explains what this value is:

```
document.getElementById('getValues').onclick = function() {
  alert('Current Zoom level is ' + map.getZoom());
}
```

If you run the page now and click the getValue button, the alert shown in Figure 4-16 will trigger.

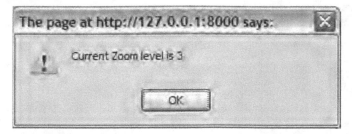

Figure 4-16. An alert with the current zoom level

Next you're going to add an `alert` that will display the current center of the map. To do this, you will need to use the `getCenter()` method.

```
document.getElementById('getValues').onclick = function() {
  alert('Current Zoom level is ' + map.getZoom());
  alert('Current center is ' + map.getCenter());
}
```

Now when you reload the page and click the button, two alerts will trigger. The second one will display the current center of the map (Figure 4-17).

Figure 4-17. An alert with the current center

If you haven't panned the map, the value that will be displayed is the one you provided in the `MapOptions` object. But if you try panning the map and click the button again, you will notice that the value has been updated with the value for the new center of the map.

Lastly you're going to add an alert that will display the current `mapType`:

```
document.getElementById('getValues').onclick = function() {
  alert('Current Zoom level is ' + map.getZoom());
  alert('Current center is ' + map.getCenter());
  alert('The current mapType is ' + map.getMapTypeId());
}
```

Now when you click the button, a third alert is triggered that will display the current map type (see Figure 4-18).

Figure 4-18. An alert that displays the current mapType

If you change the `mapType` and click the `getValues` button again, you will notice that it displays the new value.

Dynamically Changing the MapOptions Object

OK, now you've built the functionality to retrieve the values, and that's good. But even better is to be able to change the values. It's time to build the functionality for this. You're going to make the following things happen when you click the button:

- Set the center of the map on the Statue of Liberty in New York City.

- Zoom in to zoom level 17.

- Change the map type to satellite.

You're going to do this both by utilizing the generic `setOptions()` method and by using the specific "setter" methods. But first you need to attach a click event to the `changeValues` button. Insert this code right after the event handler for `getValues`:

```
document.getElementById('changeValues').onclick = function() {
  // Insert code
}
```

Changing the Center

You're going to use the `setCenter()` method to change the center of the map. Since this method takes a `LatLng` object as its argument, you first need to find out what coordinates to use. You're going to set the center on the Statue of Liberty, and its position is at latitude 40.6891 and longitude -74.0445. Let's use those values to create a `LatLng` object:

```
document.getElementById('changeValues').onclick = function() {
  var latLng = new google.maps.LatLng(40.6891, -74.0445);
}
```

With the `LatLng` object ready, all you need to do is to pass it as the argument to the `setCenter()` method.

```
document.getElementById('changeValues').onclick = function() {
  var latLng = new google.maps.LatLng(40.6891, -74.0445);
  map.setCenter(latLng);
}
```

There! The functionality for setting the correct center is in place. But let's make the code a bit more compact by moving the creation of the LatLng object inside the setCenter() method.

```
document.getElementById('changeValues').onclick = function() {
  map.setCenter(new google.maps.LatLng(40.6891, -74.0445));
}
```

That's better! Now that this functionality is in place, let's add the zoom-in functionality.

COORDINATE PRECISION

How many decimals should be used for the coordinates? First, even though the Google Maps API can handle more than six decimals, it can't render positions more precise than that. So, using more than six decimals is just a waste of numbers. If you're using the toUrlValue() method of the LatLng object, you will notice that it returns the coordinates with only six decimals, and now you know the reason why. But when is a certain precision enough? Esa Sijainti, a Finnish Google Maps developer, has made a test page to see what precision that is sufficient in different circumstances. The test is done in Google Maps API v2, but the same applies for API v3. In this test he comes to the following conclusions:

- **Five to six decimals** are the most decimals you should use ever.

- **Four decimals** are appropriate for detail maps.

- **Three decimals** are good enough for centering on cities.

- **Two decimals** are appropriate for countries.

Check out the test yourself at http://koti.mbnet.fi/ojalesa/exam/decimal.html.

Zooming in

This one is very straightforward. You want to set the zoom level to 17. To do that, all you need to do is to call the setZoom() method and pass 17 as its argument:

```
document.getElementById('changeValues').onclick = function() {
  map.setCenter(new google.maps.LatLng(40.6891, -74.0445));
  map.setZoom(17);
}
```

That was easy! Now let's change the map type. This is done by using the setMapTypeId() method and passing a mapTypeId to it. You want the mapType to be satellite, which means that you need to use google.maps.MapTypeId.SATELLITE as an argument.

```
document.getElementById('changeValues').onclick = function() {
  map.setCenter(new google.maps.LatLng(40.6891, -74.0445));
  map.setZoom(17);
  map.setMapTypeId(google.maps.MapTypeId.SATELLITE);
}
```

All the functionality is in place! When you click the changeValues button, the map zooms in on the Statue of Liberty and changes the map type to satellite view (see Figure 4-19).

Figure 4-19. When the `changeValues` button is clicked, the map zooms in on the Statue of Liberty.

You have working functionality, and that's good, but I still don't feel completely satisfied. You're doing three separate API calls. What if you could do just one? Remember the setOptions() method? It enables you to change several of the map settings at the same time. Let's use that to reduce the number of calls to the API.

Remove the three method calls you've already done, and replace them with the setOptions() methods. You then create an object literal with the properties center, zoom, and mapTypeID and pass the appropriate values to them.

```
document.getElementById('changeValues').onclick = function() {
  map.setOptions({
    center: new google.maps.LatLng(40.6891, -74.0445),
    zoom: 17,
    mapTypeId: google.maps.MapTypeId.SATELLITE
  });
}
```

The map behaves exactly the same way as before, but you need to make only one API call to make it happen. Although there's nothing wrong with making several calls, this is a pretty convenient way of changing several properties of the MapOptions object at once.

The Complete Code

Here's the complete code for this example.

HTML

Listing 4-18 shows the HTML.

Listing 4-18. *The Complete HTML*

```
<!DOCTYPE html PUBLIC "-//W3C//DTD XHTML 1.0 Strict//EN"
        "http://www.w3.org/TR/xhtml1/DTD/xhtml1-strict.dtd">

<html xmlns="http://www.w3.org/1999/xhtml" lang="en">
  <head>
    <meta http-equiv="Content-Type" content="text/html; charset=utf-8" />
    <title>Chapter 4 - Google Maps API 3</title>
    <link rel="stylesheet" href="css/style.css" type="text/css" media="all" />
    <script type="text/javascript"
      src="http://maps.google.com/maps/api/js?sensor=false"></script>
    <script type="text/javascript" src="js/map.js"></script>
  </head>
  <body>

    <input type="button" value="getValues" id="getValues" />
    <input type="button" value="changeValues" id="changeValues" />

    <div id="map"></div>

  </body>
</html>
```

CSS

Listing 4-19 shows the CSS.

Listing 4-19. *The Complete CSS*

```
#map {
  width: 100%;
  height: 500px;
  border: 1px solid #000;
}
```

JavaScript

Listing 4-20 shows the JavaScript.

Listing 4-20. The Complete JavaScript

```javascript
(function() {
  window.onload = function() {

    // Creating a MapOptions object with the required properties
    var options = {
      zoom: 3,
      center: new google.maps.LatLng(37.09, -95.71),
      mapTypeId: google.maps.MapTypeId.ROADMAP
    };

    // Creating the map
    var map = new google.maps.Map(document.getElementById('map'), options);

    // Attaching click events to the buttons

    // Getting values
    document.getElementById('getValues').onclick = function() {
      alert('Current Zoom level is ' + map.getZoom());
      alert('Current center is ' + map.getCenter());
      alert('The current mapType is ' + map.getMapTypeId());
    }

    // Changing values
    document.getElementById('changeValues').onclick = function() {
      map.setOptions({
        center: new google.maps.LatLng(40.6891, -74.0445),
        zoom: 17,
        mapTypeId: google.maps.MapTypeId.SATELLITE
      });
    }

  };
})();
```

Summary

In this chapter, you examined all the available map settings. They provide simple means to tweak the map to meet your requirements. You also examined the setOptions() method and the specific methods and looked at how they provide a convenient way to retrieve or change most of the map settings after the map has been created.

With this knowledge, you are ready for bigger challenges, namely, to put the map to use by plotting locations on it.

CHAPTER 5

■■■

X Marks the Spot

The most common use of maps on the Internet is to visualize the geographic position of something. The Google Maps marker is the perfect tool for doing this.

A *marker* is basically a small image that is positioned at a specific place on a map. Its most frequent incarnation is the familiar drop-shaped marker that is the default marker in Google Maps (Figure 5-1).

Figure 5-1. The default map marker

Setting a Starting Point

Before you start learning how to use markers, let's set a starting point for this example. It contains nothing new. It's just a plain map that's centered on Manhattan in New York City (Listing 5-1).

Listing 5-1. A Starting Point

```
(function() {
 window.onload = function() {

    // Creating an object literal containing the properties
    // we want to pass to the map
    var options = {
      zoom: 12,
      center: new google.maps.LatLng(40.7257, -74.0047),
      mapTypeId: google.maps.MapTypeId.ROADMAP
    };

    // Creating the map
    var map = new google.maps.Map(document.getElementById('map'), options);

 };
})();
```

Figure 5-2 shows what this map will look like.

Figure 5-2. An empty map

A Simple Marker

If you want to put a marker on your map with the default look, it's easily achieved with only a few lines of code.

To create a marker, you need to use the google.maps.Marker object. It takes only one parameter, which is an object of type google.maps.MarkerOptions. MarkerOptions has several properties that you can use to make the marker look and behave in different ways. For now, let's settle on the only two required properties: position and map.

- **position**
  This property defines the coordinates where the marker will be placed. It takes an argument in the form of a google.maps.LatLng object.

- **map**
  The map property is a reference to the map to which you want to add your marker.

OK, so now that you know how to create a marker, let's put that knowledge to good use. Add the code in Listing 5-2 right after the code that creates the map.

Listing 5-2. Creating a Marker and Adding It to the Map

```
// Adding a marker to the map
var marker = new google.maps.Marker({
  position: new google.maps.LatLng(40.7257, -74.0047),
  map: map
});
```

This little snippet of code will put a marker on the map. It has the look of the default Google Maps marker, and you can't do anything with it really, but it dutifully marks a spot on the map, as shown in Figure 5-3.

Figure 5-3. A simple marker

Adding a Tooltip

The first thing you might want to do is to add a tooltip to the marker. A *tooltip* is a yellow box with some text in it that appears when you hold the mouse pointer over an object. To add a tooltip to a marker, you'll use the property title. It's as simple as setting the title property of the MarkerOptions object (Listing 5-3).

Listing 5-3. Adding a Title to the Marker

```
// Adding a marker to the map
var marker = new google.maps.Marker({
  position: new google.maps.LatLng(40.7257, -74.0047),
  map: map,
  title: 'Click me'
});
```

Doing this will add a nice little tooltip to the marker when you hold the mouse pointer over it, as shown in Figure 5-4.

Figure 5-4. A marker with a tooltip

Changing the Icon

If you're not satisfied with the default icon, you can change it to a custom one. The easiest way to do this is to set the `icon` property of `MarkerOptions` to an URL of a suitable image.

Google hosts a number of images that you are free to use. If you go to http://gmaps-samples.googlecode.com/svn/trunk/markers/blue/blank.png with your web browser, you will find the image shown in Figure 5-5. And that's the one you're going to use for this example (Listing 5-4).

Figure 5-5. A custom marker

Listing 5-4. Changing the Icon

```
var marker = new google.maps.Marker({
  position: new google.maps.LatLng(40.761137, -73.97674),
  map: map,
  title: 'Click me',
  icon: 'http://gmaps-samples.googlecode.com/svn/trunk/markers/blue/blank.png'
});
```

Doing this will change the look of the marker, as shown in Figure 5-6.

Figure 5-6. A simple custom icon

In this example, I've been using an icon that resides at Google's servers, and that's OK since Google is also the one providing the API. Generally, though, you should not link to images that reside at servers belonging to others; rather, you should keep them on your own server and feed them from there. One of the reasons is that it's just plain wrong to steal other people's bandwidth without permission. Another reason is that if the people running the server move the files, your application will break.

Icons Supplied by Google

Google has a collection of standard icons that you can use on your map. Most of them use a similar URL that looks like this:

```
http://gmaps-samples.googlecode.com/svn/trunk/markers/color/markerx.png
```

where color is one of the following values:

- blue
- green
- orange
- pink
- red

and x is a number between 1 and 99. If you want a marker with no number, use the filename blank.png.

Consider Listing 5-5.

Listing 5-5. Changing the Icon

```
// Adding a marker to the map
var marker = new google.maps.Marker({
  position: new google.maps.LatLng(40.7257, -74.0047),
  map: map,
  title: 'Click me',
  icon: 'http://gmaps-samples.googlecode.com/svn/trunk/markers/green/marker1.png'
});
```

Notice that this example uses the URL http://gmaps-samples.googlecode.com/svn/trunk/markers/green/marker1.png. This will display a green icon with the number 1 in it on your screen (Figure 5-7 gives you an idea of how it will look).

Figure 5-7. One of the markers that Google provides

This is an easy way to construct a custom icon, but if you look at it closely, you will notice that it doesn't have a shadow. In Chapter 6, you will look at how to create a more complex icon with a shadow, a custom shape, and a defined clickable area. You will also learn about a really clever way to deal with scenarios where you need lots of different marker icons.

The Complete Code So Far

At this point, before you start adding more functionality to the map, I think it's best to stop for a minute and review the complete code of this example so far (Listing 5-6).

What you've done is to add a marker to the map and add a tooltip to it. You've also changed the default icon.

Listing 5-6. The Complete Code for Example 5-1

```
(function() {
  window.onload = function() {

    // Creating an object literal containing the properties
    // we want to pass to the map
    var options = {
      zoom: 12,
      center: new google.maps.LatLng(40.7257, -74.0047),
      mapTypeId: google.maps.MapTypeId.ROADMAP
    };

    // Creating the map
    var map = new google.maps.Map(document.getElementById('map'), options);

    // Adding a marker to the map
    var marker = new google.maps.Marker({
      position: new google.maps.LatLng(40.7257, -74.0047),
      map: map,
      title: 'Click me',
      icon: 'http://gmaps-samples.googlecode.com/svn/trunk/markers/blue/blank.png'
    });

  };
})();
```

■ **Tip** Remember that the code is available for download from the book's web site at www.svennerberg.com/bgma3. The name of the example is always mentioned in the code caption.

Adding an InfoWindow

Often when marking places on a map, you will want to show additional information related to that place. The Google Maps API offers a perfect tool for this, and that's the InfoWindow. It looks like a speech bubble and typically appears over a marker when you click it (Figure 5-8).

Figure 5-8. An InfoWindow

A Simple InfoWindow

Much like the `Marker` object, the `InfoWindow` object resides in the `google.maps` namespace and takes only one argument, and that argument is an object called `InfoWindowOptions`.

Like the `MarkerOptions` object, the `InfoWindowOptions` object has several properties, but the most important one is content. This property controls what will show inside the `InfoWindow`. It can be plain text, HTML, or a reference to an HTML node. For now, you will stick with plain text, but do note that you can use full HTML if you like (Listing 5-7). That also means that you can include any HTML element, image, or video and then style it any way you want.

Listing 5-7. Creating an InfoWindow with the Text "Hello World"

```
// Creating an InfoWindow with the content text: "Hello World"
var infowindow = new google.maps.InfoWindow({
  content:'Hello world'
});
```

Now you've created an InfoWindow object that will contain the text "Hello world," but it doesn't automatically appear on the map. What you want to do is to connect it with the marker so that when you click the marker, the `InfoWindow` appears. To do this, you need to attach a click event to the marker.

CONTROLLING THE SIZE OF THE WINDOW

To control the size of the `InfoWindow`, you can add an HTML element with a specific `class` attribute as its content. This way, you can control its size in your CSS.

Here's the JavaScript:

```
var infowindow = new google.maps.InfoWindow({
content:'<div class="info">Hello world</div>'
});
```

Here's the CSS:

```
.info {
  width: 250px;
}
```

A Word or Two About Events

Every time you interact with something on a web page, an *event* is triggered. For example, when you click a link, a *click event* is triggered. When you press a button on the keyboard, a *keypress event* is triggered.

These are all active events that are triggered by the user. But there are also other types of events, such as passive events, that is, events that happen in the background. You've already looked at the *load event* of the window object. It's triggered when the web page in a browser window has finished loading. Another example is the *focus event*, which triggers when an object gets focus. In the Google Maps API, there are lots of these passive events, such as `tilesloaded`, `bounds_changed`, and `center_changed`, which are all events of the `Maps` object.

■ **Note** Actually, when you click something, three events happen. They are click, mousedown, and mouseup. You can choose which one of these you want to capture. What you should know is that mousedown happens first, right when you hold down the mouse button. The mouseup event happens when you release the depressed mouse button, and click happens after mouseup and mousedown both have occurred. Similarly, when you press a key on the keyboard, three events happen. These are besides keypress, keydown, and keyup. Of these, keydown happens first, then keyup, and lastly keypress.

Listen for the Events

What these events have in common is that you can catch them in your code and do stuff when they are triggered. To do this, you need to add *listeners*. A listener is connected to an object and a certain event. It just sits quietly and waits for the event to happen. When the event does happen, the listener pops into action and runs some code. In the Google Maps API, there's a method for adding a listener that's called google.maps.events.addListener(). It takes three arguments:

- The object it's attached to.
- The event it should listen for.
- A function that is executed when the event is triggered. This function is called an *event handler*.

Adding a Click Event to the Marker

To add a click event to your marker, you need to extend the code with an event listener (Listing 5-8).

Listing 5-8. Adding an Event Listener

```
// Creating an InfoWindow with the content text: "Hello World"
var infowindow = new google.maps.InfoWindow({
  content: 'Hello world'
});

// Adding a click event to the marker
google.maps.event.addListener(marker, 'click', function() {
  // Code to be run...
});
```

This code will attach a click event to the marker that will run some code when it's being triggered. Now all you have left to do is to write some code that will open the InfoWindow.

The InfoWindow object has a method called open() that will open the InfoWindow and make it visible on the map. The open() method takes two arguments. The first argument is a reference to the map object that it will be added to (in case you have more than one map on the page). The second argument is the object that the InfoWindow will attach itself to. In our case, you want to attach it to the marker being clicked. The reason you need to do this is that you want the InfoWindow to know where it should position itself on the map. If you provide it with an object, it will automatically position itself so that the tip of the stem of the speech bubble will point at the object. This argument is actually optional. You could, if you wanted, skip this and instead set the position property of the InfoWindowOptions object to the correct position, but that's not what you're going to do here (Listing 5-9).

Listing 5-9. Opening an InfoWindow

```
// Creating an InfoWindow with the content text: "Hello World"
var infowindow = new google.maps.InfoWindow({
  content: 'Hello world'
});

// Adding a click event to the marker
google.maps.event.addListener(marker, 'click', function() {
  // Calling the open method of the infoWindow
  infowindow.open(map, marker);
});
```

Now you have all the components in place, and if you try this code, the map will initially display your marker. When you click the marker, the InfoWindow will display (Figure 5-9). Notice how it points at the marker.

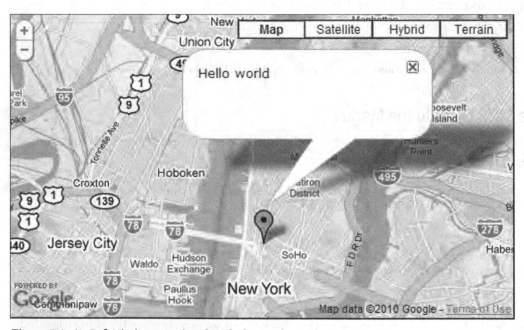

Figure 5-9. An InfoWindow associated with the marker

The Complete Code

Listing 5-10 shows the complete code so far in the process. What it does is to create a map, put a marker on it, and attach a click event to the marker that will open an InfoWindow.

Listing 5-10. The Complete Code for Example 5-2

```javascript
(function() {
  window.onload = function() {

    // Creating an object literal containing the properties
    // we want to pass to the map
    var options = {
      zoom: 12,
      center: new google.maps.LatLng(40.7257, -74.0047),
      mapTypeId: google.maps.MapTypeId.ROADMAP
    };

    // Creating the map
    var map = new google.maps.Map(document.getElementById('map'), options);

    // Adding a marker to the map
    var marker = new google.maps.Marker({
        position: new google.maps.LatLng(40.7257, -74.0047),
      map: map,
      title: 'Click me'
    });

    // Creating an InfoWindow with the content text: "Hello World"
    var infowindow = new google.maps.InfoWindow({
      content: 'Hello world'
    });

    // Adding a click event to the marker
    google.maps.event.addListener(marker, 'click', function() {
      // Calling the open method of the infoWindow
      infowindow.open(map, marker);
    });

  };
})();
```

More Markers

Now you know how to put a single marker on the map. You also have some rudimentary knowledge of how to tweak the marker a little bit and how to attach an InfoWindow to it. But what if you want to put more markers on the map? You could of course add them one by one, but eventually that's going to add up to a whole lot of code. A much smarter thing to do is to use arrays and loops.

JavaScript Arrays

A JavaScript *array* is basically a collection of variables. It can contain whatever you want to put in it.

There are two ways of creating an array in JavaScript. The first one is to call the constructor of the Array object:

```javascript
var myArray = new Array();
```

The other way is to create an array literal:

```
var myArray = [];
```

These two do exactly the same thing, but the second one is the preferred method these days and is also the method that I will stick to throughout this book.

With the array literal method, you can easily instantly fill the array with different things, such as, for example, a list of fruit.

```
var myArray = ['apple', 'orange', 'banana'];
```

Each of the items in the array list gets an individual index number. The first item gets number 0, the second item gets number 1, and so on. So to retrieve an item from an array, you simply use its index number.

```
myArray[0]    // returns apple
myArray[1]    // returns orange
myArray[2]    // returns banana
```

Another way of adding items to an array is with the array's native method push(). What push() does is take the passed value and add it to the end of the array. So, creating the same array as used earlier with this technique would look like this:

```
// First we create the array object
var myArray = [];

//Then we add items to it
myArray.push('apple');
myArray.push('orange');
myArray.push('banana');
```

This will produce exactly the same array as previously. This method is handy when you don't have all the values up front and instead need to add them as you go along.

Arrays also have a native length property that returns the number of items that it contains. In our case, length will return the value 3 since myArray contains three items:

```
myArray.length    // returns 3
```

Knowing this, you can loop through the array to extract its items.

ARRAY CONFUSION

The index of each array item and the array's length are a source of confusion for most novice programmers. When counting the items in an array, you start from 1; therefore, an array that contains three items has a length of 3. Nothing confusing about that! The confusion starts when you start looking at each item's index number. The index number of the last item is not 3, but 2. But why is that? It's because the index always starts at 0; thus, if you have three items, that last one will have the index 2 (0, 1, 2).

Introducing Loops

There are two kinds of loops in JavaScript. There are ones that execute a specified number of times called for loops, and there are ones that execute while a specific condition is true called while loops. We're going to focus on for loops.

Loops are good for executing the same code several times. This is very handy when you, for example, want to put lots of markers on a map. You then want to run the same code over and over but insert different data each time. For this task, a for loop is perfect.

The basic construction of a for loop looks like this:

```
for (var i = 0; i < 3; i++) {
  document.writeln(i + ',');
}
```

This loop will produce the following result:

```
0, 1, 2,
```

This is what happens:

1. The first statement (var i = 0) defines the variable i and assigns it the value 0. This will be done only before the first iteration.

2. Before each iteration, the loop will check the second statement (i < 3) and see if it's true. If it's true, it will run one more time and then check it again. This will go on until it eventually isn't true anymore, and then the loop will stop.

3. The third statement will add 1 to i at the end of each iteration. So, eventually i will be 3, and when it is, the second statement will no longer be true, and the loop will stop.

Now that you understand the mechanics of the for loop, you can get started using them to add markers to the map.

Adding U.S. Cities to the Map

In this example, you're going to put a few U.S. cities on the map. First you're going to store the coordinates for the cities in an array. Then you're going to loop through that array to put each one of those on a map.

Before you start learning how to do this, let's start with a clean plate. I'm going to use the code in Listing 5-11 as a starting point for this example.

Listing 5-11. A Fresh Start

```
(function() {
  window.onload = function() {

    // Creating an object literal containing the properties
    // we want to pass to the map
    var options = {
      zoom: 3,
      center: new google.maps.LatLng(37.09, -95.71),
```

```
    mapTypeId: google.maps.MapTypeId.ROADMAP
};

// Creating the map
var map = new google.maps.Map(document.getElementById('map'), options);

};
})();
```

Since you're going to put U.S. cities on the map, you need it to be zoomed out and to display all of the United States (Figure 5-10).

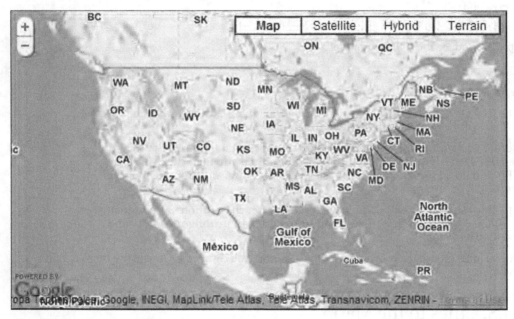

Figure 5-10. A clean plate

OK, let's get started! First you have to create an array containing the coordinates. Since you can store any object you want to in an array, let's store a google.maps.LatLng object containing the coordinates for each city in each spot in the array. This way, you can use the array items right away when you create the markers (Listing 5-12).

Listing 5-12. Creating the places Array

```
// Creating an array that will contain the coordinates
// for New York, San Francisco, and Seattle
var places = [];

// Adding a LatLng object for each city
places.push(new google.maps.LatLng(40.756, -73.986));
places.push(new google.maps.LatLng(37.775, -122.419));
places.push(new google.maps.LatLng(47.620, -122.347));
```

You now have an array containing all the data you need to put markers on the map. The next step is to loop through the array to extract this data (Listing 5-13).

Listing 5-13. Looping Through the places Array

```
// Looping through the places array
for (var i = 0; i < places.length; i++) {

  // Creating a new marker
  var marker = new google.maps.Marker({
    position: places[i],
    map: map,
    title: 'Place number ' + i
  });

}
```

This code loops through the array, and each iteration creates a new marker. Notice when you set the value for the property position, you call the array by its index number, places[i]. Also notice that you set a tooltip for each marker with the property title. It will get the text "Place number" followed by the current number of the iteration. The marker in the first iteration will get the tooltip "Place number 0," the marker in the second iteration will get the tooltip "Place number 1," and so on (Figure 5-11).

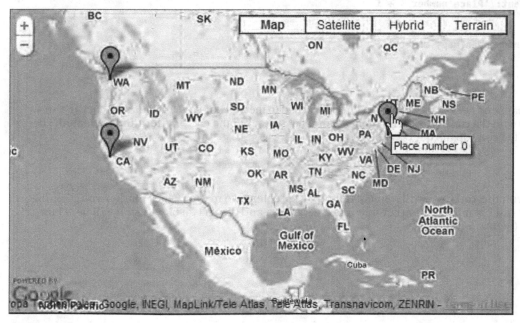

Figure 5-11. Displaying several markers at the same time

CHAPTER 5 ■ X MARKS THE SPOT

Adding InfoWindows

Next you want to add InfoWindow objects to the marker so that when you click them, an InfoWindow pops up. You do this by adding the code in Listing 5-14 inside your loop, just beneath the code that creates the marker.

Listing 5-14. Adding an Event Listener

```
// Looping through the places array
for (var i = 0; i < places.length; i++) {

  // Creating a new marker
  var marker = new google.maps.Marker({
    position: places[i],
    map: map,
    title: 'Place number ' + i
  });

  // Adding an event-listener
  google.maps.event.addListener(marker, 'click', function() {
    // Creating a new infowindow
    var infowindow = new google.maps.InfoWindow({
      content: 'Place number ' + i
    });

    infowindow.open(map, marker);

  });
}
```

What happens here is that a click event is attached to the marker so that when you click it, a new InfoWindow with the content "Place number," and the number of the current iteration is created. The last line of the code opens the InfoWindow.

Problem

When you run this code, you will immediately spot a problem. No matter which marker you click, the InfoWindow will open for the marker that was created last, and the text displayed in it will be "Place number 3" (Figure 5-12).

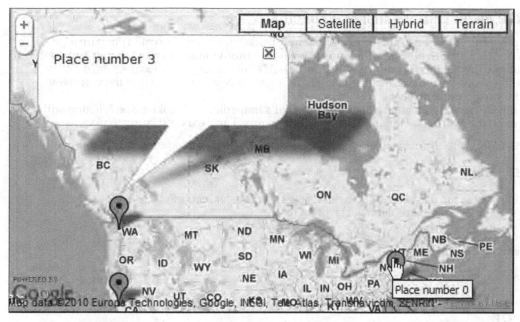

Figure 5-12. *Even though place number 0 is clicked, place number 2 is opened with the text "Place number 3"*

This is a problem that is common when dealing with event listeners. Instead of passing the *values of the variables* to the event handler of the event listener, you pass the *variables* themselves. Since the variable marker, after the code has run, contains the last marker created, that's the marker you're going to get, and that's why the InfoWindow is attached to it. This happens because event listeners are invoked at a later time than the time of their creation. In this case, it happens when a marker is clicked.

Also notice that the text in the InfoWindow shows "Place number 3" even though it's place number 2. That's because 3 is the last value assigned to i before the loop exits.

To solve this problem, you need to use something called *closure*. I think Douglas Crockford is the one defining it best in his article "Private Members in JavaScript" at http://www.crockford.com/javascript/private.html:

> *"This pattern of public, private, and privileged members is possible because JavaScript has closures. What this means is that an inner function always has access to the vars and parameters of its outer function, even after the outer function has returned. This is an extremely powerful property of the language..."*

What he says is that the inner function has access to the variables and parameters of outer functions. But if you look at it from the other end, you see that outer functions *do not* have access to the parameters and variables of its inner functions.

And that's exactly what happens here. The inner function, in this case the event handler, has access to the outer variables, but you want it to have its own persistent variables. So, how are you going to find a way around this?

Nesting the Event Listener Inside a Function

To fix your problem, you need to put the event listener inside a function. You could put it inside a named function, but a more elegant solution is to create an anonymous function to wrap around it. You will immediately invoke this function, passing the variables of the loop, i and marker, as its parameters. This way, you ensure that the event handler has access to the values of the variables instead of the variables themselves.

You do this by creating an anonymous function that's immediately invoked. The function will be wrapped around the event listener and takes two parameters, i and marker (Listing 5-15).

Listing 5-15. Adding an Self-invoking Anonymous Function That Takes i and marker as Its Parameter

```
(function(i, marker) {

  // Creating the event listener. It now has access to the values of
  // i and marker as they were during its creation
  google.maps.event.addListener(marker, 'click', function() {
    var infowindow = new google.maps.InfoWindow({
      content: 'Place number ' + i
    });
    infowindow.open(map, marker);
  });

})(i, marker);
```

You probably recognize this pattern since it's the Module pattern you've been using all along to wrap your code in. The difference here is that instead of merely invoking it at the end using (), you now also pass parameters to it (i, marker).

As you can probably see, the code for creating the event listener is identical to what you had before. The difference is that it now has access to the values of the outer variables i and marker, in its own inner variables i and marker.

This takes care of the previous problem! Now when you click the markers, the correct InfoWindow objects are displayed (Figure 5-13).

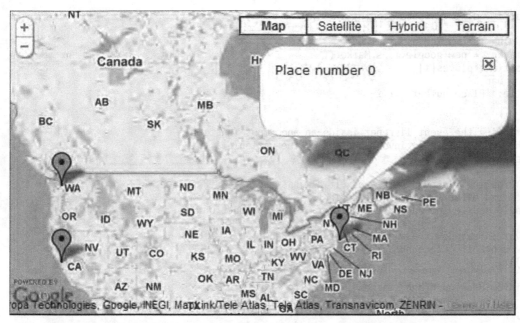

Figure 5-13. Clicking the first marker now displays the correct InfoWindow.

Listing 5-16 shows the complete code so far.

Listing 5-16. The Complete Code for Example 5-3

```
(function() {
  window.onload = function() {

    // Creating an object literal containing the properties
    // we want to pass to the map
    var options = {
      zoom: 3,
      center: new google.maps.LatLng(37.09, -95.71),
      mapTypeId: google.maps.MapTypeId.ROADMAP
    };

    // Creating the map
    var map = new google.maps.Map(document.getElementById('map'), options);

    // Creating an array that will contain the coordinates
    // for New York, San Francisco, and Seattle
    var places = [];

    // Adding a LatLng object for each city
    places.push(new google.maps.LatLng(40.756, -73.986));
    places.push(new google.maps.LatLng(37.775, -122.419));
    places.push(new google.maps.LatLng(47.620, -122.347));

    // Looping through the places array
```

```
for (var i = 0; i < places.length; i++) {

    // Adding the marker as usual
    var marker = new google.maps.Marker({
      position: places[i],
      map: map,
      title: 'Place number ' + i
    });

    // Wrapping the event listener inside an anonymous function
    // that we immediately invoke and passes the variable i to.
    (function(i, marker) {

      // Creating the event listener. It now has access to the values of
      // i and marker as they were during its creation
      google.maps.event.addListener(marker, 'click', function() {

        var infowindow = new google.maps.InfoWindow({
          content: 'Place number ' + i
        });

        infowindow.open(map, marker);

      });

    })(i, marker);

  }

}
})();
```

Did you get all that? Don't worry if you didn't. Closure is an advanced topic and is pretty hard to really wrap your head around. Just remember this pattern when creating event listeners in loops, and you'll be fine.

If you want to learn more about how closures work, here are a couple of articles to get you started:

- **Closure article on Wikipedia**
  http://en.wikipedia.org/wiki/Closure_(computer_science)

- **"Closures, finally explained!"**
  http://reprog.wordpress.com/2010/02/27/closures-finally-explained/

- **"A Graphical Explanation of JavaScript Closures in a jQuery Context"**
  http://www.bennadel.com/blog/1482-A-Graphical-Explanation-Of-Javascript-Closures-In-A-jQuery-Context.htm

Dealing with Several Windows

In Google Maps API 2, only one InfoWindow could be displayed at a time. The default behavior was that every time you opened an InfoWindow, if another InfoWindow was open, it would close. This is not the case in version 3 of the API where you instead can open an infinite number of them. In some situations, that's great, but most of the time you'll probably want to have only one InfoWindow open at a time (Figure 5-14). An easy way to fix that is to simply have one InfoWindow that you reuse over and over again.

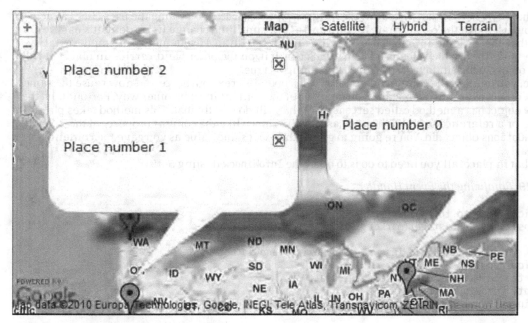

Figure 5-14. Several InfoWindow objects

To do this, you first need to declare a global variable that will hold the InfoWindow object (Listing 5-17). This will be your reusable object. Be sure to create this outside of the loop so that it's readily available. (If you declare it inside the loop, it would be re-created each time the loop iterates.)

Listing 5-17. Declaring the infowindow Variable

```
// Declare infowindow as a global variable This will be at placed
// outside the for-loop just above it
var infowindow;
```

Next you need to add a check to see whether your variable already contains an InfoWindow object. If it does, you just use it; if it doesn't, you create it (Listing 5-18).

Listing 5-18. Checking for the InfoWindow

```
// Add a click event to the marker
google.maps.event.addListener(marker, 'click', function() {

  // Check to see if the infowindow already exists
  if (!infowindow) {
    // Create a new InfoWindow object
    infowindow = new google.maps.InfoWindow();
  }

});
```

What happens here is that instead of creating a new InfoWindow every time the user clicks a marker, you just move the existing one around and at the same time change its content. It's easy to check whether the variable infowindow is carrying an object with an if statement. An empty variable will return undefined, which means false in JavaScript. If it, on the other hand, carries an object, it will return the object, which in JavaScript is the same thing as true.

Before, you defined the content of the InfoWindow upon its creation. Since you now reuse the same InfoWindow object over and over again, you need to set the content in some other way. Fortunately, the InfoWindow object has a method called setContent() that will do exactly that. This method takes plain text, HTML, or a reference to an HTML node as its value, much like the content property of the InfoWindowOptions object did. You're going to give it the exact same value as you gave the content property early.

With that in place, all you need to do is to open the InfoWindow (Listing 5-19).

Listing 5-19. Finalizing the Event Handler

```
// Add click event to the marker
google.maps.event.addListener(marker, 'click', function() {

  // Check to see if the infowindow already exists and is not null
  if (!infowindow) {
    // if the infowindow doesn't exist, create an
    // empty InfoWindow object
    infowindow = new google.maps.InfoWindow();
  }

  // Setting the content of the InfoWindow
  infowindow.setContent('Place number ' + i);

  // Tying the InfoWindow to the marker
  infowindow.open(map, marker);
});
```

Now the code will produce a map that will display only one InfoWindow at a time. Listing 5-20 shows the complete code.

Listing 5-20. The Complete Code for Example 5-4

```
(function() {
  window.onload = function() {

    // Creating an object literal containing the properties
    // you want to pass to the map
    var options = {
      zoom:3,
      center: new google.maps.LatLng(37.09, -95.71),
      mapTypeId: google.maps.MapTypeId.ROADMAP
    };

    // Creating the map
    var map = new google.maps.Map(document.getElementById('map'), options);

    // Creating an array which will contain the coordinates
```

```
    // for New York, San Francisco and Seattle
    var places = [];

    // Adding a LatLng object for each city
    places.push(new google.maps.LatLng(40.756, -73.986));
    places.push(new google.maps.LatLng(37.775, -122.419));
    places.push(new google.maps.LatLng(47.620, -122.347));


    // Creating a variable that will hold the InfoWindow object
    var infowindow;

    // Looping through the places array
    for (var i = 0; i < places.length; i++) {

      // Adding the markers
      var marker = new google.maps.Marker({
        position: places[i],
        map: map,
        title: 'Place number ' + i
      });

      // Wrapping the event listener inside an anonymous function
      // that we immediately invoke and passes the variable i to.
      (function(i, marker) {

        // Creating the event listener. It now has access to the values of
        // i and marker as they were during its creation
        google.maps.event.addListener(marker, 'click', function() {

          if (!infowindow) {
            infowindow = new google.maps.InfoWindow();
          }

          // Setting the content of the InfoWindow
          infowindow.setContent('Place number ' + i);

          // Tying the InfoWindow to the marker
          infowindow.open(map, marker);

        });

      })(i, marker);

    }

  };
})();
```

Automatically Adjusting the Viewport to Fit All Markers

Sometimes you know beforehand which markers are going to be added to the map and can easily adjust the position and zoom level of the map to fit all the markers inside the viewport. But more than often, you're dealing with dynamic data and don't know exactly where the markers are going to be positioned. You could, of course, have the map zoomed out so far out that you're certain that all the marker will fit, but a better solution is to have the map automatically adjust to the markers added. There's when the LatLngBounds object will come in handy.

Introducing the LatLngBounds Object

A bounding box is a rectangle defining an area. Its corners consist of geographical coordinates, and everything that's inside it is within its *bounds*. It can be used to calculate the viewport of the map, but it's also useful for calculating whether an object is in a certain area.

The bounding box in Google Maps is represented by the google.maps.LatLngBounds object. It takes two optional arguments, which are the *southwest* and the *northeast* corners of the rectangle. Those arguments are of the type LatLng.

To manually create a LagLngBounds object to fit the markers, you have to first determine the coordinates for its corners and then create it. This code is typically inserted just after the code that creates the map (Listing 5-21 and Figure 5-15).

Listing 5-21. Creating a LatLngBounds Object

```
var bounds = new google.maps.LatLngBounds(
  new google.maps.LatLng(37.775,-122.419),
  new google.maps.LatLng(47.620,-73.986)
);
```

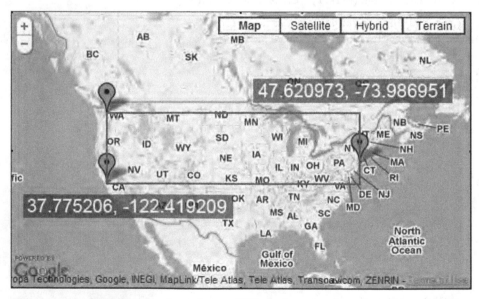

Figure 5-15. A bounding box is made up of the southwest and northeast corners of the rectangle fitting all of the markers inside it

Let the API Do the Heavy Lifting

To extend the example to automatically adjust the viewport to fit the markers inside it, you need to add a LatLngBounds object to it.

First you create an empty LatLangBounds object (Listing 5-22). It needs to be placed somewhere outside the for loop.

Listing 5-22. Creating an Empty LatLngBounds Object

```
// Creating a LatLngBounds object
var bounds = new google.maps.LatLngBounds();
```

Then you're going to extend the bounds with each marker added to the map (Listing 5-23). This will automatically give you a bounding box of the correct dimensions.

Listing 5-23. Extending the bounds Object

```
// Looping through the places array
for (var i = 0; i < places.length; i += 1) {

  […]

  // Extending the bounds object with each LatLng
  bounds.extend(places[i]);

}
```

Lastly, when you've iterated through all the markers, you're going to adjust the map using the fitBounds() method of the map object (Listing 5-24). It takes a LatLngBounds object as its argument and then uses it to determine the correct center and zoom level of the map.

Listing 5-24. Adjusting the Map According to the Bounds

```
// Looping through the places array
for (var i = 0; i < places.length; i += 1) {

  […]

  // Extending the bounds object with each LatLng
  bounds.extend(places[i]);

}

// Adjusting the map to new bounding box
map.fitBounds(bounds)
```

Ta-da! You now have a map that perfectly fits all the markers inside the viewport. If you were to add additional cities to the map, they would automatically be taken into account when calculating the viewport.

Now if you add Rio de Janeiro in Brazil to your array of cities and run the map (Listing 5-25), you will see that it automatically adjusts to the new bounding box (Figure 5-16).

Listing 5-25. Adding Rio de Janeiro to the places Array

```
places.push(new google.maps.LatLng(-22.933, -43.184));
```

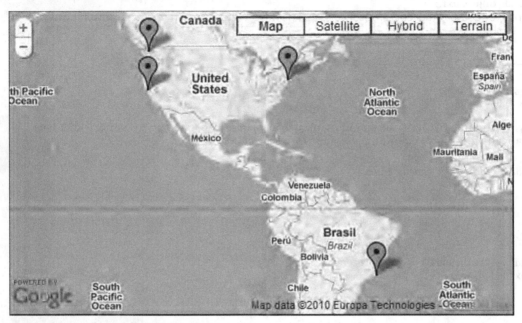

Figure 5-16. Now that Rio de Janeiro is added to the map, you can see that the map adjusts the viewport to fit it as well.

The Complete Code

You've done quite a lot in this chapter and kept adding more and more functionality to your map. You now have a pretty capable map that utilizes a lot of the built-in functionality in the Google Maps API. Listing 5-26 shows the complete code.

Listing 5-26. The Complete Code for Example 5-5

```
(function() {

  // Creating a variable that will hold the InfoWindow object
  var infowindow;

  window.onload = function() {

    // Creating an object literal containing the properties
    // we want to pass to the map
    var options = {
      zoom: 3,
      center: new google.maps.LatLng(37.09, -95.71),
```

```
    mapTypeId: google.maps.MapTypeId.ROADMAP
};

// Creating the map
var map = new google.maps.Map(document.getElementById('map'), options);

// Creating a LatLngBounds object
var bounds = new google.maps.LatLngBounds();

// Creating an array that will contain the coordinates
// for New York, San Francisco, and Seattle
var places = [];

// Adding a LatLng object for each city
places.push(new google.maps.LatLng(40.756, -73.986));
places.push(new google.maps.LatLng(37.775, -122.419));
places.push(new google.maps.LatLng(47.620, -122.347));
places.push(new google.maps.LatLng(-22.933, -43.184));

// Creating a variable that will hold
// the InfoWindow object
var infowindow;

// Looping through the places array
for (var i = 0; i < places.length; i++) {

  // Adding the markers
  var marker = new google.maps.Marker({
    position: places[i],
    map: map,
    title: 'Place number ' + i
  });

  // Wrapping the event listener inside an anonymous function
  // that we immediately invoke and passes the variable i to.
  (function(i, marker) {

    // Creating the event listener. It now has access to the values of
    // i and marker as they were during its creation
    google.maps.event.addListener(marker, 'click', function() {

      // Check to see if we already have an InfoWindow
      if (!infowindow) {
        infowindow = new google.maps.InfoWindow();
      }

      // Setting the content of the InfoWindow
      infowindow.setContent('Place number ' + i);

      // Tying the InfoWindow to the marker
      infowindow.open(map, marker);

    });
```

```
    })(i, marker);

    // Extending the bounds object with each LatLng
    bounds.extend(places[i]);

  }

  // Adjusting the map to new bounding box
  map.fitBounds(bounds)

 };

})();
```

Summary

In this chapter, you examined markers and what you can do with them. You also looked at some basic usage of InfoWindow objects. These are some of the things you learned:

- How to put a marker on the map

- How to change the marker icon

- How to associate an InfoWindow with a marker

- How to attach events to objects

- How to put several markers on the map

- How to automatically adjust the viewport to fit the markers

With this knowledge you will be able to cope with most of the challenges of designing maps with a reasonable amount of markers. However, when the markers start adding up to hundreds or maybe even thousands, you will run into problems. But don't worry; in Chapter 9, you will take a look at different strategies for dealing with a lot of markers. But first you will examine how to create better marker icons, which is the topic for the next chapter.

CHAPTER 6

■■■

Marker Icons

Sometimes the default icon is just not good enough, and you want something else. A carefully selected icon can convey lots of information and can make your maps more appealing and more usable. In the previous chapter, you looked at one way to change the appearance of a marker, but it was a basic approach, enabling you only to use a simple image that has no shadow. In this chapter, you will examine how to use custom icons and how to create an advanced marker that not only has a shadow but other useful enhancements such as different states and improved performance.

Setting a Starting Point

Before you start looking at how to use marker icons, it's a good idea to create a clean new map to start from. The code that you'll be adding later in the chapter will be placed right below the code that creates a new map (see Listing 6-1).

Listing 6-1. A Starting Point

```
(function() {
  window.onload = function() {

    // Creating a map
    var options = {
      zoom: 3,
      center: new google.maps.LatLng(37.09, -95.71),
      mapTypeId: google.maps.MapTypeId.ROADMAP
    };

    var map = new google.maps.Map(document.getElementById('map'), options);

    // Put new code here

  }
})();
```

Changing the Marker Icon

You've already examined how to change the default marker icon to a simple image without a shadow. That's as simple as setting the `icon` property of `MarkerOptions` to a URL pointing to a suitable image. Now, if you want to have a little more sophisticated icon with a shadow, give `icon` a `MarkerImage` object as its value instead of setting it to a URL.

Introducing the MarkerImage Object

`MarkerImage` is an object that contains information about the image and shadow being used for the marker's icon (see Table 6-1). That means you need to define one `MarkerImage` object for the main image and one for the shadow. Then why, you might ask, not simply use a URL to an image like you did before? That, my friend, is because using a `MarkerImage` object will enable you to define not only the image file being used but also its size, its visible area, and which part of the image will be positioned at a certain location of the map. The latter is very useful for getting the icon positioned at the exact right position of the map. Having these settings at your disposal also enables you to use something called *sprites*. I will explain sprites thoroughly later in this chapter, but for now you only need to know that using sprites is a useful technique for enhancing the performance of your map.

Table 6-1. Definition of MarkerImage

Constructor	Description
`MarkerImage(url:string, size?:Size, origin?:Point, anchor?:Point, scaledSize?:Size)`	Defines an image that is to be used as the icon or shadow for a marker

MarkerImage's Five Properties

Although `MarkerImage` has five properties, only the first one is required.

- **url**
  A URL pointing to an image. This property is required.

- **size**
  The size of the marker icon. This takes a `Size` object.

- **origin**
  The part of the image being used. (Does that sound cryptic? Don't worry, I'll explain it a little later when I talk about sprites.) This takes a `Point` object.

- **anchor**
  The part of the icon that is pointing at a location in the map. For the default marker it's the tip of the stem. If you don't set this value, it will be at the center at the bottom of the image. This takes a `Point` object.

- **scaledSize**
  This argument lets you display the image smaller or bigger than its original size. Note that if you use this property, you need to adjust the anchor to the scaled size of the image.

■ **Note** After a `MarkerImage` object has been created, it can't be changed. Therefore, if you need to change it, you have to discard it and create a new one.

Adding a Custom Icon to a Marker

Although the `MarkerImage` object contains properties that let you tweak it in different ways, in its simplest form, you need to provide only the first property, `url`. Let's call this variable `recycle` since it will have a recycle icon.

```
var recycle = new google.maps.MarkerImage('img/recycle.png');
```

What you get is a plain icon (Figure 6-1). It's nothing fancy, but you have a custom image.

Figure 6-1. A plain icon

Adding a Shadow

`MarkerOptions` has an additional property called `shadow` that works like `icon`. It also takes a `MarkerImage` object as its value. You will add a link to an image of a shadow to the `url` property. The image looks like Figure 6-2.

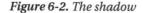

Figure 6-2. The shadow

It looks like it will fit nicely beneath the new marker icon. Let's name this variable `shadow` and point it to the image of the shadow:

```
var shadow = new google.maps.MarkerImage('img/shadow.png');
```

Putting It Together

Now that you've created objects for the marker and the shadow images, you can put it all together by using them as values for the icon and shadow properties of the `Marker` object. This will create a marker with a nice shadow that gives a 3D feel to the map (Figure 6-3).

```
var marker = new google.maps.Marker({
  position: new google.maps.LatLng(40.756054, -73.986951),
  map: map,
  icon: recycle,
  shadow: shadow
});
```

Figure 6-3. The shadow doesn't align nicely with the icon.

But wait, there's something wrong with how this looks. The shadow doesn't fit nicely beneath the icon at all. It looks like it's too far to the left.

Adjusting the Shadow

Let's examine the recycle marker more closely (Figure 6-4).

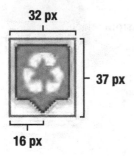

Figure 6-4. The dimensions of the icon

This icon is pretty symmetrical. Its anchor point, the point that will be anchored at a certain location in the map, is located at the bottom center. This position also happens to be the default anchor position of the MarkerImage object. This means that you don't need to give it special treatment for its anchor point to be at the right position.

Let's examine the shadow a bit closer (Figure 6-5).

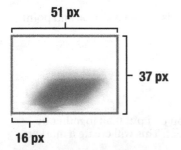

Figure 6-5. The dimensions of the shadow

The dimensions of this image are a bit different from the icons. It's wider and higher, but more importantly, the "tip" of the shadow is not in the center of the image but rather to the left. Since the default position of the anchor point is at the bottom center of the image, 26 pixels from the left, and the tip is positioned 16 pixels from the left, it will be positioned slightly (10 pixels) to the left (Figure 6-6).

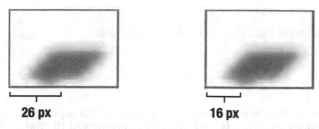

Figure 6-6. *The center point of the shadow*

You could fix this by changing the image so that the shadow's "tip" is in fact at the center and thereby at the same place as the default anchor position (Figure 6-7).

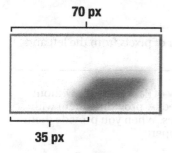

Figure 6-7. *Fixing the shadow image*

That's one way of doing it, but a better way is to use the property anchor of the "shadow" MarkerImage object. You know that the anchor point of the recycle icon is 16 pixels from the left and 37 pixels from the top. With this knowledge, you're set to make the appropriate adjustment.

What you need to do is to tell the MarkerImage object for the shadow to align its anchor point with the anchor point of the MarkerImage object of the marker icon. This is where the magic happens. By setting it to the same as the marker icon, it automatically positions the shadow at the correct position.

While you're at it, also move the shadow 2 pixels lower by setting the anchor point at 35 pixels from the top instead of 37 pixels (Figure 6-8).

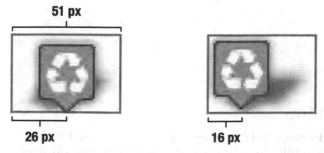

Figure 6-8. *Aligning the shadow*

■ **Note** The anchor point of the marker image and the anchor point of the shadow will always align.

Setting the Anchor Point

The anchor property takes a Point as its value. A Point is defined with an x and y value, which represents a two-dimensional plane (see Table 6-2). These values are in pixels. So if you give it a value x of 16, that means it will set the anchor at 16 pixels from the left edge of the image. Consequently, setting the value y to 35 will set the anchor point to 35 pixels down from the top of the image.

Table 6-2. Definition of Point

Constructor	Description
Point(x:number, y:number)	Defines a point in pixels where x is number of pixels from the left and y is number of pixels from the top

Now, how can you use the anchor property, which is the fourth property of MarkerImage, without using the preceding two properties, size and origin? Well, that's easily solved by providing them with the value null, which essentially means "nothing" in programming languages. When you provide them with that value, it's like they don't exist, but it enables you to set that last property.

Enough said. Let's take a look at the code for this:

```
// Creating a shadow
var shadow = new google.maps.MarkerImage(
  'img/shadow.png',
  null,
  null,
  new google.maps.Point(16, 35)
);
```

There! You've now defined the anchor point properly. And if you look at how the icon is displayed the shadow sits beautifully underneath the marker icon right where it should be (Figure 6-9).

Figure 6-9. The shadow is perfectly aligned with the icon.

Enabling and Disabling the Shadow

To enable or disable the shadow of the marker, the property flat of MarkerOptions can be used. If you set it to true, no shadow will be displayed. It's set to false by default, so use it only if you explicitly want to disable any use of a shadow.

Defining a Clickable Area

Sometimes the whole icon shouldn't be clickable. Often this is true when it has an irregular shape. Take, for example, the icons in Figure 6-10. The transparent parts of them shouldn't be clickable.

Figure 6-10. Examples of irregular-shaped icons

MarkerOptions has a property called shape. It is used to define which area of the icon is clickable and/or draggable. This is an optional attribute, and if it's not set, the API presumes that all parts of the marker image are clickable. It can, however, be used to explicitly define an area of the marker that is clickable/draggable (Figure 6-11).

Figure 6-11. The clickable area of the icon

shape takes an object literal with two properties: type and coord. The first one, type, defines what kind of shape is being used, and the second one, coord, is an array of points marking out the shape. The shape property actually works the same way as the attributes type and coord of the <area> element that are used to create clickable areas in an HTML image map. So if you familiar with them, you already know how to use this property. There are three shapes to choose from, and each one is provided to the type property as a string value. Depending on which one you choose, the coord property works a bit differently.

- **Rectangles (rect)**
  Rectangles are defined with the string value 'rect'. If you choose this one, you'll need to provide the coord property with two points, which marks the top-left and bottom-right corners of the rectangle.

- **Circlular (circ)**
  Circles are defined with the value 'circ'. Choosing this shape requires the coord property to have three values: x, y, and r where x and y marks the center of the circle and r defines its radius.

- **Polygons (poly)**
  Polygons are defined with the value 'poly' and consist of several points connected with lines, just like one of those connect-the-dots figures from a child's painting book. If you choose this shape, you'll have to provide the coord property with a series of x and y values that define each "dot." You can use as many as you like, and since polygons are a closed figure, the last point you define will be connected with the first.

The most useful of these shapes are probably the polygon, and in this example you're going to use just that. To define a polygon, you need a number of points that are defined with coordinate pairs of x and y values. They are in pixels and correspond to points in the image of the visible area of the icon. They are calculated in relation to the top-left corner of the image, which is always defined with 0,0.

A point located 4 pixels down and 4 pixels to the left is defined with 4,4. A point located 29 pixels to the left and 4 pixels down is defined with 29,4 and so on. Now you just plot each point in a comma-separated sequence of numbers until you have plotted the whole image, as shown in Figure 6-12.

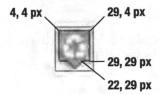

Figure 6-12. Some of the points for the shape

```
var shape = {
  type: 'poly',
  coord: [4,4, 29,4, 29,29, 22,29, 17,35, 16,35, 10,29, 4,29, 4,4]
}
```

Now you've defined the shape. To apply it to the custom marker, you add it using the shape property of the `MarkerImage` object:

```
// Adding a marker to the map
var marker = new google.maps.Marker({
  position: new google.maps.LatLng(40.756054, -73.986951),
  map: map,
  icon: wifi,
  shadow: shadow,
  shape: shape
});
```

Looking at the result that this code produces, you now have a map with a complex marker that has both a shadow and a defined clickable area (Figure 6-13).

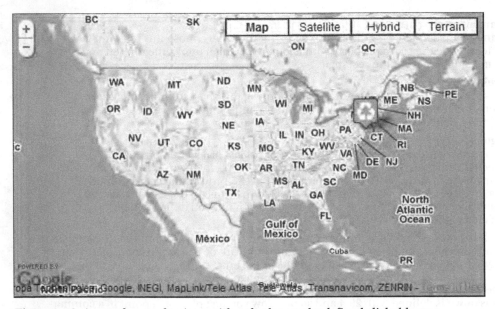

Figure 6-13. A complex marker icon with a shadow and a defined clickable area

The Complete Code

Listing 6-2 shows the complete code for this example.

Listing 6-2. Complete JavaScript Code for Example 6-1

```
(function() {
  window.onload = function() {

    // Creating a map
    var options = {
      zoom: 3,
      center: new google.maps.LatLng(37.09, -95.71),
      mapTypeId: google.maps.MapTypeId.ROADMAP
    };

    var map = new google.maps.Map(document.getElementById('map'), options);

    // Creating the recycle icon
    var recycle = new google.maps.MarkerImage('img/recycle.png');

    // Creating the shadow
    var shadow = new google.maps.MarkerImage(
      'img/shadow.png',
      null,
      null,
      new google.maps.Point(16, 35)
    );

    // Creating a shape
    var shape = {
      type: 'poly',
      coord: [4,4, 29,4, 29,29, 22,29, 17,35, 16,35, 10,29, 4,29, 4,4]
    }

    // Creating the marker
    var marker = new google.maps.Marker({
      position: new google.maps.LatLng(40.756054, -73.986951),
      map: map,
      icon: recycle,
      shadow: shadow,
      shape: shape
    });

  }
})();
```

Using Sprites

Using sprites is a technique that originally came from the early computer games. It's the practice of using one image that contains several small images. You display only part of the whole image at a time, which gives the illusion that it is actually just one image (Figure 6-14). This technique was first introduced in a web context by Dave Shea in the A list apart article "CSS Sprites: Image Slicing's Kiss of Death" (www.alistapart.com/articles/sprites).

Figure 6-14. A sprite. Only part of the image is displayed at a time.

This is a practice that is pretty common on the Web these days, and the Google Maps API uses it extensively (Figure 6-15). All the images for the standard controls that are used in the map are in sprites.

Figure 6-15. A sprite containing the control elements of a standard Google map

One of the biggest reasons for using sprites is something called *latency*.

Latency

It takes longer to download several small files than one big one. There are several reasons for this. The first reason is that it takes the browser a while from requesting a file to actually start downloading it. So if it has to do that only once, time is saved. The second reason is that browsers have a built-in limitation in how many files they can download simultaneously from the same domain. Most browsers are limited to three simultaneous downloads. What this means is that it can't start downloading new files until one of those slots gets freed up. Therefore, a great way to enhance performance is to reduce the number of files it has to download.

Sprite Support

`MarkerImage` objects supports the use of sprites, so instead of using one icon for each marker icon, you can use one sprite image containing several icons. You do this by using the second argument of `MarkerImage`, `size`, in conjunction with the third argument, `origin`.

The `size` argument defines how big the visible part of the image should be. When you used a regular image for the marker icon, this property wasn't necessary since you wanted to use the entire image. But now when you just want to use part of the entire image, it becomes really important. It's defined by using an object of type `Size`.

■ **Note** Actually, it's a good idea to always define the `size` property since it provides a small performance boost. The reason for this is that the browser doesn't need to calculate the size of the image.

A `Size` object is always a rectangle, and a rectangle has two dimensions, a width and a height (see Table 6-3). Consequently, the `Size` object has two properties, `width` and `height`. Width defines the x-axis of the rectangle, and height defines the y-axis. By default these values are measured in pixels, but you could use other units if you like. To construct a `Size` object, you have to provide it with the two required arguments, `width` and `height`, but you could also provide it with two optional arguments, which are the units you want to use for each axis.

Table 6-3. Definition of Size

Constructor	Description
`Size(width:number, height:number, widthUnit?:string, heightUnit?:string)`	Defines a size

Origin takes a google.maps.Point as its value, and it defines where the starting point of the "hole" in the sprite that will be displayed is located. Did that make sense to you? Well, consider this example.

If you have one image per marker icon, you probably want to set origin to 0,0, since that is the top-left corner of the image. But if you have a sprite, like the one shown in Figure 6-14 earlier, and want to display a green Wi-Fi icon, which is the one in the middle, you want to set it to something else.

First you need to define the size of the image. This defines a box. Then you need to define where to position that box inside the sprite, which is done with origin. In this case, it's 34 pixels from the left edge of the image and 0 pixels from the top (Figure 6-16).

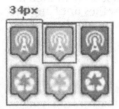

Figure 6-16. The position in the sprite for the green Wi-Fi icon

```
var image = new google.maps.MarkerImage(
  'img/markers.png',
  new google.maps.Size(32, 37),  // The size
  new google.maps.Point(34, 0),  // The origin
  new google.maps.Point(16, 35)  // The anchor
);
```

You also need to change the value for the icon property in the code that creates the marker to image:

```
// Creating the marker
  var marker = new google.maps.Marker({
  position: new google.maps.LatLng(40.756054, -73.986951),
  map: map,
  icon: image,
  shadow: shadow
});
```

This code will just take the part with the middle Wi-Fi icon and use it as the marker icon, as shown in Figure 6-17.

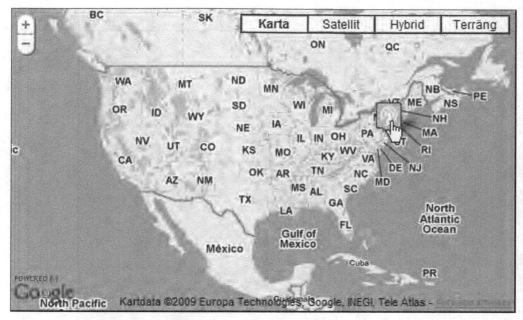

Figure 6-17. *A sprite being used as a marker icon*

If you change the origin parameter to a square that starts at 65 pixels from the left, you will get the right-most icon instead (Figure 6-18).

```
var image = new google.maps.MarkerImage(
  'img/markers.png',
  new google.maps.Size(32, 37),  // The Size
  new google.maps.Point(65, 0),  // The origin
  new google.maps.Point(16, 35)  // The anchor
);
```

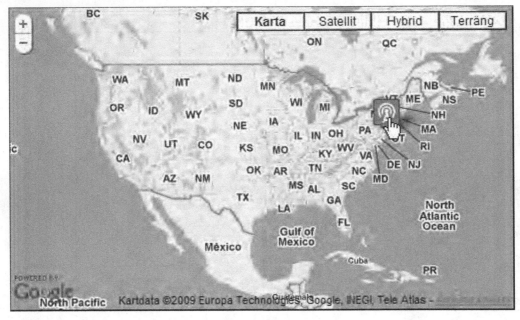

Figure 6-18. A different Wi-Fi icon in the sprite is visible.

■ **Note** Shape objects (if used) have to be created separately for each sprite position.

The Complete Code

Listing 6-3 shows the complete code for the example using sprites.

Listing 6-3. Complete JavaScript Code for Example 6-2

```
(function() {
  window.onload = function() {

    // Creating a map
    var options = {
      zoom: 3,
      center: new google.maps.LatLng(37.09, -95.71),
      mapTypeId: google.maps.MapTypeId.ROADMAP
    };

    var map = new google.maps.Map(document.getElementById('map'), options);

    // Creating the icon using a sprite
    var image = new google.maps.MarkerImage(
```

```
    'img/markers.png',
    new google.maps.Size(32, 37),   // The Size
    new google.maps.Point(65, 0),   // The origin
    new google.maps.Point(16, 35)   // The anchor
  );

  // Creating the shadow
  var shadow = new google.maps.MarkerImage(
    'img/shadow.png',
    null,
    null,
    new google.maps.Point(16, 35)
  );

  // Creating the marker
  var marker = new google.maps.Marker({
    position: new google.maps.LatLng(40.756054, -73.986951),
    map: map,
    icon: image,
    shadow: shadow
  });

  }
})();
```

Where to Find Icons

There are several resources on the Web for finding icons. Here's a few that I've found useful, but there are many more out there.

google-maps-icons

This is a collection of more than 900 map icons to use as markers for points of interests. The creator of this collection is Nico Mollet. Most of the icons used in this chapter are taken from this collection (Figure 6-19).

```
http://code.google.com/p/google-maps-icons/
```

Figure 6-19. A few of the icons found in the Tourism & Nature set of google-maps-icons

Google Maps: Colored Markers

This is a collection of Google Maps marker like icons but in different colors and with letters and numbers in them (Figure 6-20).

`http://www.benjaminkeen.com/?p=105`

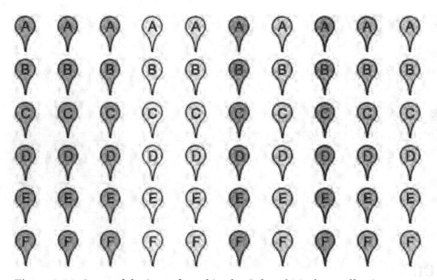

Figure 6-20. Some of the icons found in the Colored Markers collection

Mapito Map Marker Icons

This collection features a very compact marker icon with a number in it ranging from 1 to 99 (Figure 6-21). They come in two shades of blue and can be used freely if you provide a link to its page somewhere on your web site.

`http://www.mapito.net/map-marker-icons.html`

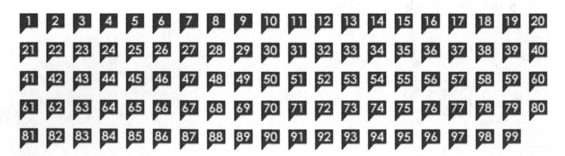

Figure 6-21. One of the two icon sets provided by Mapito

Changing the Marker Icon According to Mouse Events

Changing the look of something when the user hovers with the mouse over it is a great way to provide the user with additional feedback. It enhances the feeling of a responsive user interface and gives the user nice little clues that he can interact with an object.

With the help of mouse events, you can alter the state of the marker. This can be used to change how the marker looks by changing its icon.

As already mentioned, a marker can have different states. The most common are the following:

- **Normal**
  This is its normal look.

- **Hover**
  This happens when the user holds the mouse pointer over the marker. This is actually two events, mouseover and mouseout. Mouseover happens when the mouse pointer enters the area above the marker, and mouseout happens when it leaves.

- **Click**
  This is when the user presses the left mouse button while holding the pointer over the marker and is fetched with the mousedown event.

- **Selected**
  This typically happens when the user has clicked the marker. It's fetched with the mouseup event. As the name implies, mouseup happens when the user releases the mouse button while still holding the pointer over the marker and always happens after a mousedown event.

To change the look of the marker according to its current state, you need to use events. But first you need to define how the marker will look in its different states (see Table 6-4). I'm going to change the color of the marker. So, its normal color will be orange. When the user hovers with the mouse pointer over it, it will be green, and on a click it will turn blue.

Table 6-4. States of the Marker

Icon	State	Event
	Normal	(mouseout)
	Hover	mouseover
	Click	mousedown

You will start by defining the icons. Since a MarkerImage cannot be changed once it's been created, you will have to make three different ones, one for each state.

Defining the MarkerImages

You're going to use the same sprite that you created a few pages ago for this example too.

Normal state

This is the way the marker will normally look. Since this part of the sprite is in the top-left corner, you're going to set the origin parameter to google.maps.Point(0, 0).

```
var wifi = new google.maps.MarkerImage(
  'img/markers.png',
  new google.maps.Size(32, 37),
  new google.maps.Point(0, 0),
  new google.maps.Point(16, 35)
);
```

Hover State

This is the MarkerImage that will be used when the user holds the mouse pointer over the marker. Name it wifiHover so that it's clear what it's for. It will be the green part of the sprite. The only difference from the normal state is that you're changing the origin parameter to google.maps.Point(33, 0).

```
var wifiHover = new google.maps.MarkerImage(
  'img/markers.png',
  new google.maps.Size(32, 37),
  new google.maps.Point(33, 0),
  new google.maps.Point(16, 35)
);
```

Click State

Call this MarkerImage wifiClick. The only difference from the others is the origin parameter, which you will set to google.maps.Point(66, 0).

```
var wifiClick = new google.maps.MarkerImage(
  'img/markers.png',
  new google.maps.Size(32, 37),
  new google.maps.Point(66, 0),
  new google.maps.Point(16, 35)
);
```

Adding the Events

There, you've defined three MarkerImage objects for the different states of the marker. The next step is to add the events.

Hover

To add the hover state to the marker, you need to use two events, mouseover and mouseout. Mouseover is activated when the user moves the mouse pointer over the clickable area of the marker. It's added with the google.maps.event.addListener() method. What it does is to run some code when it's activated.

The code you will run is to call the markers setIcon() method. It changes the icon of the marker, and you will pass wifiHover as its parameter.

```
google.maps.event.addListener(marker, 'mouseover', function() {
  this.setIcon(wifiHover);
});
```

This will change the look of the marker to the green Wi-Fi icon. The problem is that it will stay that way even if the user moves the mouse pointer away from the marker. To remedy this, you need to add another event, the mouseout event:

```
google.maps.event.addListener(marker, 'mouseout', function() {
  this.setIcon(wifi);
});
```

This pretty much does the same thing as the mouseover event; the main difference is that it changes the MarkerImage back to the original one. With that in place, the hover state is working and provides the user with a subtle signal that this is a marker that he can interact with.

Click

The next thing you want to do is to add a click event to the marker. The purpose is to provide the user with feedback that he actually clicked the marker. It's done by using the mousedown event.

```
google.maps.event.addListener(marker, 'mousedown', function() {
  this.setIcon(wifiClick);
});
```

After the user has released the mouse button (mouseup), you want to the marker to return to its original state that in this case is mouseover state.

```
google.maps.event.addListener(marker, 'mouseup', function() {
  this.setIcon(wifiHover);
});
```

And that's it! You now have a marker that provides visual feedback while the user is interacting with it (Figure 6-22).

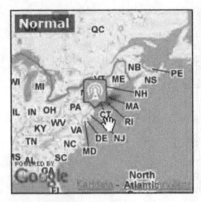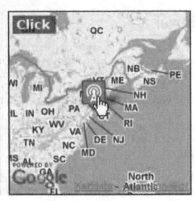

Figure 6-22. The different states of the marker

The Complete Code

Listing 6-4 shows the complete code for doing this.

Listing 6-4. Complete JavaScript Code for Example 6-3

```
(function() {
  window.onload = function() {
    // Creating a LatLng object containing the coordinate for the center of the map
    var latlng = new google.maps.LatLng(37.09, -95.71);

    // Creating an object literal containing the properties you want to pass to the map
    var options = {
      zoom: 3,
      center: latlng,
      mapTypeId: google.maps.MapTypeId.ROADMAP
    };

    // Calling the constructor, thereby initializing the map
    var map = new google.maps.Map(document.getElementById('map'), options);

    // Defining different MarkerImages for different states
    var wifi = new google.maps.MarkerImage(
      'img/markers.png',
      new google.maps.Size(32, 37),
      new google.maps.Point(0, 0),
      new google.maps.Point(16, 35)
    );

    var wifiHover = new google.maps.MarkerImage(
      'img/markers.png',
      new google.maps.Size(32, 37),
      new google.maps.Point(33, 0),
      new google.maps.Point(16, 35)
    );
```

```
var wifiClick = new google.maps.MarkerImage(
  'img/markers.png',
  new google.maps.Size(32, 37),
  new google.maps.Point(66, 0),
  new google.maps.Point(16, 35)
);

// Defining the shadow image for the marker
var shadow = new google.maps.MarkerImage(
  'img/shadow.png',
  new google.maps.Size(51, 37),
  new google.maps.Point(0, 0),
  new google.maps.Point(16, 35)
);

// Adding a marker to the map
var marker = new google.maps.Marker({
  position: new google.maps.LatLng(40.756054, -73.986951),
  map: map,
  icon: wifi,
  shadow: shadow
});

// Adding events that will alter the look of the marker


// Hover
google.maps.event.addListener(marker, 'mouseover', function() {
  this.setIcon(wifiHover);
});

google.maps.event.addListener(marker, 'mouseout', function() {
  this.setIcon(wifi);
});

// Click
google.maps.event.addListener(marker, 'mousedown', function() {
  this.setIcon(wifiClick);
});

google.maps.event.addListener(marker, 'mouseup', function() {
  this.setIcon(wifiHover);
});

  }
})();
```

A Clever Way of Dealing with Lots of Different Marker Icons

In some applications that use a lot of different marker icons on the map, managing these icons can be a problem. You have to define a new MarkerImage for each different marker type, and you will have a massive if clause to handle which MarkerImage to use in each particular case.

One technique to make all of this more manageable is to store all your MarkerImage objects in an array.

You previously learned that each item in an array has an index. In JavaScript it's possible to use a more descriptive label than an index to mark each item. This is called an *associative array*. What it means is that instead of getting an array item by its index number, you can get it by its label.

```
var fruit = [];
fruit['apples'] = 20;
fruit['oranges'] = 10;
fruit['bananas'] = 15;
```

To access the number of oranges, you simply call the array with the label oranges.

```
fruit['oranges']; // returns 10
```

You'll utilize this to manage your MarkerImage objects. In this example, you're going to plot weather onto a map. To do this, you'll need several different icons that indicate what the weather is like (see Table 6-5). You're just going to use three different weather types for the brevity of the example, but as you can imagine, if this were a real weather map, you would need a lot more.

Table 6-5. Weather Icons

Icon	Weather	Filename
	Cloudy weather	clouds.png
	Rainy weather	rain.png
	Sunny weather	sun.png

These are just a few of the icons available in the Tango Weather Icon pack, which is free for commercial use. You can download it from http://darkobra.deviantart.com/art/Tango-Weather-Icon-Pack-98024429.

You start by defining the array that will contain the icons:

```
var weatherIcons = [];
```

Now that you have an array, you will start adding MarkerImage objects to it. Let's start with the clouds icon:

```
// Adding the clouds icon
weatherIcons['clouds'] = new google.maps.MarkerImage(
  'img/clouds.png',
  new google.maps.Size(48, 48),
  null,
  new google.maps.Point(24, 24)
);
```

Notice how you create a new MarkerImage at the same time as you pass it to the array. The value of this particular array item is now a fully fledged MarkerImage object.

Creating the MarkerImage contains no surprises. You pass the four parameters to the constructor of the MarkerImage object just like you did in the previous examples. To recap what they are, the first parameter is the URL to the image file. The second parameter is the size of the icon, which in this case is 48 × 48 pixels. The third parameter is the origin, which is used only with sprites, so you pass a null value to it since you don't need it here. The fourth parameter sets the anchor, and you want to set it to the center of the icon so that it centers nicely over the correct point in the map.

Let's add the other two weather icons as well:

```
// Adding the rain icon
weatherIcons['rain'] = new google.maps.MarkerImage(
  'img/rain.png',
  new google.maps.Size(48, 48),
  null,
  new google.maps.Point(24, 24)
);

// Adding the sun icon
weatherIcons['sun'] = new google.maps.MarkerImage(
  'img/sun.png',
  new google.maps.Size(48, 48),
  null,
  new google.maps.Point(24, 24)
);
```

You now have all three marker types set up and ready to use. To create a marker and add it to the map, you call the constructor of the Marker object as normal and define the properties position and map. The interesting part is how you pass the value for the icon property. In this case, you want to use the MarkerImage that represents cloudy weather.

```
// Adding a "cloud" marker over New York
var marker = new google.maps.Marker({
  position: new google.maps.LatLng(40.756054, -73.986951),
  map: map,
  icon: weatherIcons['clouds']
});
```

Look how you simply call the weatherIcons array and use the "clouds" label for it to return the right MarkerImage.

Adding Dynamic Data

This type of data is probably dynamic. Let's say that the weather data is fetched from a weather web service that returns that data in JSON format. Since it will provide different kinds of weather, it will most likely have a property containing the weather type. If you make sure to have the same labels in your arrays as the values for the data object's weatherType, you can automatically get the correct MarkerImage by passing that value directly to the array.

Did that sound confusing? Let me show you what I mean. Assume that you make an Ajax call to a weather service that will return the following data:

```
{'weather': [
  {
    'lat': 40.756054,
    'lng': -73.986951,
    'weatherType': 'clouds'
  },
  {
    'lat': 47.620973,
    'lng': -122.347276,
    'weatherType': 'rain'
  },
  {
    'lat': 37.775206,
    'lng': -122.419209,
    'weatherType': 'sun'
  }
]};
```

As you can see, this is an object that contains a property called weather. The value of weather is an array that contains a list of weather objects. These weather objects each have three properties: lat, lng, and weatherType. lat and lng define the center for the weather observation, and weatherType defines what kind of weather it is. Notice its values: clouds, rain, and sun. It's the same names that you used as labels in the associative array. Since they are the same, you can use these values straightaway to determine which MarkerImage to use.

■ **Note** If you want to learn more about JSON, http://json.org is a great starting point.

Faking an Ajax Call

You're going to fake the Ajax call that fetches the weather data. You're going to do this by defining it directly it in the code instead of grabbing it from a web service. Create a variable called weatherData that will hold the data. (Imagine that you make an Ajax call to a weather service that returns this data.)

```
// Creating a JSON object with weather data
var weatherData = {'weather': [
  {
    'lat': 40.756054,
    'lng': -73.986951,
    'weatherType': 'clouds'
  },
```

```
  {
    'lat': 47.620973,
    'lng': -122.347276,
    'weatherType': 'rain'
  },
  {
    'lat': 37.775206,
    'lng': -122.419209,
    'weatherType': 'sun'
  }
]};
```

With this data available, you now need to create a loop that iterates through all the weather objects and adds them to the map. Let's do this by creating a for loop that will iterate through all the weather objects in the weatherData array. For convenience, you're going to create a variable called weather at the top of the loop that will hold the current weather object.

```
for (var i = 0; i < weatherData.weather.length; i++) {
  // creating a variable that will hold the current weather object
  var weather = weatherData.weather[i];
}
```

This isn't strictly necessary, but by creating the variable weather, the code will be a little tidier. Instead of having to write weatherData.weather[i] for each place you want to use its properties, you can now simply write weather.

The next step is to actually create the marker.

```
for (var i = 0; i < weatherData.weather.length; i++) {
  // creating a variable that will hold the current weather object
  var weather = weatherData.weather[i];

  // Creating marker
  var marker = new google.maps.Marker({
    position: new google.maps.LatLng(weather.lat, weather.lng),
    map: map,
    icon: weatherIcons[weather.weatherType]
  });
}
```

Pay particular attention to the value of the icon property. By simply inserting weather.weatherType as the label to weatherIcons, it automatically returns the correct MarkerImage object. There's no need for lengthy if statements to determine what MarkerImage to use. It makes the code both more succinct and in my opinion more beautiful.

Figure 6-23 shows what the map will look like.

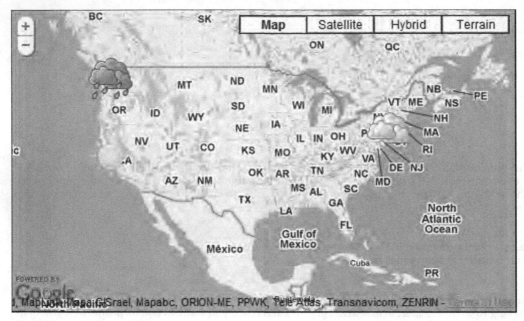

Figure 6-23. The weather map

The Complete Code

Listing 6-5 shows the complete code for this example.

Listing 6-5. Complete JavaScript Code for Example 6-4

```
(function() {

// Creating an array that will contain all of our weather icons
var weatherIcons = [];

weatherIcons['clouds'] = new google.maps.MarkerImage(
  'img/clouds.png',
  new google.maps.Size(48, 48),
  null,
  new google.maps.Point(24, 24)
);

weatherIcons['rain'] = new google.maps.MarkerImage(
  'img/rain.png',
  new google.maps.Size(48, 48),
  null,
  new google.maps.Point(24, 24)
);

weatherIcons['sun'] = new google.maps.MarkerImage(
```

```
      'img/sun.png',
      new google.maps.Size(48, 48),
      null,
      new google.maps.Point(24, 24)
  );

  window.onload = function() {

    // Creating a map
    var options = {
      zoom: 3,
      center: new google.maps.LatLng(37.09, -95.71),
      mapTypeId: google.maps.MapTypeId.ROADMAP
    };
    var map = new google.maps.Map(document.getElementById('map'), options);

    // Creating a JSON object with weather data
    var weatherData = {'weather': [
      {
        'lat': 40.756054,
        'lng': -73.986951,
        'weatherType': 'clouds'
      },
      {
        'lat': 47.620973,
        'lng': -122.347276,
        'weatherType': 'rain'
      },
      {
        'lat': 37.775206,
        'lng': -122.419209,
        'weatherType': 'sun'
      }
    ]};

    // Looping through the weather array in weatherData
    for (var i = 0; i < weatherData.weather.length; i++) {

      // creating a variable that will hold the current weather object
      var weather = weatherData.weather[i];

      // Creating marker
      var marker = new google.maps.Marker({
        position: new google.maps.LatLng(weather.lat, weather.lng),
        map: map,
        icon: weatherIcons[weather.weatherType]
      });

    }

  }
})();
```

Benefits

By taking this approach, you gain two things:

- You need to define each MarkerImage in one place. Imagine that you have a web application that has maps on different pages that uses the same icons. To change an icon, you need to do it in only one place.

- Instead of using a big if clause to determine which MarkerImage to use, you can pass the type name to the array and automatically get the right MarkerImage back.

Since the example contained only three weather observations and three different kinds of weathers, it would have been pretty easy to write even without using this approach. But imagine having hundreds of weather observations and 20 different weather types; then the true value of this approach becomes apparent.

Creating a Custom Marker Icon

If you can't find suitable premade icons, you can create your own. Several tools are available online to create marker icons or for creating shadows for your icons, or you could create one all by yourself using some image-editing software, such as Adobe Photoshop.

If you do decide to create your own icons, you should keep two things in mind:

- The icon should be a 24-bit PNG image with alpha transparency.

- The shadow should be in a 45-degree direction leaning up to the right.

Online Tools

If you don't want to create your own icons from scratch, there are several online tools available. A few of them are listed next.

Google Map Custom Marker Maker

This tool is for Google Maps API v2, but it can still be used to create marker shadows for your icons. It also generates some other Google Maps API v2–specific images and example code. By using common sense, I'm sure you'll be able to use this information to incorporate in your Google Maps API v3 solutions.

```
http://www.powerhut.co.uk/googlemaps/custom_markers.php
```

Google Maps Icon Shadowmaker

This is a great tool that automatically creates a shadow for your images. You upload your image, and it creates a shadow and previews of how it will look. Do note, however, that the example code it generates for adding the MarkerImage is code for Google Maps API v2. But you can easily extract the information to use in your Google Maps API v3 code.

```
http://www.cycloloco.com/shadowmaker/shadowmaker.htm
```

mapicon Factory

With this tool you can create a wide variety of marker icons. To get access to all features, you have to pay an annual fee, but if you can get by using only the basic features, it's free of charge.

`http://www.cartosoft.com/mapicons/`

Summary

In this chapter, you learned how to use complex icons. You also looked at how to use sprites to increase performance and to add a greater level of interactivity to your maps. Toward the end of the chapter, you also examined a technique for managing lots of different map icons.

Markers are great for marking locations on a map. But when you need to provide more information about that location, InfoWindow objects are an invaluable tool. In Chapter 5, you looked at how to create basic InfoWindow objects. In the next chapter, you will dig deeper into the API to see what's possible with them.

InfoWindow Tips and Tricks

In the old Google Maps API (version 2), you could do all sorts of things with InfoWindows. It has features such as tabbed windows, showing a detail map of the place you clicked, a maximize function, and so on. In Google Maps API 3 you basically have only the absolute minimum feature set, such as opening an InfoWindow and filling it with content. In this chapter, I will, however, show you how to build some of the functionality that the old API has. But first you'll look at how to fill the InfoWindow with rich content using HTML.

Setting a Starting Point

Before getting into the actual examples, you will set a starting point for all of them. This is the code that all the examples will start with. It will provide you with a page that contains a basic map with a marker on it.

No surprises here. It's a plain ol' HTML page, just like the ones you've been using in the previous chapters (Listing 7-1).

Listing 7-1. The HTML

```
<!DOCTYPE html PUBLIC "-//W3C//DTD XHTML 1.0 Strict//EN"
    "http://www.w3.org/TR/xhtml1/DTD/xhtml1-strict.dtd">

<html xmlns="http://www.w3.org/1999/xhtml" lang="en">
  <head>
    <meta http-equiv="Content-Type" content="text/html; charset=utf-8" />
    <title>Chapter 7 - InfoWindows Tips and Tricks</title>
    <link rel="stylesheet" href="css/style.css" type="text/css" media="all" />
    <script type="text/javascript"
      src="http://maps.google.com/maps/api/js?sensor=false"></script>
    <script type="text/javascript" src="js/7-x.js"></script>
  </head>
  <body>
    <div id="map"></div>
  </body>
</html>
```

The map will be filling the entire page (Figure 7-1).

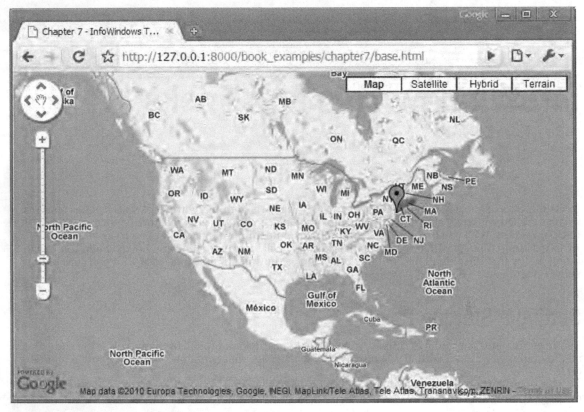

Figure 7-1. The base map as it will look in Google Chrome

Style Sheet

The style sheet provides some basic styling (Listing 7-2). What's different from the previous examples is that the map will span the whole page. Worth mentioning is that to make this work across most browsers, the height must be set to 100 percent for the HTML, body, and map.

Listing 7-2. The CSS

```
html, body {
  height: 100%;
  font-family: Verdana, Geneva, Arial, Helvetica, sans-serif;
  font-size: small;
  margin: 0;
}
#map {
  width: 100%;
  height: 100%;
}
```

JavaScript

The JavaScript creates a map and adds a marker with a click event to it (Listing 7-3).

Listing 7-3. The Initial JavaScript

```
(function() {

  // Defining variables that need to be available to some functions
  var map, infoWindow;

  window.onload = function() {

    // Creating a map
    var options = {
      zoom: 3,
      center: new google.maps.LatLng(37.09, -95.71),
      mapTypeId: google.maps.MapTypeId.ROADMAP
    };

    map = new google.maps.Map(document.getElementById('map'), options);

    // Adding a marker
    var marker = new google.maps.Marker({
      position: new google.maps.LatLng(40.756054, -73.986951),
      map: map,
      title: 'Click me'
    });

    google.maps.event.addListener(marker, 'click', function() {
      // Code that happens after click
    });

  };

})();
```

With the base set, you can move on to the examples.

Adding Rich Content to the InfoWindow

In Chapter 5, you looked at some basic usage of InfoWindows. You looked at how to create them and how to fill them with basic text. Now you're going to take this one step further by adding full HTML to them.

There's nothing magical about InfoWindows; they're really just HTML containers. Think of them as just another part of the web page. And just like all other parts of a web page, you can fill this part with whatever content you like.

There are two ways of adding content to an InfoWindow. The first, and perhaps most straightforward way, is to provide an InfoWindow with a string that contains all the HTML. The other way is to provide it with a reference to an existing HTML node. This HTML node can either already exist in the document or be one that you create with JavaScript.

In this first example, you're going to add content to an InfoWindow using a string.

Providing the HTML As a String

In this example, you will create an InfoWindow that will contain an image a heading, some text, and a link. The image you will use is of a squirrel with the dimensions 100 × 100 pixels. It's included in the code that comes with the book. The final HTML will look like this:

```
<div id="info">
  <img src="img/squirrel.jpg" alt="" />
  <h2>Maps are awesome</h2>
  <p>Some sample text</p>
  <p><a href="http://www.svennerberg.com">A sample link</a></p>
</div>
```

Notice that the HTML elements are enclosed inside <div id="info">. You're doing this because you want to be able to pinpoint this content from the style sheet.

The end result will look like Figure 7-2.

Figure 7-2. *An InfoWindow with styled HTML in it*

Before you create the content, you will have to make sure that you have a InfoWindow object. You will use the same approach as described in Chapter 5 where you define a global variable called infoWindow that you reuse for each window that is opened. Each time the user clicks a marker, you check whether the variable infoWindow contains an InfoWindow object. If it doesn't contain one, you create it. You've already defined the infoWindow variable at the top of the code. You now need to check whether it exists:

```
// Check to see if an InfoWindow already exists
if (!infoWindow) {
  infoWindow = new google.maps.InfoWindow();
}
```

Now that you have an InfoWindow object in place, you can create the content for it. First you create a string that will contain all the HTML. Store this string in a variable called content:

```
var content = '<div id="info">' +
  '<img src="img/squirrel.jpg" alt="" />' +
  '<h2>Maps are awesome</h2>' +
  '<p>Some sample text</p>' +
  '<p><a href="http://www.svennerberg.com">A sample link</a></p>' +
  '</div>';
```

■ **Note** Notice how you add the different string fragments using +. This is called *concatenation* and is an easy way of connecting strings with each other.

Next you will set the content of the InfoWindow to the variable content and open it. This is done by using its setContent() method. Finally, you will open it using the open() method.

```
// Setting the content of the InfoWindow
infoWindow.setContent(content);

// Opening the InfoWindow
infoWindow.open(map, marker);
```

The final event listener code will look like this:

```
google.maps.event.addListener(marker, 'click', function() {

  // Check to see if an InfoWindow already exists
  if (!infoWindow) {
    infoWindow = new google.maps.InfoWindow();
  }

  // Creating the content
  var content = '<div id="info">' +
    '<img src="img/squirrel.jpg" alt="" />' +
    '<h2>Maps are awesome</h2>' +
    '<p>Some sample text</p>' +
    '<p><a href="http://www.svennerberg.com">A sample link</a></p>' +
    '</div>';

  // Setting the content of the InfoWindow
  infoWindow.setContent(content);

  // Opening the InfoWindow
  infoWindow.open(map, marker);
});
```

Styling the Content

You need to do some styling to make the content look a bit nicer. You will do this by modifying `style.css` that resides in the `css` folder.

First you want the image to float to the left of the other content. You also want to add some whitespace to the right of the image:

```
#info img {
  float: left;
  margin-right: 10px;
}
```

This will float the image to the left just as expected, but it will also break the heading. See Figure 7-3.

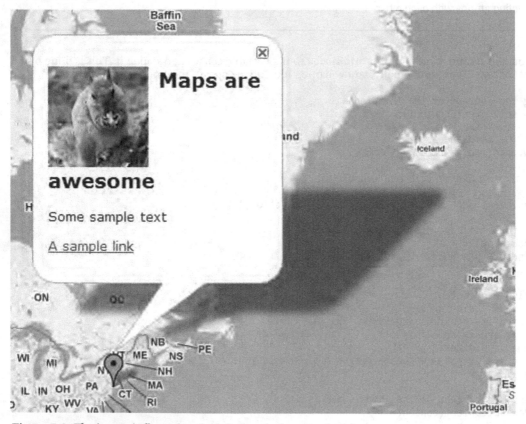

Figure 7-3. The image is floated to the left, but the heading breaks.

To fix this, you need to increase the width of the `InfoWindow`. You're going to do that by setting the width of `<div id="info">` to 350 pixels. While you're at it, you also going to make sure that the heading sits at the top of the `InfoWindow` by setting its upper margin to 0.

```
#info {
  width: 350px;
}

#info h2 {
  margin-top: 0;
}
```

This will fix the issues and make the InfoWindow look just the way you want it to look.

■ **Note** The size of the InfoWindow is determined with a combination of your styled size, the content of the InfoWindow, and the size of the map. So, for example, if the map is too small to fit the InfoWindow nicely, the API will reduce the size of it. The consequence of this is that the InfoWindow now might have scrollbars because the content no longer fits inside it.

Triggering Events

Even though the InfoWindow now looks the way you want it, let's add one extra thing: the InfoWindow will open automatically as the page loads.

It's possible to trigger events by using the google.maps.event.trigger() method. It takes two required arguments; the first argument is the object you want to trigger, and the second argument is the event type (see Table 7-1). To trigger your marker's click event, you'll need to pass the marker variable and the string 'click' to the method.

```
google.maps.event.trigger(marker, 'click');
```

This will cause the InfoWindow to open when the page is loaded.

Table 7-1. Definition of the trigger() Method

Method	Return value	Description
trigger(target:Object, eventName:string, args?:*)	None	Triggers an event at the targeted object. All arguments passed after the eventName are passed to the listeners. These are all optional.

The Complete Code

The following sections show the complete code.

The JavaScript Code

Listing 7-4 shows the JavaScript.

Listing 7-4. The Complete JavaScript Code for Example 7-1

```
(function() {

  // Defining variables that need to be available to some functions
  var map, infoWindow;

  window.onload = function() {

    // Creating a map
    var options = {
      zoom: 3,
      center: new google.maps.LatLng(37.09, -95.71),
      mapTypeId: google.maps.MapTypeId.ROADMAP
    };

    map = new google.maps.Map(document.getElementById('map'), options);

    // Adding a marker
    var marker = new google.maps.Marker({
      position: new google.maps.LatLng(40.756054, -73.986951),
      map: map,
      title: 'Click me'
    });

    google.maps.event.addListener(marker, 'click', function() {

      // Check to see if an InfoWindow already exists
      if (!infoWindow) {
        infoWindow = new google.maps.InfoWindow();
      }

      // Creating the content
      var content = '<div id="info">' +
        '<img src="img/squirrel.jpg" alt="" />' +
        '<h2>Maps are awesome</h2>' +
        '<p>Some sample text</p>' +
        '<p><a href="http://www.svennerberg.com">A sample link</a></p>' +
        '</div>';

      // Setting the content of the InfoWindow
      infoWindow.setContent(content);

      // Opening the InfoWindow
      infoWindow.open(map, marker);

    });

    // Triggering the click event
    google.maps.event.trigger(marker, 'click');

  };

})();
```

The Complete CSS for the InfoWindow

Listing 7-5 shows the CSS.

Listing 7-5. The Complete CSS for the InfoWindow

```
#info {
  width: 350px;
}

#info h2 {
  margin-top: 0;
}

#info img {
  float: left;
  margin-right: 10px;
}
```

Inserting a Video Using HTML5

With HTML 5 you will be able to do a lot of things that you need third-party plug-ins for now. One of these things is video playback. Today the dominant technique is to use Flash or Silverlight. But because HTML5 has native support for video, there's no need for that. It's no harder inserting a video than it is inserting an image.

Browser Support

It's important to note that the HTML 5 specification is still in draft form, so it can't be used as a full-fledged alternative yet. There is, however, surprisingly widespread support for it in most modern web browsers. Because of this, you can use it right now. You must be aware, though, that it will only work in browsers that support it.

As of the time of writing, which is summer 2010, the web browsers that support HTML video are Google Chrome 4 and 5, Firefox 3.6, Opera 10.5, and Safari 4. Not surprisingly, the current versions of Internet Explorer do not support this, but it looks like IE9 will have support for it.

The site findmebyIP features a great page for checking browser support for HTML5 (and CSS3). It can be found at www.findmebyip.com/litmus (see Figure 7-4).

Figure 7-4. Browser support for HTML5 video, taken from http://findmebyip.com/litmus

---

■ **Tip** The site findmebyip.com is great for checking browser support for all the HTML 5 features.

Altering the HTML

For this example, you're going to do a slight adjustment of the HTML file. You will need to change the doctype declaration from XHTML 1.0 to HTML5. At the top of the HTML file, exchange the existing doctype for the following:

```
<!DOCTYPE html>
```

Having done that, you're done editing the HTML file. This is one of the beauties of HTML5. The XHTML 1.0 code run as HTML5 is perfectly valid, so you don't have to redo anything. Still, you get a whole lot of new elements and capabilities to play around with. Let's check out the <video> element.

Examining the <video> Element

The <video> element works a lot like the <img> element but has a few extra attributes. The minimum you have to define is the src attribute.

```
<video src="movie.ogv"></video>
```

This will insert a video in the web page, but the user will have to right-click it and choose Play from the context menu. If you want the video to start playing right away and provide the user with a better control panel, you can use the attributes autoplay and controls.

```
<video src="movie.ogv" autoplay="autoplay" controls="controls"></video>
```

Now you have a video that starts right away and has a control panel. The control panel will look different in different browsers depending on how they've implemented it. Figure 7-5 shows how it will look in Google Chrome.

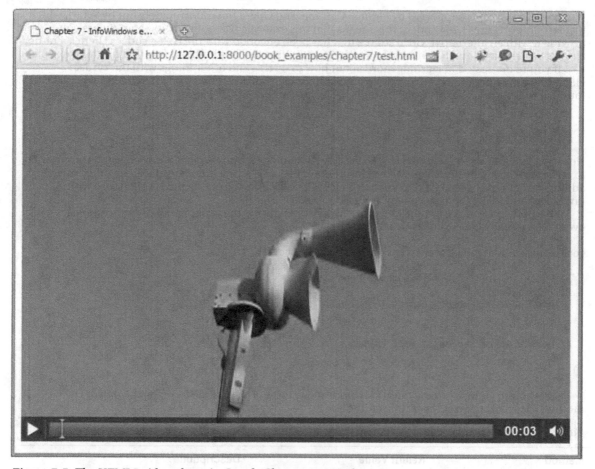

Figure 7-5. The HTML5 video player in Google Chrome on Windows

Two other useful attributes are width and height. With these you control the size of the video. If you omit them, the video player will default to the size of the video being played.

Supported Video Formats

You might have noticed the name of the video file being used. It's of the type Ogg Theora video codec, which is why it has the suffix .ogv, for Ogg Vorbis Video. It's an open source format.

> *"Theora is a free and open video compression format from the Xiph.org Foundation. Like all our multimedia technology it can be used to distribute film and video online and on disc without the licensing and royalty fees or vendor lock-in associated with other formats."*

—From http://theora.org/

This file format is supported by Firefox, Chrome, and Opera but unfortunately not by Safari, which instead supports the H.264 codec. This means that this example will not work in Safari unless you provide it with an alternative video source that has been encoded with the H.264 codec. There's a rather elegant way of handling this with the <video> element, but I will not bother doing that for this example.

If you're interested in learning more about how to do this and other things with the <video> element, I recommend that you read the excellent article "Introduction to HTML5 Video," which is found at http://dev.opera.com/articles/view/introduction-html5-video/.

The Example

Now that you know a little about HTML5 <video>, it's time that you use that knowledge to insert a video in an InfoWindow. This time, you will not insert the HTML as a string but instead use the other way of adding content by inserting a reference to an HTML node. You will create the HTML nodes with JavaScript and inject them as content in the InfoWindow.

Like in the previous example, the magic will happen inside the event handler for the marker's click event. You already have some code in place:

```
google.maps.event.addListener(marker, 'click', function() {

  // Check to see if an InfoWindow already exists
  if (!infoWindow) {
    infoWindow = new google.maps.InfoWindow();
  }

  // Here's where the magic will happen

});
```

First you're going to create the HTML node for <video>. This is done by using the native DOM method document.createElement() (see Table 7-2).

Table 7-2. Definition of document.createElement()

Method	Return Value	Description
document.createElement (tagName:string)	A reference to the new element	Creates an HTML element and returns it

```
google.maps.event.addListener(marker, 'click', function() {

  // Check to see if an InfoWindow already exists
  if (!infoWindow) {
    infoWindow = new google.maps.InfoWindow();
  }

  // Creating a video element and setting its attributes
  var video = document.createElement('video');

});
```

Next you need to add the src attribute. You will do this by using the setAttribute() method. The video file you're going to use is one featuring a siren. It's supplied by Wikimedia and is found at http://en.wikipedia.org/wiki/File:ACA_Allertor_125_video.ogv.

```
google.maps.event.addListener(marker, 'click', function() {

  // Check to see if an InfoWindow already exists
  if (!infoWindow) {
    infoWindow = new google.maps.InfoWindow();
  }

  // Creating a video element and setting its attributes
  var video = document.createElement('video');

  // Setting the attributes for the <video> element
  video.setAttribute('src',
      'http://upload.wikimedia.org/wikipedia/commons/3/3f/ACA_Allertor_125_video.ogv');

});
```

That's the least you will have to provide to create the <video> element, but let's add a few more attributes. First let's set the size of the video so that it fits inside the InfoWindow. This is done by using the width and height properties. Second, let's automatically start the video as the InfoWindow is being opened and add a control bar so that the user can easily control it.

```
google.maps.event.addListener(marker, 'click', function() {

  // Check to see if an InfoWindow already exists
  if (!infoWindow) {
    infoWindow = new google.maps.InfoWindow();
  }

  // Creating a video element and setting its attributes
  var video = document.createElement('video');
  video.setAttribute('src',
      'http://upload.wikimedia.org/wikipedia/commons/3/3f/ACA_Allertor_125_video.ogv');
  video.setAttribute('width', '300');
  video.setAttribute('height', '200');
  video.setAttribute('controls', 'controls');
  video.setAttribute('autoplay', 'autoplay');

});
```

Now the video is ready. All that's left to do is to add the video as the InfoWindow content and to open the InfoWindow. Adding the video as content is simply done by passing the video variable as the parameter for the setContent() method of the InfoWindow object. Opening the InfoWindow is done the same way as before, by calling its open() method.

```
google.maps.event.addListener(marker, 'click', function() {

  // Check to see if an InfoWindow already exists
  if (!infoWindow) {
```

```
    infoWindow = new google.maps.InfoWindow();
}

// Creating a video element and setting its attributes
var video = document.createElement('video');
video.setAttribute('src',
    'http://upload.wikimedia.org/wikipedia/commons/3/3f/ACA_Allertor_125_video.ogv');
video.setAttribute('width', '300');
video.setAttribute('height', '200');
video.setAttribute('controls', 'controls');
video.setAttribute('autoplay', 'autoplay');

// Passing the video variable as the content for the InfoWindow
infoWindow.setContent(video);

// Opening the InfoWindow
infoWindow.open(map, marker);

});
```

That's it! You now have a map that, when you click the marker, opens an InfoWindow with the video playing in it. It will look something like Figure 7-6.

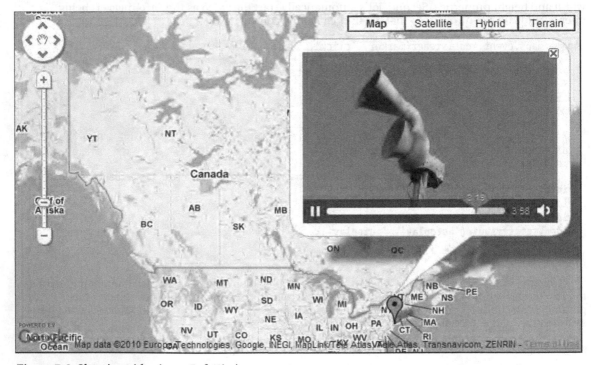

Figure 7-6. *Showing video in an InfoWindow*

For good measure, you're going to do one last thing and that's to create a trigger for the marker's click event when the map loads. This is placed right after the code for the marker event listener.

```
google.maps.event.trigger(marker, 'click');
```

The Complete Code for Adding a Video to an InfoWindow

Listing 7-6 shows the complete JavaScript code for this example.

Listing 7-6. The Complete JavaScript Code for Example 7-2

```
(function() {

  // Defining variables that need to be available to some functions
  var map, infoWindow;

  window.onload = function() {

    // Creating a map
    var options = {
      zoom: 3,
      center: new google.maps.LatLng(37.09, -95.71),
      mapTypeId: google.maps.MapTypeId.ROADMAP
    };

    map = new google.maps.Map(document.getElementById('map'), options);

    // Adding a marker to the map
    var marker = new google.maps.Marker({
      position: new google.maps.LatLng(40.756054, -73.986951),
      map: map,
      title: 'Click me'
    });

    // Adding a click-event to the marker
    google.maps.event.addListener(marker, 'click', function() {

      // Check to see if an InfoWindow already exists
      if (!infoWindow) {
        infoWindow = new google.maps.InfoWindow();
      }

      // Creating a video element and setting its attributes
      var video = document.createElement('video');
      video.setAttribute('src',
          'http://upload.wikimedia.org/wikipedia/commons/3/3f/ACA_Allertor_125_video.ogv');
      video.setAttribute('width', '300');
      video.setAttribute('height', '200');
      video.setAttribute('controls', 'controls');
      video.setAttribute('autoplay', 'autoplay');

      // Passing the video variable as the content for the InfoWindow
```

```
        infoWindow.setContent(video);

        // Opening the InfoWindow
        infoWindow.open(map, marker);

    });

    // Opening the InfoWindow when the map loads
    google.maps.event.trigger(marker, 'click');

  };
})();
```

Creating a Detail Map

In some circumstances, the possibility of displaying a detail map will greatly enhance the user experience. In the old API, it was just a simple function call, but in the new API you have to do a little more than that. The final result will look something like Figure 7-7.

Figure 7-7. An InfoWindow with a detail map

So, how is this done? It's quite simple really. All you need to do is to create a second map and, instead of putting it directly on the web page, put it inside the InfoWindow. I will guide you through the code of doing this.

You start with a map that already has a marker in it and then add a click event for the marker. You can, for example, use the code that you set as a starting point at the beginning of this chapter:

```
google.maps.event.addListener(marker, 'click', function() {
  // Code that will run on click
});
```

Now you have a click event attached to the marker so that when it's clicked, some code will run.

The first thing you need to do is to create a container for the new map. This is done by using the generic DOM method document.createElement().

You also need to define the size of the container since it will determine the size of the map. This can be done either by setting its style properties directly or by giving it a class and putting the definition of its size in an external style sheet. Generally, it's best practice to keep style and behavior separated, but for the sake of simplicity in this example, I will set the size directly on the element.

```
// Create the div that will act as a container for the detail map
var detailDiv = document.createElement('div');

// Set the size of the div
detailDiv.style.width = '200px';
detailDiv.style.height = '200px';
```

Having created the detailDiv, you need to somehow add it to the document. This is done by using the DOM method appendChild(), which does exactly that (see Table 7-3). It adds a child element to a parent element.

You can actually add the detailDiv to any part of the document, but in this case you're going to add it to the map container.

```
// Appending the detailDiv to the map container
document.getElementById('map').appendChild(detailDiv);
```

Table 7-3. Definition of appendChild()

Method	Return value	Description
appendChild(childNode:DOMnode)	A reference to the child node	This method appends a child node to a DOM node

The next step is to create the new map. You start by defining the options for the new map. First you need to set the zoom property. Since you want the detail map to be fairly zoomed in, you set it to 14. It is, after all, a *detail* map.

Next you need to set the center of the map. Since the map will show a detailed view of the area where the marker is placed, you want it to center on the location of it. This is done by calling the getPosition() method of the marker. It will return a LatLng that you can use to define the center of the map.

You set the mapTypeId to the same as the surrounding map. You could do this by setting it explicitly with google.maps.MapTypeId.ROADMAP, but a more clever thing to do is to set it the same as the big map using its getMapTypeId() method. This way, if the user changes the map type, you will still get the same map type in the detail map.

That's the three required properties that you always have to set. In this case, however, you'll want to set one more property. Since this will be a very small map, I don't want it cluttered by the zoom and pan control or by any other control. To get rid of those, you set the `disableDefaultUI` property to `true`. This way, there will be no controls obscuring the view on the map.

```
var overviewOpts = {
  zoom: 14,
  center: marker.getPosition(),
  mapTypeId: map.getMapTypeId(),
  disableDefaultUI: true
};
```

Now you're all set to initialize the detail map. You have a container for it, and you have defined its properties. All that's left to do is to create it.

```
var detailMap = new google.maps.Map(detailDiv, overviewOpts);
```

Now the map is created, but you also want a marker in it marking the spot.

First you set the position. Now, you can do this in one of two ways. You could get it from your newly created detail map or from the clicked marker. In this example, I've chosen to get it from the latter.

Next you need to define what map the marker should be added to. In this case, it's the newly created detail map.

That's it for the required properties, but I'm going to add one more property. Since you don't want this marker to be clickable, you want to somehow disable that. You can do this by setting the property `clickable` to `false`. This way, the cursor won't change when the user hovers with the mouse over it, and the user can't interact with it.

OK, you're set to create the marker. Here's the code to do that:

```
var detailMarker = new google.maps.Marker({
  position: marker.getPosition(),
  map: detailMap,
  clickable: false
});
```

That's it for the map. It has been created, and the marker has been added to it. But you still can't see anything if you try to click the marker. That's because a crucial part is still missing, creating the InfoWindow.

Creating the InfoWindow

First you check to see whether you already have an InfoWindow. If not, you create one.

```
if (!infoWindow) {
  infoWindow = new google.maps.InfoWindow();
}
```

Next you're going to set its content and then add it to the map. You probably know how to do this by now, but I'll explain it anyway. First you'll set the content by using its `setContent()` method. Then you call its `open()` method and pass a map object and a marker to it. The only thing you have to keep in mind is to pass it the right map and the right marker. In this case, it's the big map and the clicked marker.

```
// Setting the content of the InfoWindow
infoWindow.setContent(detailDiv);

// Adding the InfoWindow to the map
infoWindow.open(map, marker);
```

That's it! You now have a map with a detail map inside an InfoWindow. To recap, you've just done the following:

1. Added a click event to the marker on the map
2. Created a detail map by first creating a <div> and then putting a map in it
3. Added a nonclickable marker in the detail map's center
4. Created or reused an InfoWindow and added the detail map to it

The Complete Code

Listing 7-7 shows the complete code.

Listing 7-7. The Complete JavaScript Code for Example 7-3

```
(function() {

  // Defining variables that need to be available to some functions
  var map, infoWindow;

  window.onload = function() {

    // Creating a map
    var options = {
      zoom: 3,
      center: new google.maps.LatLng(37.09, -95.71),
      mapTypeId: google.maps.MapTypeId.ROADMAP
    };

    map = new google.maps.Map(document.getElementById('map'), options);

    // Adding a marker to the map
    var marker = new google.maps.Marker({
      position: new google.maps.LatLng(40.756054, -73.986951),
      map: map,
      title: 'Click me'
    });


    google.maps.event.addListener(marker, 'click', function() {

      // Creating the div that will contain the detail map
      var detailDiv = document.createElement('div');
      detailDiv.style.width = '200px';
      detailDiv.style.height = '200px';
      document.getElementById('map').appendChild(detailDiv);

      // Creating MapOptions for the overview map
```

```
    var overviewOpts = {
      zoom: 14,
      center: marker.getPosition(),
      mapTypeId: map.getMapTypeId(),
      disableDefaultUI: true
    };

    var detailMap = new google.maps.Map(detailDiv, overviewOpts);

    // Create a marker that will show in the detail map
    var detailMarker = new google.maps.Marker({
      position: marker.getPosition(),
      map: detailMap,
      clickable: false
    });

    // Check to see if an InfoWindow already exists
    if (!infoWindow) {
      infoWindow = new google.maps.InfoWindow();
    }

    // Setting the content of the InfoWindow to the detail map
    infoWindow.setContent(detailDiv);

    // Opening the InfoWindow
    infoWindow.open(map, marker);

  });

  };
})();
```

Creating a Zoom-In Link

Sometimes you can provide users with shortcuts to make the user experience more pleasurable. One simple shortcut is to provide a zoom-in link in the InfoWindow. This way, the user can easily zoom in on an object without having to use the zoom controls.

In this example, you will use the marker centered on Manhattan. Initially the map is zoomed out so all the United States is visible. When the zoom-in link in the InfoWindow is clicked, the map zooms in on the marker. See Figure 7-8.

Figure 7-8. *The map before and after the "Zoom in" link has been clicked*

Adding the Event Handler

You start this example by reverting to the starting code in the beginning of this chapter. The first thing you need to do next is to add an event handler to the marker that will open the InfoWindow.

```
google.maps.event.addListener(marker, 'click', function(e) {
  // Insert code for InfoWindow
}
```

Now that you have the event handler in place, you need to add the logic to it that will do the following things:

- Create the content of the InfoWindow
- Create the InfoWindow
- Open the InfoWindow

You start with the content, which will consist of some text and a link that when clicked will center the map on the marker and zoom in. You will use a slightly different approach than the one that you used in the first example when you added HTML to the InfoWindow. Then you just created a string that contained the entire HTML and inserted it into the InfoWindow. Now you will create the HTML elements using native DOM methods.

Let's start by creating a `<div>` that will contain the content and two `<p>` elements that will contain the text and the link.

```
// First we create the container for the content
// of the InfoWindow
var content = document.createElement('div');

// We then create a paragraph element that will contain
// some text
var p = document.createElement('p');
p.innerHTML = 'This marker is positioned on Manhattan.';

// We then create a second paragraph element that will contain
// the clickable link
var p2 = document.createElement('p');
```

Now you need to create the link. You start by creating a `<a>` element and give it a text and a value to its `href` attribute.

```
// Creating the clickable link
var a = document.createElement('a');
a.innerHTML = 'Zoom in';
a.href = '#';
```

■ **Note** The standard way of assigning values to HTML elements is the DOM method `setAttribute()`. But since there are some differences in implementation in different browsers (mainly IE), I stick with the attributes `innerHTML` and `href` since they are supported by all browsers. Another approach could be to use a JavaScript framework such as jQuery or prototype to do this. They will take care of the browser inconsistencies for you.

OK, so now that the `<a>` element is created, it's time to add the magic that will zoom the map. You will do this by assigning an anonymous function to its `onclick` event. In the anonymous function, you will add the code that will do the heavy work in this example.

```
a.onclick = function() {
  // Code goes here
}
```

You probably recognize this syntax since it's the same as the one you've been using all along when attaching an onload event to the windows object.

■ **Note** There are other ways of attaching click events to an element than using the `onclick` property. The benefit of using `onlick` is that it's cross-browser compatible. The standard way of doing it, using the method `addEventListener()`, involves having to provide a separate method for IE called `attachEvent()` since it doesn't support it.

Next you need to add some functionality inside the event handler. You will use the setCenter() and setZoom() method of the map object. You might recall them from Chapter 4, where I discussed them in detail.

Let's start with the setCenter() method; it takes a LatLng object as its argument and centers the map on that location. You want the map to center on the position of the marker and will therefore use the marker object's getPosition() method. This method returns a LatLng that represents the markers position, so it's perfect for this scenario.

```
a.onclick = function() {
  map.setCenter(marker.getPosition());
};
```

Now the map centers on the marker, but you also want the map to zoom in. Let's do it by using the setZoom() method. setZoom() takes a number representing the desired zoom level as its argument. In this case, I think the zoom level 15 is an appropriate, so let's set it to that.

```
a.onclick = function() {
  map.setCenter(marker.getPosition());
  map.setZoom(15);
};
```

Now there's just one more thing you'll want to do, and that is to cancel out the default behavior of the link being clicked. If you don't do this, the browser will try to follow the link. It's easily canceled by returning false.

```
a.onclick = function() {
  map.setCenter(marker.getPosition());
  map.setZoom(15);
  return false;
};
```

Now all the elements of the content are created, and you want to assemble them all inside the content <div>. You're going to do this by using the appendChild() method.

```
// Appending the link to the second paragraph element
p2.appendChild(a);
```

```
// Appending the two paragraphs to the content container
content.appendChild(p);
content.appendChild(p2);
```

Opening the InfoWindow

Lastly, you want to create the InfoWindow object if it's not already created and open it. This code should be familiar to you by now.

```
// Check to see if infoWindow already exists
// if not we create a new
if (!infoWindow) {
  infoWindow = new google.maps.InfoWindow();
}
```

```
// We set the content of the InfoWindow to our content container
infoWindow.setContent(content);

// Finally we open the InfoWindow
infoWindow.open(map, marker);
```

The Complete Code

Listing 7-8 shows the complete code for this example.

Listing 7-8. The Complete JavaScript Code for Example 7-4

```
(function() {

  // Defining variables that need to be available to some functions
  var map, infoWindow;

  window.onload = function() {
    // Creating a map
    var options = {
      zoom: 3,
      center: new google.maps.LatLng(37.09, -95.71),
      mapTypeId: google.maps.MapTypeId.ROADMAP
    };

    var map = new google.maps.Map(document.getElementById('map'), options);

    // Adding a marker
    var marker = new google.maps.Marker({
      position: new google.maps.LatLng(40.756054, -73.986951),
      map: map,
      title: 'Click me'
    });

    // Add event handler for the markers click event
    google.maps.event.addListener(marker, 'click', function() {


      // First we create the container for the content of the InfoWindow
      var content = document.createElement('div');

      // We then create a paragraph element that will contain some text
      var p = document.createElement('p');
      p.innerHTML = 'This marker is positioned on Manhattan.';

      // We then create a second paragraph element that will contain the clickable link
      var p2 = document.createElement('p');

      // Creating the clickable link
      var a = document.createElement('a');
      a.innerHTML = 'Zoom in';
      a.href = '#';
```

```
    // Adding a click event to the link that performs
    // the zoom in, and cancels its default action
    a.onclick = function() {

      // Setting the center of the map to the same as the clicked marker
      map.setCenter(marker.getPosition());

      // Setting the zoom level to 15
      map.setZoom(15);

      // Canceling the default action
      return false;
    };

    // Appending the link to the second paragraph element
    p2.appendChild(a);

    // Appending the two paragraphs to the content container
    content.appendChild(p);
    content.appendChild(p2);

    // Check to see if infoWindow already exists, if not we create a new
    if (!infoWindow) {
      infoWindow = new google.maps.InfoWindow();
    }
    // We set the content of the InfoWindow to our content container
    infoWindow.setContent(content);

    // Lastly we open the InfoWindow
    infoWindow.open(map, marker);

  });

  };
})();
```

Further Refinements

You now have a working example for zooming in on a spot on the map. A suggestion for further refinement is to change the link in the InfoWindow to a "Zoom out" link once it's been clicked. I will, however, leave it up to you to work out how to implement it.

Summary

In this chapter, you examined a few things that can be accomplished with InfoWindows. First, you learned how to add full HTML as the content of an InfoWindow. Then you looked at how to add video to it using HTML5. Lastly you looked at how to create a detail map and a "Zoom in" link in the InfoWindow.

Knowing these concepts, you're equipped with the knowledge to create a lot of functionality. Your own imagination sets the limit.

CHAPTER 8

■ ■ ■

Creating Polylines and Polygons

The Google Maps API has two classes for dealing with geometric shapes. These are *polylines* and *polygons.* These shapes provide you with the necessary tools for marking roads, borders, and other areas. One area where polylines are particularly useful is to track different paths, such as creating driving directions or tracking a jogging path. Polygons, on the other hand, are very useful when you want to highlight a certain geographic area, such as a state or a country.

In this chapter, you'll learn how to harness the power of polylines and polygons and how to do some pretty amazing stuff with them.

Creating Polylines

Polylines are made up of several connected lines. A line consists of two points: a starting point and an end point. These points are made up of coordinates. Therefore, at its core, a polyline is a collection of points with lines between them, much like a connect-the-dots sketch (Figure 8-1).

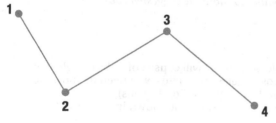

Figure 8-1. A polyline is essentially dots connected with lines.

When using the Google Maps Driving Directions service, which calculates a route for you to drive (or walk), a polyline is being used to display the route on the map (Figure 8-2). This polyline is very complex since it consists of a large number of points, probably thousands of them. The polylines that you're going to create in this chapter are a lot simpler and will consist of a very few points. The principles are still the same, though, regardless of how many points you use.

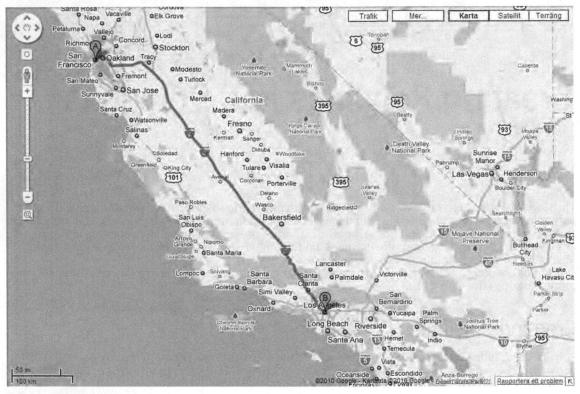

Figure 8-2. *The Google Maps Driving Directions uses polylines to show the suggested route.*

Creating a Simple Polyline

You're going to start easy and create the smallest possible polyline. It will consist of only a single line. Specifically, you will draw a line from San Francisco to Los Angeles. To do this, you need to know the coordinates for the starting point (San Francisco) and for the end point (Los Angeles).

To set a starting point for this example, you will use the JavaScript code shown in Listing 8-1.

Listing 8-1. *The Starting JavaScript Code*

```
(function() {
  window.onload = function() {

    // Creating a map
    var options = {
      zoom: 5,
      center: new google.maps.LatLng(36.1834, -117.4960),
      mapTypeId: google.maps.MapTypeId.ROADMAP
    };
```

```
    var map = new google.maps.Map(document.getElementById('map'), options);

  };

})();
```

There's nothing new in this code at all. All it does is create a blank Google map that is centered somewhere on the West Coast of the United States.

Preparing the Coordinates

As you now know, a polyline consists of several coordinates (points on the map). In this case, you're going to create a very small polyline with just two points. To get started, you need to find out what these coordinates are.

Fortunately, I have already found out the correct coordinates (see Table 8-1).

Table 8-1. The Coordinates for San Francisco and Los Angeles

City	Latitude	Longitude
San Francisco	37.7671	-122.4206
Los Angeles	34.0485	-118.2568

To use these coordinates, you need to convert them to objects of the type google.maps.LatLng and add them to an array. Create an array called route to store them in:

```
var route = [
  new google.maps.LatLng(37.7671, -122.4206),
  new google.maps.LatLng(34.0485, -118.2568)
];
```

That's really all the information you need to create a polyline. Now all you have to do is call the constructor for the Polyline class, add the route arrays to it, and then add the polyline to the map. Let's take it step-by-step and start with creating the Polyline object (see Table 8-2).

Table 8-2. Definition of the Polyline Constructor

Constructor	Description
Polyline(options?:PolylineOptions)	Creates a Polyline object

The Polyline object takes one argument, and that is an object of type PolylineOptions. PolylineOptions has several properties, but only one is required. That's the property path. The path property takes an array of google.maps.LatLng objects. That's exactly what you have in the route array that you just prepared.

```
var polylineOptions = {
 path: route
};
```

With the `option` object prepared, you add it as an argument to the `Polyline` object constructor like this:

```
var polyline = new google.maps.Polyline(polylineOptions);
```

You now have a `Polyline` object in place, so there's really only one thing left to do, and that is to add it to the map. But before you do that, I want you to change the code slightly. For brevity, I usually don't bother creating a variable to hold the `polylineOptions` object. Instead, I just add the object on the fly to the constructor.

The code will look like this:

```
var polyline = new google.maps.Polyline({
  path: route
});
```

It does the exact the same thing, but you save a few lines of code. The only drawback is if you want to reuse the `PolylineOptions` object for another polyline. To do that, you'll need to have it stored in a variable. I rarely find that to be the case, though.

Let's get back on track. You've created the polyline but haven't yet added it to the map. The `Polyline` object has a method called `setMap()`, which is used to add the polyline to the map. This method takes one argument, which is the `Map` object to which you want to add the polyline.

```
polyline.setMap(map);
```

As soon as the method is called, the polyline is added to the map. When you look at the result, you see a black line connecting San Francisco with Los Angeles (Figure 8-3).

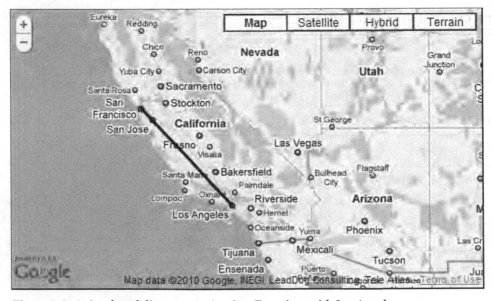

Figure 8-3. A simple polyline connecting San Francisco with Los Angeles

Another Way of Adding the Polyline

There is another way of adding the polyline to the map, and that is to use the map property of the PolylineOptions object. It takes a reference to the map that the polyline is being added to as its value.

```
var polyline = new google.maps.Polyline({
  path: route,
  map: map
});
```

If you use that code, the polyline will be instantly added to the map, and there's no need to use the setMap() method. It's mostly a matter of preference which way you do it. One case where the setMap() method is useful is for removing a polyline from the map. It's done by passing null as its parameter:

```
polyline.setMap(null);
```

Adding a Bit More Flare to the Line

Although your newly created polyline does the job, it looks a bit boring. Fortunately, you can easily add a bit more flare to it by using the other properties of the PolylineOptions object. These properties control the color, opacity, and size of the line.

- **strokeColor**
  This property defines the color of the line. The value used is a string in hex format, so the color red will be #ff0000. The default value is #000000, which is black.

- **strokeOpacity**
  This property is a number that defines the opacity of the line. 1.0 means that it's 100 percent opaque, and 0 means that it's 0 percent opaque, in other words, completely transparent. Anything in between, such as 0.5, will render a semi-transparent line. The default value is 1.0.

- **strokeWeight**
  This property is a number and defines the width of the line in pixels. To create a 5 pixel wide line, pass it the value 5. The default value is 3.

Let's make the line a bit wider, color it red, and make it semi-transparent. To do this, you have to add these properties to the PolylineOptions object and assign them the appropriate values. Having done that, the code will look like this:

```
var polyline = new google.maps.Polyline({
  path: route,
  strokeColor: "#ff0000",
  strokeWeight: 5,
  strokeOpacity: 0.6
});
```

Now you have a nice semi-transparent red line instead of the boring black line you had before (Figure 8-4 gives you the idea). The line being semi-transparent is a nice touch since it makes it easier to read the map underneath it, thereby enhancing the usability of the map.

Figure 8-4. A nice semi-transparent line now connects the two cities.

The Complete Code

Listing 8-2 shows the complete code for this example.

Listing 8-2. The Complete JavaScript for Example 8-1

```
(function() {
  window.onload = function() {

    // Creating a map
    var options = {
      zoom: 5,
      center: new google.maps.LatLng(36.1834, -117.4960),
      mapTypeId: google.maps.MapTypeId.ROADMAP
    };
    var map = new google.maps.Map(document.getElementById('map'), options);

    // Creating an array that will contain the points for the polyline
    var route = [
      new google.maps.LatLng(37.7671, -122.4206),
      new google.maps.LatLng(34.0485, -118.2568)
    ];

    // Creating the polyline object
    var polyline = new google.maps.Polyline({
      path: route,
```

```
        strokeColor: "#ff0000",
        strokeOpacity: 0.6,
        strokeWeight: 5
    });

    // Adding the polyline to the map
    polyline.setMap(map);

    };
})();
```

■ **Note** Don't forget that you can download the example code from the book's web site at
http://svennerberg.com/bgma3.

Polyline Arrays

As you probably remember, the path property of the PolylineOptions object was the one you fed with
the route array. This property plays a dual role since it can also take another kind of array called an
MVCArray. This is an object in the Google Maps API that is an array in the sense that it can contain
objects. It differs from a regular array by having some special methods to retrieve, remove, and insert
new objects on the fly.

Why use this special array instead of a regular one? I mean, a regular array also has methods to
retrieve, remove, and add new objects on the fly, right?

The reason is that if you use an MVCArray, the map instantly updates with the changes you make to it.
For instance, if you use an MVCArray to feed the path property, it behaves just as normal, and the polyline
is displayed properly on the map. But if you then, after the map is initialized and the polyline has been
rendered, add a new point to the MVCArray, the polyline on the map will instantly extend to that point.

Let's try this by building a simple map that by clicking it dynamically adds points to a polyline.

■ **Note** When we're using a regular array to store the coordinates, it's actually being converted to an MVCArray
internally in the API.

Plotting Your Own Path

In this example, you will build upon the previous example. You will modify it slightly by replacing the
array holding the points with an empty MVCArray. You will also add a click event to the map that will add
a point to the MVCArray each time it's being triggered.

Let's start by replacing the existing route array with an empty MVCArray:

```
var route = new google.maps.MVCArray();
```

You now have an MVCArray object that will enable you to dynamically add points to the polyline.
Now let's add the code that creates the Polyline object and then call the setMap() method on it. This
code will look exactly as in the previous example:

```
// Creating the Polyline object
var polyline = new google.maps.Polyline({
  path: route,
  strokeColor: "#ff0000",
  strokeOpacity: 0.6,
  strokeWeight: 5
});

// Adding the polyline to the map
polyline.setMap(map);
```

With this code, the polyline is in place and is attached to the map. But since the MVCArray doesn't yet contain any points, the polyline will not be visible.

What you need to do now is to create a click event and attach it to the map. The click event returns an object of type google.maps.MouseEvent, which contains a property called latLng, which contains a google.maps.LatLng object that represents the position clicked. In other words, the click returns the position in the map that's being clicked, and you can use that information to create a point for the polyline.

First you attach a click event to the map object using the addListener() method of the google.maps.event object. You will pass three arguments to it; the first one is the map, and the second one is the type of event you want to catch, in this case the click event. The last argument is an anonymous function that will execute when the event is being triggered. You will pass a reference to the event (e) to this function. It is that reference that is the MouseEvent object.

```
// Adding a click event to the map object
google.maps.event.addListener(map, 'click', function(e) {
  // Code that will be executed once the event is triggered
});
```

Now you have the event listener in place. The next step is to actually do something when it's being triggered.

So, you need to get a reference to the MVCArray. This is done by calling the getPath() method of the polyline. Once you have that reference, you can call its methods. The method you want to use is the push() method, which inserts a new item in the end of the array. You pass the LatLng object as an argument to this method, and once that's done, a new point is added to the polyline.

```
// Adding a click event to the map object
google.maps.event.addListener(map, 'click', function(e) {

  // Getting the MVCArray
  var path = polyline.getPath();

  // Adding the position clicked which is in fact
  // a google.maps.LatLng object to the MVCArray
  path.push(e.latLng);

});
```

There! Everything is in place, and you now have a dynamic polyline (Figure 8-5). Each click in the map will extend the polyline to the point being clicked. Since a polyline must contain at least two points to show, it will not be visible until after the second click in the map.

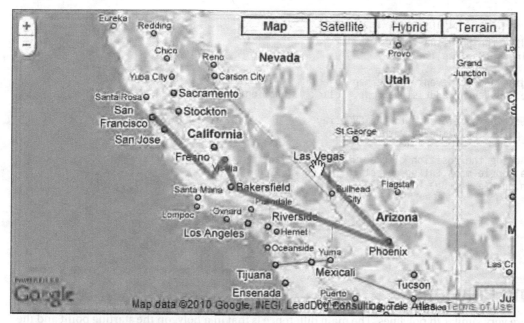

Figure 8-5. A dynamic polyline. Each click in the map adds a point to it.

The Complete Code

Listing 8-3 shows the complete code for this example:

Listing 8-3. The Complete JavaScript Code for Example 8-2

```
(function() {
  window.onload = function(){

    // Creating a map
    var options = {
      zoom: 5,
      center: new google.maps.LatLng(36.1834, -117.4960),
      mapTypeId: google.maps.MapTypeId.ROADMAP
    };
    var map = new google.maps.Map(document.getElementById('map'), options);

    // Creating an empty MVCArray
    var route = new google.maps.MVCArray();

    // Creating the Polyline object
    var polyline = new google.maps.Polyline({
      path: route,
      strokeColor: "#ff0000",
      strokeOpacity: 0.6,
      strokeWeight: 5
```

```
    });

    // Adding the polyline to the map
    polyline.setMap(map);

    // Adding a click event to the map object
    google.maps.event.addListener(map, 'click', function(e) {

        // Getting a reference to the MVCArray
        var path = polyline.getPath();

        // Adding the position clicked which is in fact
        // a google.maps.LatLng object to the MVCArray
        path.push(e.latLng);

    });

  };
})();
```

Creating Polygons

Polygons are very similar to polylines. The main difference is that in a polygon the starting point and the end point are always connected, making it into a closed figure (Figure 8-6). So ,where polylines mark routes, polygons mark areas. This makes them the perfect choice for marking areas such as countries or other geographic regions in a map.

Figure 8-6. In a polygon, the end point is always connected to the starting point.

Creating a Simple Polygon

Let's start by creating a very simple polygon. It will consist of only three points, making it a triangle. Just like the Polyline object, it has a constructor that takes an options object as its only argument. For polygons, this is a PolygonOptions object. It's very similar to the PolyLine object but introduces some differences. Table 8-3 shows the definition of its constructor.

Table 8-3. Definition of the Polygon Constructor

Constructor	Description
`Polygon(options?:PolygonOptions)`	Creates a Polygon object

To create a very simple polygon, you need to use two of its properties, `paths` and `map`. The `paths` property takes the points of the polygons as its value, and the `map` property takes the map that it's being added to as its value.

Creating a Triangle

You're going to create a triangle that connects San Francisco, Las Vegas, and Los Angeles. Let's start by creating an array called `points` that will contain the coordinates for the cities:

```
var points = [
  new google.maps.LatLng(37.7671, -122.4206),
  new google.maps.LatLng(36.1131, -115.1763),
  new google.maps.LatLng(34.0485, -118.2568),
];
```

These points will each mark a corner of the triangle. Do you remember that in polygons the starting point and end point are always connected? Because of this, you don't need to explicitly provide the end point, since it will be the first point in the array.

The next step is to create the polygon:

```
var polygon = new google.maps.Polygon({
  paths: points,
  map: map
});
```

Now the polygon is created and added to the map. It will look like the polygon shown in Figure 8-7.

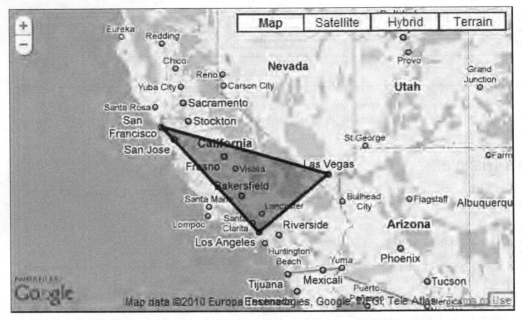

Figure 8-7. A basic polygon connecting San Francisco, Las Vegas, and Los Angeles

This is how a basic polygon looks, but the polygonOptions object also provides a number of properties to style it with. The properties are the same as for the polylineOptions object, but there are two additional properties, which are fillColor and fillOpacity.

- **fillColor**
  Defines the color of the area inside the polygon. The value used is a string in hex format, so the color red will be #ff0000. The default value is #000000, which is black.

- **fillOpacity**
  This property is a number that defines the opacity of the filled area. 1.0 means that it's 100 percent opaque, and 0 means that it's 0 percent opaque. The default value is 1.0.

Let's use these properties to style the polygon. We'll make it have a blue semi-transparent look with a very thin border.

```
var polygon = new google.maps.Polygon({
  paths: points,
  map: map,
  strokeColor: '#0000ff',
  strokeOpacity: 0.6,
  strokeWeight: 1,
  fillColor: '#0000ff',
  fillOpacity: 0.35
});
```

The polygon will now look like the polygon in Figure 8-8.

Figure 8-8. A styled polygon

Controlling the Stack Order

The polygonOptions object actually has one additional property that you haven't used, and that is zIndex. This property is useful only if you have several polygons on the map since it controls their stack order. The higher zIndex is, the further up in the stack the polygon is rendered. So, a polygon with zIndex of 2 will be rendered on top of a polygon with the zIndex 1.

If you don't use zIndex, they will be stacked in the order they're being added to the map. The first one added will be at the bottom, and the last one will be at the top.

The Complete Code

Listing 8-4 shows the complete JavaScript code for this example.

Listing 8-4.The Complete JavaScript Code for Example 8-3

```
(function() {
  window.onload = function() {

    // Creating a map
    var options = {
      zoom: 5,
      center: new google.maps.LatLng(36.6, -118.1),
      mapTypeId: google.maps.MapTypeId.ROADMAP
    };
    var map = new google.maps.Map(document.getElementById('map'), options);
```

```
    // Creating an array with the points for the polygon
    var points = [
      new google.maps.LatLng(37.7671, -122.4206),
      new google.maps.LatLng(36.1131, -115.1763),
      new google.maps.LatLng(34.0485, -118.2568),
    ];

    // Creating the polygon
    var polygon = new google.maps.Polygon({
      paths: points,
      map: map,
      strokeColor: '#0000ff',
      strokeOpacity: 0.6,
      strokeWeight: 1,
      fillColor: '#0000ff',
      fillOpacity: 0.35
    });

  };

})();
```

Creating Donuts

Polygons that contain other polygons are often called *donuts*. The name comes from the idea that a donut has a hole in it, and that's exactly what a donut polygon has.

The paths property of the PolygonOptions object differs from the PolylineOptions object's path property by being able to take more than one array of points as its value. To create a donut, you will have to create a wrapper array that contains other arrays that contain the actual points.

Let's start by creating two arrays. The first one polyOuter will contain the outline of the polygon, and the other one, polyInner, will contain the "hole" in the polygon.

```
// Creating an array with the points for the outer polygon
var polyOuter = [
  new google.maps.LatLng(37.303, -81.256),
  new google.maps.LatLng(37.303, -78.333),
  new google.maps.LatLng(35.392, -78.333),
  new google.maps.LatLng(35.392, -81.256)
];

// Creating an array with the points for the inner polygon
var polyInner = [
  new google.maps.LatLng(36.705, -80.459),
  new google.maps.LatLng(36.705, -79),
  new google.maps.LatLng(35.9, -79),
  new google.maps.LatLng(35.9, -80.459)
];
```

Having done that, you need to create one additional array that will contain both of these arrays. Let's call it points:

```
var points = [polyOuter, polyInner];
```

Now you have all you need to create the donut. You'll provide the points array as the value for the paths property. You'll also provide the map property with the map object as its value.

```
var polygon = new google.maps.Polygon({
  paths: points,
  map: map
});
```

This will provide you with a donut polygon with the default look. To add some final touches, you'll also style it a bit.

```
var polygon = new google.maps.Polygon({
  paths: points,
  map: map,
  strokeColor: '#ff0000',
  strokeOpacity: 0.6,
  strokeWeight: 3,
  fillColor: '#ff0000',
  fillOpacity: 0.35
});
```

This will provide you with a polygon that looks like the one in Figure 8-9. Note that the map center is changed in this example to be centered on (36.6, -118.1); otherwise, the donut will not be visible when the map loads. You'll see this change in the section "The Complete Code."

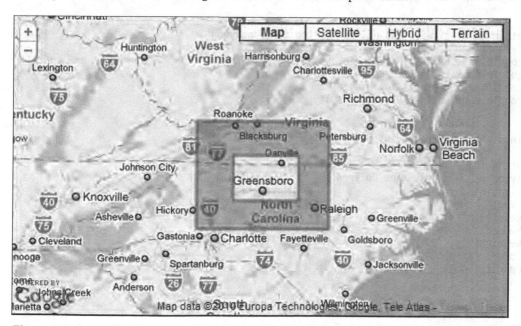

Figure 8-9. *A so-called donut, a polygon with a hole in it*

In this example, the polygon has only one hole in it, but it's entirely possible to have several holes in it.

171

The Complete Code

Listing 8-5 shows the complete JavaScript code for this example.

Listing 8-5. The Complete JavaScript Code for Example 8-4

```
(function() {

  window.onload = function() {

   // Creating a map
    var options = {
      zoom: 6,
      center: new google.maps.LatLng(36.5, -79.8),
      mapTypeId: google.maps.MapTypeId.ROADMAP
    };
    var map = new google.maps.Map(document.getElementById('map'), options);

    // Creating an array with the points for the outer polygon
    var polyOuter = [
      new google.maps.LatLng(37.303, -81.256),
      new google.maps.LatLng(37.303, -78.333),
      new google.maps.LatLng(35.392, -78.333),
      new google.maps.LatLng(35.392, -81.256)
    ];

    // Creating an array with the points for the inner polygon
    var polyInner = [
      new google.maps.LatLng(36.705, -80.459),
      new google.maps.LatLng(36.705, -79),
      new google.maps.LatLng(35.9, -79),
      new google.maps.LatLng(35.9, -80.459)
    ];

    var points = [polyOuter, polyInner];

    // Creating the polygon
    var polygon = new google.maps.Polygon({
      paths: points,
      map: map,
      strokeColor: '#ff0000',
      strokeOpacity: 0.6,
      strokeWeight: 3,
      fillColor: '#FF0000',
      fillOpacity: 0.35
    });

  };

})();
```

Creating a Polygon with a Highlight Effect

In this example, you'll create a polygon that features a highlight effect when the user moves the mouse over it.

A Starting Point

Listing 8-6 shows the JavaScript code that you will start this example from. It creates a map that is centered over part of the Atlantic Ocean.

Listing 8-6. The Starting Point for Example 8-5

```
(function() {

  window.onload = function(){

    // Creating a map
    var options = {
      zoom: 4,
      center: new google.maps.LatLng(25.5, -71.0),
      mapTypeId: google.maps.MapTypeId.ROADMAP
    };
    var map = new google.maps.Map(document.getElementById('map'), options);


  };

})();
```

The Bermuda Triangle

The first thing you will do is to create a polygon that will mark the infamous Bermuda Triangle. The Bermuda Triangle stretches from Miami to Bermuda and Puerto Rico. You'll find the coordinates for these locations in Table 8-4.

Table 8-4. The Coordinates for the Bermuda Triangle

City	Latitude	Longitude
Miami	25.7516	-80.1670
Bermuda	32.2553	-64.8493
Puerto Rico	18.4049	-66.0578

Having these coordinates available, you can start creating the polygon. You start by creating an array called bermudaTrianglePoints that will contain the coordinates:

```
var bermudaTrianglePoints = [
  new google.maps.LatLng(25.7516, -80.1670),
  new google.maps.LatLng(32.2553, -64.8493),
  new google.maps.LatLng(18.4049, -66.0578)
];
```

Next you create the polygon. Style it to have a semi-transparent red color.

```
var bermudaTriangle = new google.maps.Polygon({
  paths: bermudaTrianglePoints,
  map: map,
  strokeColor: '#ff0000',
  strokeOpacity: 0.6,
  strokeWeight: 1,
  fillColor: '#ff0000',
  fillOpacity: 0.35
});
```

You now have a map that clearly marks the Bermuda Triangle, as shown in Figure 8-10.

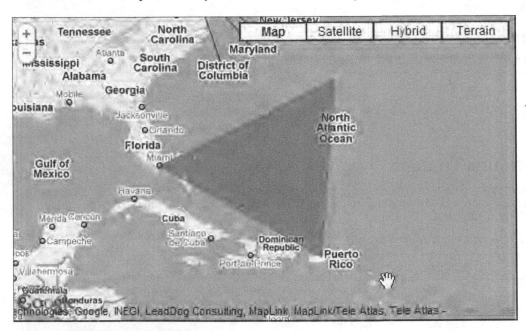

Figure 8-10. The Bermuda Triangle

Adding a Highlight Effect

The next step is to add a highlight effect to the triangle. This is done by changing the color of the polygon when the user moves the mouse over it. To detect when the user does this, you'll use the Polygon object's mouseover event.

```
google.maps.event.addListener(bermudaTriangle, 'mouseover', function() {
  // Add code that will run on mouseover
});
```

Now you are listening for the mouseover event. The next thing you need to do is to change the color of the polygon when that event triggers. To do this, you will use the Polygon object's setOptions() method. With this method, you can change any of the properties of the PolygonOptions object. It takes a PolygonOptions object as its parameter.

What you want to do is to change the color of the polygon. Therefore, you will create a PolygonOptions object that will change the values for fillColor and strokeColor. Let's set them to #0000ff, which will give the polygon a blue color.

```
google.maps.event.addListener(bermudaTriangle, 'mouseover', function() {
  bermudaTriangle.setOptions({
    fillColor: '#0000ff',
    strokeColor: '#0000ff'
  });
});
```

Now when you try the map, the polygon will switch color to blue when you move the mouse pointer over it.

This works fine, but when you move the mouse away from the polygon, it doesn't switch back to the original color. To fix this, you need to listen for the mouseout event. When that event triggers, you'll set the color back to red.

```
google.maps.event.addListener(bermudaTriangle, 'mouseout', function(e) {
  bermudaTriangle.setOptions({
    fillColor: '#ff0000',
    strokeColor: '#ff0000'
  });
});
```

Now you have a working example that features a nice hover effect.

The Complete Code

Listing 8-7 shows the complete JavaScript code for this example.

Listing 8-7. The Complete JavaScript Code for Example 8.5

```
(function() {

  window.onload = function() {

    // Creating a map
    var options = {
      zoom: 4,
      center: new google.maps.LatLng(25.5, -71.0),
      mapTypeId: google.maps.MapTypeId.ROADMAP
    };
    var map = new google.maps.Map(document.getElementById('map'), options);
```

```
// Creating an array with the points for the Bermuda Triangle
var bermudaTrianglePoints = [
  new google.maps.LatLng(25.7516, -80.1670),
  new google.maps.LatLng(32.2553, -64.8493),
  new google.maps.LatLng(18.4049, -66.0578)
];

// Creating the polygon
var bermudaTriangle = new google.maps.Polygon({
  paths: bermudaTrianglePoints,
  map: map,
  strokeColor: '#ff0000',
  strokeOpacity: 0.6,
  strokeWeight: 1,
  fillColor: '#ff0000',
  fillOpacity: 0.35
});

// Adding mouseover event to the polygon
google.maps.event.addListener(bermudaTriangle, 'mouseover', function(e) {

  // Setting the color of the polygon to blue
  bermudaTriangle.setOptions({
    fillColor: '#0000ff',
    strokeColor: '#0000ff'
  });

});

// Adding a mouseout event for the polygon
google.maps.event.addListener(bermudaTriangle, 'mouseout', function(e) {

  // Setting the color of the polygon to red
  bermudaTriangle.setOptions({
    fillColor: '#ff0000',
    strokeColor: '#ff0000'
  });

});

};

})();
```

Summary

In this chapter, you looked at polylines and polygons. They provide the means to mark different things in a map such as roads and areas. With the things you learned in this chapter, you'll be able to create maps that incorporate these effects in different ways, including dynamic behavior such as plotting your own paths or adding hover effects.

■ ■ ■

CHAPTER 9

Dealing with Massive Numbers of Markers

A common problem that most maps developers run into sooner or later is that they need to add a large number of markers to a map. There are a few problems related to this. The first problem that becomes painfully apparent as soon as you start adding a lot of markers is that the performance of the map quickly degrades. A second big problem is with the usability of the map. It can be hard to make sense of a map that is crammed with markers.

In the first part of this chapter, I will discuss different approaches for dealing with these problems. In the second part, you will do some coding using third-party libraries.

Too Many Markers?

First of all the question is, how many markers are too many? Well, that depends on several things. First, there's the performance issue. The more markers you add, the slower the map will be. Exactly at what point the number of markers makes the map too slow is hard to say since it depends on which browser is used to view the map and on the speed of the computer being used. A map that performs really fast in Google Chrome could, for example, be painfully slow in Internet Explorer.

Another issue is the usability aspect. The more markers you use, the harder it is for the user to make sense of them and find the relevant ones (see Figures 9-1 and 9-2). The ideal number depends on different factors. For example, are the markers positioned very close to each other, or are they scattered over a larger area? If they are scattered over a large area, you can probably get away with using a lot more markers than if they are close together.

Figure 9-1. Ten markers is no problem, but even when we increase the number to 50, there's a risk of overlap.

Figure 9-2. Probably 100 markers is really unusable...not to mention 1,000 markers.

Generally speaking, if you're using fewer than 100 markers, you rarely have a problem. But if you have more, you have to ask yourself these questions:

- Is the map slow?
- Is it hard to get an overview of the map because of all markers?
- Is it hard to make sense of the data being shown on the map?

If the answer is no to all of these questions, you probably don't have a problem. But if the answer is yes to any of them, you probably have to think about how to improve the way you're visualizing the data.

Reducing the Number of Markers Being Displayed

One obvious way of to get around this problem is to not display all the markers all the time. Before getting into how to code actual solutions to this problem, I'll explain some possible approaches for reducing the number of markers being shown. Since v3 is still in beta at the time of writing this book, I've had problems finding relevant examples implemented with v3. So, the examples shown here are implemented using Google Maps API v2. These concepts can, however, just as well be implemented using v3. Also, since most of these solutions involve server-side coding, which is beyond the scope of this book, I'm not going to get into how to actually implement them. Let these first examples just serve as inspiration for how you can approach the too-many-markers problem.

Searching

One way of reducing the number of markers being displayed is to provide a search function. This way, even if you have thousands of locations, only the ones that match the search criteria are visible. One example of this is the search function in Google Maps. If you search for Starbucks, it will only display the Starbucks available in the visible map (see Figure 9-3).

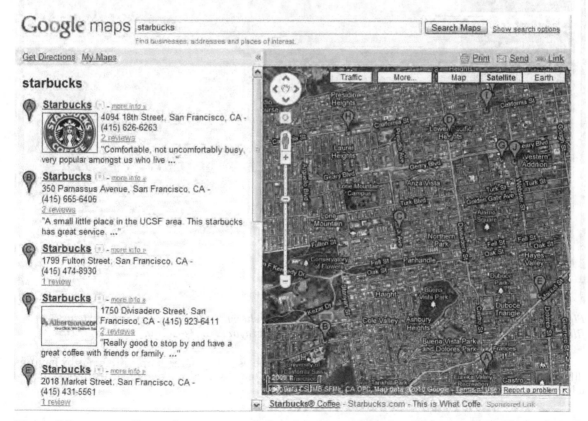

Figure 9-3. maps.google.com features a search function that searches the visible map and adds markers of the locations found.

Also notice that the markers are displayed with labels that correspond to the search result to the left of the map. This is a great way to enhance the maps usability since it makes it possible to understand which marker is which.

Filtering

Another way of reducing the number of markers displayed on the map is by offering a filtering function. STF (which is a Swedish Tourist Association with more than 400 hostels, mountain stations, and alpine huts) offers a map where you can find all of their accommodations as well as other things to see and do (see Figure 9-4). To make the map easier to use, they provide a filter function with which you can filter the map. This is done by marking options in the filter area to the left of the map.

Figure 9-4. STF offers a map that enables you to filter what is shown on the map by marking items in the filter area to the left of the map. The map is found at http://tinyurl.com/36ug6jw.

STF is also utilizing another great way of increasing the usability of the map, and that is by having different marker icons for different types of locations. This technique alone makes scanning the map a lot easier.

Don't Always Use Markers

This might sound like a no-brainer, but sometimes we get so focused on using markers for everything that we forget that we have other tools at our disposal. Don't forget that we also have polylines and polygons in our toolbox. If the thing you want to mark in the map is a road stretch or an area, use polylines or polygons instead. They are much better suited for the job.

Clustering

A common solution for handling the lots-of-markers-problem is to cluster them. What this means is that instead of displaying each individual marker at each time, clusters of markers are displayed. When you zoom in on a cluster, it will break up into smaller clusters or in individual markers.

Using a cluster will significantly increase the performance of the map as well as making it easier to understand (see Figure 9-5).

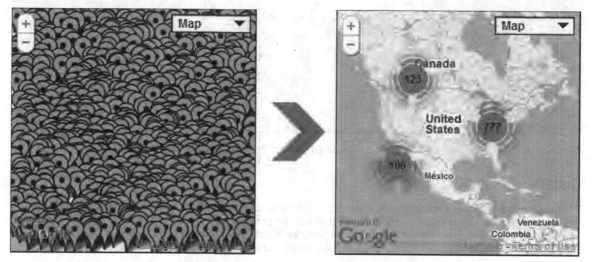

Figure 9-5. The difference between displaying 1,000 markers on a small map and using clusters to do it

Grid-Based Clustering

Grid-based clustering is probably the most common approach for clustering markers. It will divide the map into a grid and group all markers within each square into a cluster. Although an efficient technique, it has some obvious limitations since it can lead to unwanted results. Two markers that are really close together but in separate squares will, for example, not be grouped into the same cluster. See Figure 9-6.

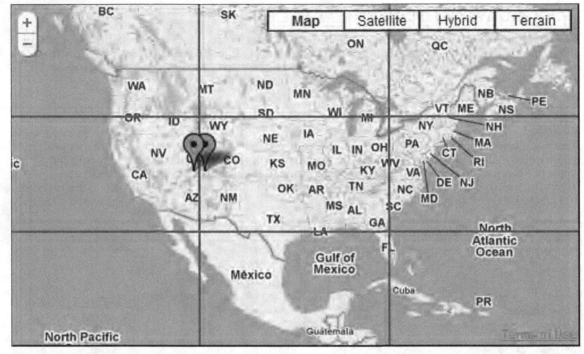

Figure 9-6. These two markers will not be clustered since they reside in different squares of the grid

Distance-Based Clustering

This technique looks at each individual marker and checks whether it's nearby other markers. If it's close enough to another marker, the two of them will be grouped into a cluster.

Distance-based clustering also has its drawbacks. Since the clusters will appear at random locations depending on where a cluster is formed they may not make sense for the user.

Regional Clustering

A third technique is regional clustering. What this means is that you define different geographical regions, such as counties or states. All markers in each region will be grouped into a cluster. You also define at which zoom level the cluster will break up into separate markers (or smaller clusters).

The advantage of this technique is that you can create clusters that make more sense to the user. The drawback is that it requires more effort and can't as easily be automated as the other clustering techniques.

Some Practical Examples

We will soon take a look at some solutions for dealing with too many markers. But before you do that, you will create a map that features a lot of markers so that you have a problem to fix. Therefore, you will write some code that will auto generate markers at random locations.

The Starting Point

As usual the starting point will be a regular map of the United States (Listing 9-1).

Listing 9-1. The Starting JavaScript Code

```
(function() {

  window.onload = function(){

    // Creating a map
    var options = {
      zoom: 3,
      center: new google.maps.LatLng(37.09, -95.71),
      mapTypeId: google.maps.MapTypeId.ROADMAP
    };
    var map = new google.maps.Map(document.getElementById('map'), options);

  };

})();
```

OK, so now that we have a starting point, let's add some functionality. What you want to do is to generate markers within the current viewport. The first thing you need to do is to find out the boundaries of the map so you know where to put the markers. The boundaries indicate what part of the map that's visible to the user, that is, what part of the map that's in the viewport.

Calculating the Current Map Boundaries

To get the current boundaries you execute the getBounds() method of the map object. It returns a LatLngBounds object. I discussed this object in greater detail in Chapter 5, but in short, it's a rectangle.

```
var bounds = map.getBounds();
```

You would think that running this line of code would return the boundaries of the map, but it doesn't. If you examine the bounds variable, you will see that it's undefined. The reason is the asynchronous nature of the Google Maps API. When you call the getBounds() method, the bounds don't yet exist. This means that you need to wait for the bounds to get ready. To do this, you need to listen for the map objects bounds_changed event. Once that event has fired, you can be certain that it's available for you.

So to make your code work, you need to add that event listener and put your code inside the event handler. Since you want this code to run only once, just when the map has finished loading, you're going to use a special method to add the event listener. It's called addListenerOnce(), and the good thing about it is that it removes itself once its event has triggered (see Table 9-1). Other than that, it works exactly as the addListener() method that you've used before.

```
google.maps.event.addListenerOnce(map, 'bounds_changed', function() {

  var bounds = map.getBounds();

});
```

Table 9-1. Definition of addListenerOnce()

Method	Return Value	Description
google.maps.event.addListenerOnce (instance:Ojbect, eventName:string, handler:Function)	MapsEventListener	Adds an event listener that will be removed after it have been triggered

Now if you examine the bounds variable, it will contain a LatLngBounds object that indicates the current map boundaries. Next you'll need to find out the southwest and northeast corners of the boundaries. You get these by calling the getSouthWest() and getNorthEast() methods for the LatLngBounds object. These methods return a LatLng object.

```
google.maps.event.addListenerOnce(map, 'bounds_changed', function() {

  var bounds = map.getBounds();

  var southWest = bounds.getSouthWest();
  var northEast = bounds.getNorthEast();

});
```

Maybe you're starting to wonder where I'm going with all of this. Just remember that you want to calculate a rectangle in the map so that you know where to create the random markers. You now know the lower-left corner of the viewport (southWest) and the upper-right corner (northEast). Next you need to find out the distance between the left and right side of the map as well as the distance between the upper and lower sides. These values will be stored in the variables latSpan and lngSpan. To get the values you need for each calculation, you will use the methods lat() and lng() of the LatLng object.

```
google.maps.event.addListenerOnce(map, 'bounds_changed', function() {

  var bounds = map.getBounds();

  var southWest = bounds.getSouthWest();
  var northEast = bounds.getNorthEast();
  var latSpan = northEast.lat() - southWest.lat();
  var lngSpan = northEast.lng() - southWest.lng();

});
```

Note that this code is not completely foolproof. If the map is zoomed out far enough so both the prime meridian and the international date line are visible, it will put the markers on the other side of the globe (Figure 9-7).

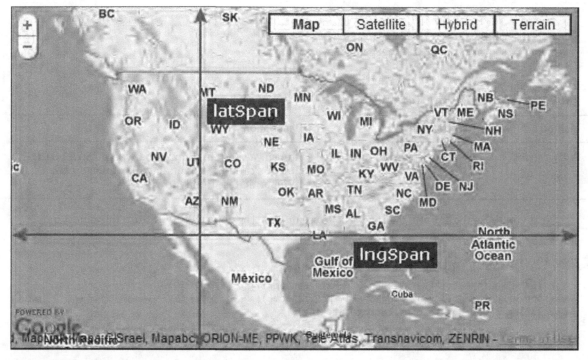

Figure 9-7. latSpan measures the distance from the top to the bottom of the map, and lngSpan measures the distance between the sides.

Now you know the distance from the lower part of the map to the upper part as well as the distance from side to side. In other words, you now know the playing field onto which you will add the markers.

Adding the Markers

You will create a loop that on each iteration will add a marker to the map at a random location within our boundaries. You will use the information that you've already calculated in combination with a random number to create the LatLng for each marker.

Let's start by creating a for loop that will iterate 100 times. The code for the loop will reside inside the event handler, but for brevity, I will display only the code for the loop here. You'll find the complete code at the end of this section.

Inside the loop you're going to calculate the LatLng for each marker. You create a variable called lat that will store the latitude and a variable called lng that will store the longitude. The latitude is calculated by taking the latitude for the lower part of the map and adding the distance from the bottom to the top multiplied by a random number between 0 and 1. To get the random number, you will use the JavaScript Math object. It has a method called random() that will return a random number between 0 and 1 each time you call it (see Table 9-2). This will provide you with a random latitude that will reside within your boundaries.

You're doing the same thing with the longitude only that you're using the longitude for the left part of the map added with the distance from side to side multiplied by a random number.

```
for (var i = 0; i < 100; i++) {

  var lat = southWest.lat() + latSpan * Math.random();
  var lng = southWest.lng() + lngSpan * Math.random();

}
```

Table 9-2. Definition of `Math.random()`

Method	Return value	Description
Math.random()	A number between 0 and 1	Returns a random number between 0 and 1 each time it's called. It never actually returns 1 but a number that is slightly lower.

Next you'll use the lat and the lng value to create a LatLng object. We will store this object in a variable called latlng.

```
for (var i = 0; i < 100; i++) {

  var lat = southWest.lat() + latSpan * Math.random();
  var lng = southWest.lng() + lngSpan * Math.random();
  var latlng = new google.maps.LatLng(lat, lng);

}
```

■ **Note** The Math object is a native JavaScript object that has several useful methods for performing mathematical tasks. Creating random numbers with the random() method is one, and round() to round numbers and max() to find out which of two numbers is the biggest are a couple of others. For a complete reference, check out the page about the Math object at w3school.com http://www.w3schools.com/js/js_obj_math.asp.

Now all that's left to do is to create a marker. You'll use the latlng variable as the position for the marker and add the marker to your map.

```
for (var i = 0; i < 100; i++) {

  var lat = southWest.lat() + latSpan * Math.random();
  var lng = southWest.lng() + lngSpan * Math.random();
  var latlng = new google.maps.LatLng(lat, lng);

  new google.maps.Marker({
    position: latlng,
    map: map
  });

}
```

The Final Code

Listing 9-2 shows the complete code. When you run this page, it will add 100 markers at random locations at the visible part of the map. If you want to try adding a different number of markers, just change the number in the for loop.

Listing 9-2. The Complete Code for Example 9-1

```
(function() {

  window.onload = function(){

    // Creating a map
    var options = {
      zoom: 3,
      center: new google.maps.LatLng(37.09, -95.71),
      mapTypeId: google.maps.MapTypeId.ROADMAP
    };
    var map = new google.maps.Map(document.getElementById('map'), options);

    google.maps.event.addListenerOnce(map, 'bounds_changed', function() {

      // Getting the boundaries of the map
      var bounds = map.getBounds();

      // Getting the corners of the map
      var southWest = bounds.getSouthWest();
      var northEast = bounds.getNorthEast();

      // Calculating the distance from the top to the bottom of the map
      var latSpan = northEast.lat() - southWest.lat();

      // Calculating the distance from side to side
      var lngSpan = northEast.lng() - southWest.lng();

      // Creating a loop
      for (var i = 0; i < 100; i++) {

        // Creating a random position
        var lat = southWest.lat() + latSpan * Math.random();
        var lng = southWest.lng() + lngSpan * Math.random();
        var latlng = new google.maps.LatLng(lat, lng);

        // Adding a marker to the map
        new google.maps.Marker({
          position: latlng,
          map: map
        });

      }

    });

  };

})();
```

Running this code will result in a map that looks something like Figure 9-8.

Figure 9-8. 100 markers at random locations

Third-Party Libraries

Although the Google Maps API has a lot of features in itself, there are external utility libraries available that add functionality to the API. A utility library is basically a collection of JavaScript files that extends the Google Maps API to include more functionality. You use them by including the JavaScript file in your HTML file, just the way you include the Google Maps API. And once you have done that, you get access to the library's objects and functionality.

Since version 3 of the Google Maps API is still so new there are not yet many of them. At the time of writing, there are two official libraries available for marker management. These are MarkerClusterer and MarkerManager.

These and all the other official libraries are found at the google-maps-utility-library-v3 repository at http://code.google.com/p/google-maps-utility-library-v3/wiki/Libraries. The number of available utility libraries is likely to grow as people are transferring from v2 to v3 of the Google Maps API.

MarkerClusterer

As the name implies, this library is used for clustering markers. It uses a grid-based clustering method, which makes it ideal for a fast solution to the many-markers problem.

The original MarkerClusterer for v2 of the Google Maps API was written by Xiaoxi Wu, but the v3 implementation was done by Luke Mahe. It's released under the Apache License version 2.0, which means that it's open source and that you can use it freely in your projects.

This library is available at its file repository at http://google-maps-utility-library-v3.googlecode.com/svn/tags/markerclusterer/1.0/. If you browse to it, you will find a page with a list of folders (Figure 9-9).

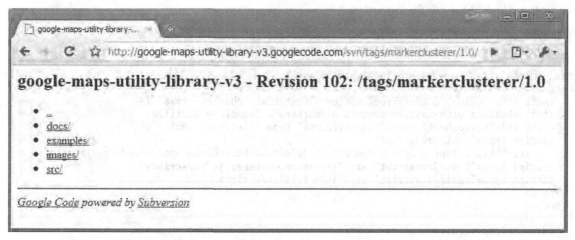

Figure 9-9. *The MarkerClusterer file repository*

The docs folder contains documentation and a complete reference on the library. The examples folder contains several examples that you can review. The images folder contains images for the examples as well as images for the clusters. Finally, the src folder contains the actual library file, which is a regular JavaScript file that you can download and put on your own server.

The original library file is called markerclusterer.js. You can examine this file to see how the library is built. There's also compressed versions of the library that is a lot smaller in file size but impossible to read (see Table 9-3). For production, I strongly suggest that you use either markerclusterer_compiled.js or markerclusterer_packed.js. Since these are much smaller they will load faster. The uncompressed version can be nice to use during development since it's possible to see what it actually contains and what the code does. Also, if you would like to extend the library, you could do that with this version.

Table 9-3. *The Different File Versions of MarkerClusterer*

Filename	File Size	Uses
markercluster.js	26KB	Use this during development since you can review and debug the code. Also useful if you want to extend the library with more functionality.
markerclusterer_compiled.js	7KB	Use for production site. Its smaller file size makes it faster to download.
markerclusterer_packed.js	7KB	Same as for the compiled version, only a different compression method.

Applying MarkerClusterer to the Example

The first thing you need to do when applying MarkerClusterer is to link in the library. To do this, you need to add a new `<script>` element to the HTML document. I have downloaded the library to my computer and placed it in the js folder, so the src attribute will point to js/markerclusterer.js. See Listing 9-3.

Listing 9-3. The HTML Code for Example 9-2

```
<!DOCTYPE html PUBLIC "-//W3C//DTD XHTML 1.0 Strict//EN"
    "http://www.w3.org/TR/xhtml1/DTD/xhtml1-strict.dtd">

<html xmlns="http://www.w3.org/1999/xhtml" lang="en">
  <head>
    <meta http-equiv="Content-Type" content="text/html; charset=utf-8" />
    <title>Dealing with massive amounts of markers - Example 9-2</title>
    <link rel="stylesheet" href="css/style.css" type="text/css" media="all" />
    <script type="text/javascript"
        src="http://maps.google.com/maps/api/js?sensor=false&language=en"></script>
    <script type="text/javascript" src="js/markerclusterer.js"></script>
    <script type="text/javascript" src="js/9-2.js"></script>
  </head>
  <body>

    <div id="map"></div>

  </body>
</html>
```

Now that you have the library linked in, it's available to use. You will start from the code you wrote in the first example of this chapter and extend it to use the MarkerClusterer library.

Reconstructing the Loop

The first thing you're going to do is to change the loop a bit. Instead of creating a marker at each iteration, you're going to add the markers to an array. Let's call the array markers and add it just above the for loop in the code.

```
var markers = [];
```

Inside the for loop, you're changing the creation of the marker so that it's not instantly added to the map. This is done by omitting the map property. You're also going to store the marker inside a variable called marker.

```
var marker = new google.maps.Marker({
  position: latlng
});
```

Finally, you're adding the marker to the markers array by using the push() method.

```
markers.push(marker);
```

Having made these adjustments to the code, the for loop should look like this:

```
// Creating an array that will store the markers
var markers = [];

for (var i = 0; i < 100; i++) {

  // Creating a random position
  var lat = southWest.lat() + latSpan * Math.random();
  var lng = southWest.lng() + lngSpan * Math.random();
  var latlng = new google.maps.LatLng(lat, lng);

  // Creating a marker. Note that we don't add it to the map
  var marker = new google.maps.Marker({
    position: latlng
  });

  // Adding the marker to the markers array
  markers.push(marker);

}
```

After the loop has run the markers array will be filled with 100 marker objects that have not yet been added to the map.

Creating a MarkerClusterer Object

In its most basic use, all you have to do to create a MarkerClusterer object is to tell it which map to use and what markers to add.

Table 9-4. Definition of the MarkerClusterer Constructor

Constructor	Description
MarkerClusterer(map:Map, markers?:Array, options?:Object)	Creates a MarkerClusterer that will cluster the markers and add them to the map.

Since you've already prepared an array with markers, all you have to do is to add one line of code. This is added right after the loop.

```
var markerclusterer = new MarkerClusterer(map, markers);
```

Doing this the markers are automatically grouped in clusters and being added to the map. If you run the code, the map should look something like Figure 9-10.

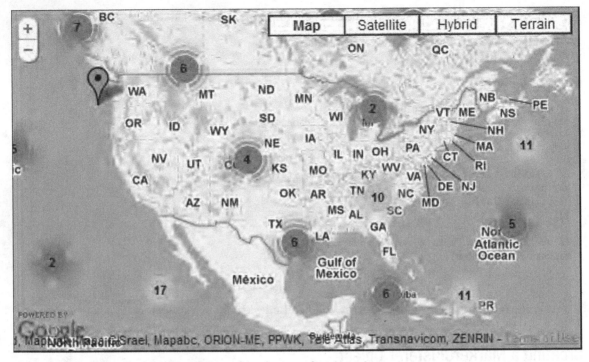

Figure 9-10. The markers are now grouped in clusters of various size.

Notice that the size of the clusters is indicated by both color and number (see Table 9-5). The number in the middle indicates the number of markers that the cluster contains. There's also a single marker on the map that has not been clustered. That's because it was too far away from other markers to be included.

Table 9-5. Cluster Sizes

Color	Size of Cluster	Comment
Blue	< 10	Clusters with less than 10 markers will look like this.
Yellow	< 100	Clusters with 10 to 100 markers will look like this.
Red	< 1000	In most cases this will be the biggest cluster you'll ever have. At this point performance is starting to degrade.
Purple	< 10.000	10.000 is a lot of markers. Probably too many to use even with clusters.
Dark purple	10.000+	This cluster will probably never be used. Using this amount of markers will be painfully slow in all browsers and will probably make IE crash.

As you probably noticed, this is a really fast and easy way to create clusters. This makes it perfect for fast solutions to the many-markers problem.

The Complete Code for This Example

Listing 9-4 shows the complete JavaScript code for this example.

Listing 9-4. The Complete JavaScript Code for Example 9-2

```
(function() {

  window.onload = function() {

    // Creating a map
    var options = {
      zoom: 3,
      center: new google.maps.LatLng(37.09, -95.71),
      mapTypeId: google.maps.MapTypeId.ROADMAP
    };
    var map = new google.maps.Map(document.getElementById('map'), options);

    google.maps.event.addListenerOnce(map, 'bounds_changed', function() {

      // Getting the boundaries of the map
      var bounds = map.getBounds();

      // Getting the corners of the map
      var southWest = bounds.getSouthWest();
      var northEast = bounds.getNorthEast();

      // Calculating the distance from the top to the bottom of the map
      var latSpan = northEast.lat() - southWest.lat();

      // Calculating the distance from side to side
      var lngSpan = northEast.lng() - southWest.lng();

      // Creating an array that will store the markers
      var markers = [];

      // Creating a loop
      for (var i = 0; i < 1000; i++) {

        // Creating a random position
        var lat = southWest.lat() + latSpan * Math.random();
        var lng = southWest.lng() + lngSpan * Math.random();
        var latlng = new google.maps.LatLng(lat, lng);

        // Creating a marker. Note that we don't add it to the map
        var marker = new google.maps.Marker({
          position: latlng
        });

        // Adding the marker to the markers array
        markers.push(marker);
```

```
        }

        // Creating a MarkerClusterer object and adding the markers array to it
        var markerclusterer = new MarkerClusterer(map, markers);

    });

  };

})();
```

Tweaking the Clustering with Options

When constructing a `MarkerClusterer` object, there's a third argument called `options` that you can pass along to change some of the behaviors of the object. It has four properties:

- **gridSize**
  The `MarkerClusterer` object divides the map into a grid. All markers within a grid are grouped into a cluster. With this property you can change the size of the grid. It takes a number representing the size in pixels as its value. The default value is 60.

- **maxZoom**
  This property determines the maximum zoom level at which a marker can be part of a cluster. It takes a number as its value, and if you don't explicitly set it, it will default to the maximum zoom level of the map.

- **zoomOnClick**
  You can control whether clicking a cluster will zoom the map in or not by using this property. It takes a Boolean as its value, and the default value is true.

- **styles**
  With this property, you can apply different styles to the clusters. It takes an array of `MarkerStyleOptions` objects as its value. The objects in the array should be ordered by cluster size. So, the first object should be the one styling the smallest cluster, and the last object should be the one styling the largest cluster. To learn more about how to set this, check out the reference documentation in the file repository.

To use the options object, you simply create an object literal and pass it as the third argument to the constructor of the `MarkerManager` object. If you would like to set the `gridSize` to 100 and `zoomOnClick` to `false`, you would write the following:

```
var markerclusterer = new MarkerClusterer(map, markers, {
  'gridSize': 100,
  'zoomOnClick': false
});
```

Further Resources

The `MarkerClusterer` object has more methods and features than I have described here. For more information, check out the reference documentation at the file repository at http://google-maps-utility-library-v3.googlecode.com/svn/tags/markerclusterer/1.0/docs/reference.html. It will provide you with a full overview of all of the features of the MarkerClusterer library.

MarkerManager

MarkerManager is another utility library for Google Maps. It's not primarily a clustering solution (although it can be used for this as you will see later in this chapter). Its primary job is to reduce the number of markers on the map by only rendering the ones that are inside the current viewport. This way, the browser isn't bogged down with markers that wouldn't be visible anyway. When the user pans or zooms the map, the MarkerManager library will recalculate which markers to render and adds those that are now inside the viewport and removes those that are outside.

The file repository for MarkerManager is found at http://google-maps-utility-library-v3.googlecode.com/svn/tags/markerclusterer/1.0/. There you will find both the source files, examples, and documentation.

Adding a Reference to the Library

First you need to add a reference in the HTML file that points to the MarkerManager library. It is inserted in the <head> section of the document, right under the reference to the Google Maps API.

```
<script type="text/javascript" src="js/markermanager_packed.js"></script>
```

In this case I've chosen to add a reference to the packed version of the library in order to reduce the file size the browser needs to download. You could of course add a reference to the unpacked version, markermanager.js, during development. Table 9-6 describes the versions of MarkerManager.

Table 9-6. The Different File Versions of MarkerManager

Filename	File Size	Uses
markermanager.js	29KB	Use this during development since you can review and debug the code. Also useful if you want to extend the library with more functionality.
markermanager_packed.js	6KB	Use for production site. Its smaller file size makes it faster to download.

The complete HTML for this example will look like Listing 9-5.

Listing 9-5. The HTML Code for Example 9-3

```
<!DOCTYPE html PUBLIC "-//W3C//DTD XHTML 1.0 Strict//EN"
    "http://www.w3.org/TR/xhtml1/DTD/xhtml1-strict.dtd">

<html xmlns="http://www.w3.org/1999/xhtml" lang="en">
  <head>
    <meta http-equiv="Content-Type" content="text/html; charset=utf-8" />
    <title>Dealing with massive amounts of markers - Example 9-3</title>
    <link rel="stylesheet" href="css/style.css" type="text/css" media="all" />
    <script type="text/javascript"
        src="http://maps.google.com/maps/api/js?sensor=false&language=en"></script>
    <script type="text/javascript" src="js/markermanager_packed.js"></script>
    <script type="text/javascript" src="js/9-2.js"></script>
  </head>
```

```
<body>

  <div id="map"></div>

</body>
</html>
```

The JavaScript

Start this example from the JavaScript code shown in Listing 9-6. It will create a map that's zoomed down somewhere in the middle of the United States.

Listing 9-6. The Starting JavaScript Code for Example 9-3

```
(function() {

  window.onload = function() {

    // Creating a map
    var options = {
      zoom: 5,
      center: new google.maps.LatLng(37.99, -93.77),
      mapTypeId: google.maps.MapTypeId.ROADMAP
    };
    var map = new google.maps.Map(document.getElementById('map'), options);

  };

})();
```

Creating a MarkerManager Object

In the JavaScript file you're now going to add code to create a `MarkerManager` object. You are then going to create several markers at random locations and add these to the object.

Let's start by creating a new `MarkerManager` object. In its simplest form, all you need to do is to pass a reference to the map to it. You will insert this code right below the code that creates the map.

```
var mgr = new MarkerManager(map);
```

The `MarkerManager` constructor does have an optional second argument, which is an object literal containing options for tweaking its default settings (see Table 9-7). For now, you will omit this and settle with the default settings, but you will come back to the options object later in this chapter.

Table 9-7. Definition of the MarkerManager Constructor

Constructor	Description
MarkerManager(map:Map, options?:Object)	Creates an empty MarkerManager object

Creating the Markers

The next step is to create all of the markers. You'll start by creating an array that will contain them. Let's call the array markers.

```
var mgr = new MarkerManager(map);
var markers = [];
```

You will use the same code as in the two previous examples for creating random markers but change it a little bit. Instead of creating markers inside the current viewport, you'll define the boundaries within which the markers will be created as a square covering most of the United States. Since you already know the boundaries, you don't have to listen for the maps bounds_changed event but can go straight to defining the boundaries and creating the markers (Figure 9-11).

```
var mgr = new MarkerManager(map);
var markers = [];

var southWest = new google.maps.LatLng(24, -126);
var northEast = new google.maps.LatLng(50, -60);
var lngSpan = northEast.lng() - southWest.lng();
var latSpan = northEast.lat() - southWest.lat();
```

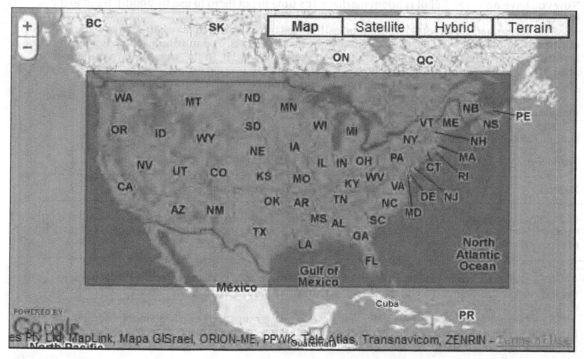

Figure 9-11. The markers will be created within these boundaries covering most of the United States.

197

Having done that, you're ready to create the loop that will create the markers. This code is identical to the code used in the previous example. It creates 100 markers at random locations within our bounds and adds them to the markers array.

```
for (var i = 0; i < 100; i++) {

    // Calculating a random location
    var lat = southWest.lat() + latSpan * Math.random();
    var lng = southWest.lng() + lngSpan * Math.random();
    var latlng = new google.maps.LatLng(lat, lng);

    // Creating a marker
    var marker = new google.maps.Marker({
        position: latlng
    });

    // Adding the marker to the array
    markers.push(marker);

}
```

Adding the Markers to the MarkerManager

Now you have an array full of random markers. It's time to put them to use by adding them to the MarkerManager object.

The MarkerManager object has a method called addMarkers(), which takes an array of markers and a minimum zoom level at which they will appear as its arguments. The minimum zoom level can be used if you don't want the markers to be visible when you go beyond it. In this case, you want them to always be visible, so you set it to 1, which is when the map is zoomed out all the way. If you have set it to 10, you would have to zoom in to zoom level 10 of the map before the markers would appear.

So, let's add the markers to the MarkerManager object. This code will appear right under the loop that you just created.

```
mgr.addMarkers(markers, 1);
```

Table 9-8. Definition of the addMarkers() Method of MarkerManager

Method	Return value	Description
addMarkers(markers:Array, minZoom:Number, maxZoom?:Number)	None	Adds an array of markers. Note that it only adds them to the MarkerManager object, not to the map.

The addMarkers() method doesn't actually add the markers to the map. It only adds them to the MarkerManager object. To add the markers to the map, you need to call a second method called refresh().

The refresh() method serves a dual purpose. If no markers are yet added to the map, it adds them. But if the MarkerManager object has already added markers to the map, the refresh() method will remove and reinsert them.

```
mgr.addMarkers(markers, 1);
mgr.refresh();
```

Now it looks like we're done, but if you try this code, it won't work. The reason for this is that just like the Google Maps API, the MarkerManager library works asynchronously. This means that you have to make sure that it has loaded before you try to use it. This is done by listening to the *loaded* event of the MarkerManager object.

```
google.maps.event.addListener(mgr, 'loaded', function() {
  mgr.addMarkers(markers, 1);
  mgr.refresh();
});
```

Now you're all set and the markers are properly added to the map. If you try to pan the map, perhaps you will notice that new markers are loaded. I say *perhaps* because if you're using a really fast browser like Google Chrome, this happens so fast that you might not even notice.

This behavior is the whole point of using the MarkerManager library. It makes sure that only the markers that matter are visible at one time, thereby providing a better overall performance of the map (Figure 9-12).

■ **Note** The MarkerManager object also has a method called addMarker() that takes a single marker and a minimum zoom level as its arguments. It instantly adds the marker to the map. The reason I'm not using it here is because the addMarkers() method provides better performance when inserting several markers at once.

Figure 9-12. 100 markers are added to the map. The MarkerManager library only displays those that are within the current viewport.

The Final Code for This Example

Listing 9-7 shows the final JavaScript code for this example.

Listing 9-7. The Final JavaScript Code for Example 9-3

```
(function() {

  window.onload = function() {

    // Creating a map
    var options = {
      zoom: 5,
      center: new google.maps.LatLng(37.99, -93.77),
      mapTypeId: google.maps.MapTypeId.ROADMAP
    };
    var map = new google.maps.Map(document.getElementById('map'), options);

    // Creating a new MarkerManager object
    var mgr = new MarkerManager(map);

    // Creating an array that will contain all of the markers
    var markers = [];

        // Setting the boundaries within where the markers will be created
        var southWest = new google.maps.LatLng(24, -126);
        var northEast = new google.maps.LatLng(50, -60);
        var lngSpan = northEast.lng() - southWest.lng();
        var latSpan = northEast.lat() - southWest.lat();

    // Creating markers at random locations
    for (var i = 0; i < 100; i++) {

      // Calculating a random location
      var lat = southWest.lat() + latSpan * Math.random();
      var lng = southWest.lng() + lngSpan * Math.random();
        var latlng = new google.maps.LatLng(lat, lng);

      // Creating a marker
      var marker = new google.maps.Marker({
        position: latlng
      });

      // Adding the marker to the array
      markers.push(marker);
    }

    // Making sure the MarkerManager is properly loaded before we use it
    google.maps.event.addListener(mgr, 'loaded', function() {

      // Adding the markers to the MarkerManager
      mgr.addMarkers(markers, 1);

      // Adding the markers to the map
```

```
        mgr.refresh();

    });

  };

})();
```

Getting in Charge of the Zoom Levels

Another way that the MarkerManager can be used is to control at which zoom level different markers are visible. This way, you can use it to create clusters. The main difference creating clusters this way instead of using a library like MarkerClusterer is that the clusters are not automatically created. You have to manually define which clusters to have and which markers will reside in them. Even though it requires more work on your part to create this kind of cluster, it also enables you to create clusters that make more sense to the user. We could for example create *regional clusters*, something that you will explore in the next example.

Regional Clustering with MarkerManager

Because of MarkerManager's ability to define the zoom levels at which certain markers will appear, you can use it to create regional clusters. Actually, these will not be proper clusters in the sense that you create a specific cluster and add markers to it. But for the user, it will appear that these are real clusters.

What you will do is to create "cluster markers" that will appear at a high zoom level. As you zoom in on the map, you will remove the cluster markers and replace them with specific markers.

In this particular example, you will create two clusters, one for Utah and one for Colorado. You will also create markers for some of the cities in these states. The Utah and Colorado markers will only appear on a high zoom-level. And the city markers will only appear at a lower zoom level.

The Starting Code

Listing 9-8 shows the starting JavaScript code for this example. It will create a map centered over the United States that is zoomed out to a pretty low zoom level.

Listing 9-8. The Starting JavaScript for Example 9-4

```
(function() {

  window.onload = function(){

    // Creating a map
    var options = {
      zoom: 3,
      center: new google.maps.LatLng(37.99, -93.77),
      mapTypeId: google.maps.MapTypeId.ROADMAP
    };
    var map = new google.maps.Map(document.getElementById('map'), options);

  };

})();
```

Creating the Clusters

Before you create the clusters, you will create a new MarkerManager object. You do this the exact same way as in the former example by passing a reference to the map to it. This code goes just below the code that creates the map.

```
var mgr = new MarkerManager(map);
```

Having done that, it's time to create the cluster markers. You will create one marker that represents Utah and one that represents Colorado and add them to an array called states. To distinguish the cluster markers from regular markers, you will give them a different look. You will do this by setting the icon property to a URL to an image called cluster.png (see Figure 9-13).

Figure 9-13. The cluster icon. It's from the map icons collection found at http://code.google.com/p/google-maps-icons/.

```
var states = [
  new google.maps.Marker({
    position: new google.maps.LatLng(39.4698, -111.5962),
    icon: 'img/cluster.png'
  }),
  new google.maps.Marker({
    position: new google.maps.LatLng(38.9933, -105.6196),
    icon: 'img/cluster.png'
  })
];
```

Next you will create another array called cities. This array will contain all the city markers. These will all have the default marker icon look, so all you need to do is to define the position property.

```
var cities = [
  // Colorado Springs
  new google.maps.Marker({position: new google.maps.LatLng(38.8338, -104.8213)}),
  // Denver
  new google.maps.Marker({position: new google.maps.LatLng(39.7391, -104.9847)}),
  // Glenwood Springs
  new google.maps.Marker({position: new google.maps.LatLng(39.5505, -107.3247)}),
  // Salt Lake City
  new google.maps.Marker({position: new google.maps.LatLng(40.7607, -111.8910)}),
  // Fillmore
  new google.maps.Marker({position: new google.maps.LatLng(38.9688, -112.3235)}),
  // Spanish Fork
  new google.maps.Marker({position: new google.maps.LatLng(40.1149, -111.6549)})
];
```

Adding the Markers to the MarkerManager

With the arrays in place, you need to add them to the MarkerManager object. But first you have to set up an event listener to listen for the loaded event of the MarkerManager object.

```
google.maps.event.addListener(mgr, 'loaded', function() {
  // Code goes here
};
```

Now you can start adding the arrays to the MarkerManager object, and you will do this by using the addMarkers() method. In the former example, you only set the minimum zoom level for when a marker would appear, but now you will also set the maximum zoom level.

Let's start by adding the overview array that contains the cluster markers. You want these two markers to appear only on a fairly high zoom level, so you set the minimum zoom level to 1 (maxed zoomed out) and the maximum zoom level to 5.

```
google.maps.event.addListener(mgr, 'loaded', function() {

  // These markers will only be visible between zoom level 1 and 5
  mgr.addMarkers(states, 1, 5);

});
```

Next you'll add the cities array to the MarkerManager object. You want these markers to appear at a zoom level that's below the zoom level that the state markers will appear. So, you set the minimum zoom level to 6. There's no need to set the maximum zoom level because if you omit it, it will default to the deepest zoom level of the map.

```
google.maps.event.addListener(mgr, 'loaded', function() {

  // These markers will only be visible between zoom level 1 and 5
  mgr.addMarkers(states, 1, 5);

  // These markers will be visible at zoom level 6 and deeper
  mgr.addMarkers(cities, 6);

});
```

Now all the markers are added to the MarkerManager object. All that's left to do is to refresh it so that the markers are added to the map.

```
google.maps.event.addListener(mgr, 'loaded', function() {

  // These markers will only be visible between zoom level 1 and 5
  mgr.addMarkers(states, 1, 5);

  // These markers will be visible at zoom level 6 and deeper
  mgr.addMarkers(cities, 6);

  // Making the MarkerManager add the markers to the map
  mgr.refresh();

});
```

You now have a map that appears to have regional clustering. When you load it, only the two cluster markers will be visible. As you zoom in, the cluster markers will disappear, and the city markers will become visible (Figures 9-14 and 9-15).

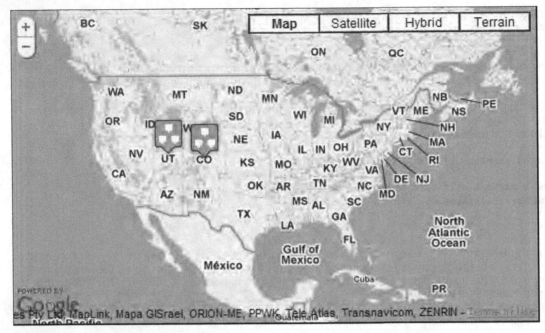

Figure 9-14. *At a high zoom level, only the two cluster markers are visible.*

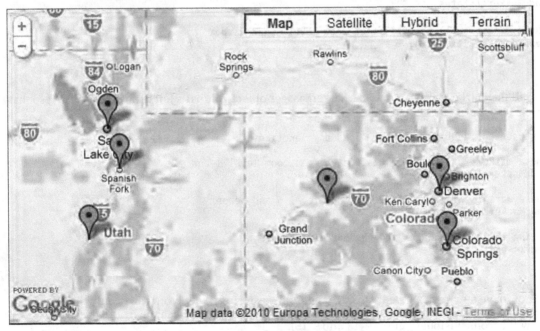

Figure 9-15. *As you zoom down past zoom level 6, only the city markers are visible.*

The Complete Code So Far

Listing 9-9 shows the complete code.

Listing 9-9. The Complete Code for Example 9-4

```
(function() {

  window.onload = function() {

    // Creating a map
    var options = {
      zoom: 3,
      center: new google.maps.LatLng(37.99, -93.77),
      mapTypeId: google.maps.MapTypeId.ROADMAP
    };
    var map = new google.maps.Map(document.getElementById('map'), options);

    // Initializing the MarkerManager
    var mgr = new MarkerManager(map);

    // Creating an array that will contain one marker for Colorado
    // and one for Utah
    var states = [
      new google.maps.Marker({
        position: new google.maps.LatLng(39.4698, -111.5962),
        icon: 'img/cluster.png'
      }),
      new google.maps.Marker({
        position: new google.maps.LatLng(38.9933, -105.6196),
        icon: 'img/cluster.png'
      })
    ];

    // Creating an array that will contain markers that is positioned
    // at cities in Colorado and Utah
    var cities = [
      // Colorado Springs
      new google.maps.Marker({position: new google.maps.LatLng(38.8338, -104.8213)}),
      // Denver
      new google.maps.Marker({position: new google.maps.LatLng(39.7391, -104.9847)}),
      // Glenwood Springs
      new google.maps.Marker({position: new google.maps.LatLng(39.5505, -107.3247)}),
      // Salt Lake City
      new google.maps.Marker({position: new google.maps.LatLng(40.7607, -111.8910)}),
      // Fillmore
      new google.maps.Marker({position: new google.maps.LatLng(38.9688, -112.3235)}),
      // Spanish Fork
      new google.maps.Marker({position: new google.maps.LatLng(40.1149, -111.6549)})
    ];

    // Making sure the MarkerManager is properly loaded before we use it
    google.maps.event.addListener(mgr, 'loaded', function() {

      // These markers will only be visible between zoom level 1 and 5
```

```
    mgr.addMarkers(states, 1, 5);

    // These markers will be visible at zoom level 6 and deeper
    mgr.addMarkers(cities, 6);

    // Making the MarkerManager add the markers to the map
    mgr.refresh();

  });

 };

})();
```

Adding Clickable Clusters

To make the clusters even more usable, you will add some additional functionality. You're going to extend the previous example by adding a click event to the cluster markers so that when they're clicked, the map will zoom in on it, revealing the city icons.

To do this, you need to change how you're adding the cluster markers to the states array. You will change this functionality, storing the markers inside an individual variable. You're then going to add the click behavior to it and finally add the variables to the states array. Let's start by creating the marker that represents Colorado.

```
var colorado = new google.maps.Marker({
  position: new google.maps.LatLng(39.4568, -105.8532),
  icon: 'img/cluster.png'
});
```

Next you want to add a click event to the marker.

```
google.maps.event.addListener(colorado, 'click', function() {
  // Code goes here
});
```

In the event handler, you will add code that will set the zoom level of the map to 7. At this zoom level, the cluster markers will be removed, and the city markers will be visible. You will also add code to center the map on the position of the clicked marker. You will recognize the methods for doing this from Chapter 4.

```
google.maps.event.addListener(colorado, 'click', function() {

  // Setting the zoom level of the map to 7
  map.setZoom(7);

  // Setting the center of the map to the clicked markers position
  map.setCenter(colorado.getPosition());

});
```

Next you'll do the same thing for the marker that represents Utah:

```
var utah = new google.maps.Marker({
  position: new google.maps.LatLng(40.0059, -111.9176),
  icon: 'img/cluster.png'
});

google.maps.event.addListener(utah, 'click', function() {
  map.setZoom(7);
  map.setCenter(utah.getPosition());
});
```

With the cluster markers all set up, it's time to create the states array and add the markers to it.

```
var states = [colorado, utah];
```

Now all the necessary changes are made, and you now have a map with clickable cluster markers. If you try it, you find that clicking one of the cluster markers will zoom the map in, revealing the city markers (Figure 9-16).

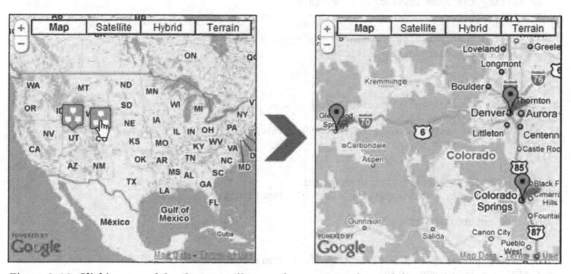

Figure 9-16. Clicking one of the clusters will zoom the map in and reveal the city clusters.

The Final Code

Listing 9-10 shows the final code for this example.

Listing 9-10. The Complete Code for Example 9-5

```
(function() {

  window.onload = function(){

    // Creating a map
```

```
var options = {
  zoom: 3,
  center: new google.maps.LatLng(37.99, -93.77),
  mapTypeId: google.maps.MapTypeId.ROADMAP
};
var map = new google.maps.Map(document.getElementById('map'), options);

// Initializing MarkerManager
var mgr = new MarkerManager(map);

// Creating a marker that represents Colorado
var colorado = new google.maps.Marker({
  position: new google.maps.LatLng(39.4568, -105.8532),
  icon: 'img/cluster.png'
});

// Adding a click event to the Colorado marker
google.maps.event.addListener(colorado, 'click', function() {

  // Setting the zoom level of the map to 7
  map.setZoom(7);

  // Setting the center of the map to the clicked markers position
  map.setCenter(colorado.getPosition());

});

// Creating a marker that represents Utah
var utah = new google.maps.Marker({
  position: new google.maps.LatLng(40.0059, -111.9176),
  icon: 'img/cluster.png'
});

// Adding a click event to the Utah marker
google.maps.event.addListener(utah, 'click', function() {
  map.setZoom(7);
  map.setCenter(utah.getPosition());
});

// Creating an array that will contain the markers forColorado and Utah
var states = [colorado, utah];

// Creating an array that will contain markers that is positioned
// at cities in Colorado and Utah
var cities = [
  // Colorado Springs
  new google.maps.Marker({position: new google.maps.LatLng(38.8338, -104.8213)}),
  // Denver
  new google.maps.Marker({position: new google.maps.LatLng(39.7391, -104.9847)}),
  // Glenwood Springs
  new google.maps.Marker({position: new google.maps.LatLng(39.5505, -107.3247)}),
  // Salt Lake City
  new google.maps.Marker({position: new google.maps.LatLng(40.7607, -111.8910)}),
  // Fillmore
```

```
    new google.maps.Marker({position: new google.maps.LatLng(38.9688, -112.3235)}),
    // Spanish Fork
    new google.maps.Marker({position: new google.maps.LatLng(40.1149, -111.6549)})
];

// Making sure the MarkerManager is properly loaded before we use it
google.maps.event.addListener(mgr, 'loaded', function() {

    // These markers will only be visible between zoom level 1 and 5
    mgr.addMarkers(states, 1, 5);

    // These markers will be visible at zoom level 6 and deeper
    mgr.addMarkers(cities, 6);

    // Making the MarkerManager add the markers to the map
    mgr.refresh();

});

};

})();
```

Tweaking the MarkerManager with Options

When creating a new `MarkerManager` object, you can pass a long an options object. These options tweak the way the `MarkerManager` object works. I'm just going to tell you which options are available and what they do:

- **maxZoom**
  This property takes a number as its value and sets the maximum zoom-level at which a marker can be part of a cluster. When you use the `addMarkers()` method to add markers and don't pass along a value for the `maxZoom` attribute, it will use this value instead. The default value is the map's maximum zoom level.

- **borderPadding**
  The `MarkerManager` object just renders the markers that are inside the current viewport, but it has a buffer zone just outside the viewport where markers also will appear. The reason for this is that when you pan the map shorter distances, you will get a better user experience since the nearest markers are already loaded. By default, this buffer zone is set to 100 pixels, but you can set it to something different using this property. As you probably already guessed, this property takes a number as its value.

- **trackMarkers**
  If you change the position of markers after you've added them to the `MarkerManager` object, you should set this property to true. If you don't, the `MarkerManager` object will not keep track of your markers, and if you move one, it will appear at two places simultaneously. Setting this option to true provides poorer performance, so you might not want to use it if you're sure you're not going to change the positions of the markers. The default value of `trackMarkers` is `false`.

The options object is an object literal that you just pass along when creating a new `MarkerManager` object. So if you want to set the `maxZoom` to 15, the `borderPadding` to 0, and the `trackMarkers` to true, you do it like this:

```
var mgr = new MarkerManager(map, {
  'maxZoom': 15,
  'borderPadding': 0,
  'trackMarkers': true
});
```

In this example, I changed all the properties, but you don't have to do that. You can just define those that you want to change. For example, if I only want to change the `trackMarkers` property to true, I write it like this:

```
var mgr = new MarkerManager(map, {
  'trackMarkers': true
});
```

Further Resources

We've been looking at some of the features of MarkerManager library, but there's even more to it. The library features a number of methods that you can use to show and hide markers, clear markers, and other useful things. For a full description of all the methods available, check out the reference documentation at the file repository at `http://google-maps-utility-library-v3.googlecode.com/svn/tags/markermanager/1.0/docs/reference.html`.

Summary

In this chapter, you learned about different ways of dealing with a lot of markers. The best solution is often to not show all markers at the same time. You can do this by adding filtering, searching or clustering capabilities. Sometimes even not using markers at all is a solution. If none of these approaches is a viable solution to the problem, then at least you can resort to using the utility library MarkerManager, which will increase the overall performance of the map by only adding those markers that are currently within the viewport.

■ ■ ■

Location, Location, Location

Often you need to find out where a location is. Maybe you have an address but don't know exactly where that address is located. Then you can turn to geocoding to get that position. This chapter will explain how geocoding and reverse geocoding work. You will learn how to look up addresses and how to show them on a map.

You will also learn about geolocation, which is different ways of getting the position of the person using a map.

Geocoding

Geocoding is an integrated part of the Google Maps API. When you send in an address, you get the coordinates for that address back. It's that simple! This is very handy in circumstances where you only have an address, but you still somehow want to automatically plot it on a map.

Restrictions

The Geocoding service if freely available, but it does have some limitations, since it's a fairly processor-intensive request. It's currently limited to 2,500 geocode requests every 24 hours from a single IP address. That's not an insignificant amount of requests, so in most cases, this will more than suffice. It's not the end of the world if you exceed that limit once or twice, but repeated abuse can result in a permanent ban.

■ **Note** The Geocoding service integrated in the Google Maps API is meant for dynamically geocoding addresses from user input. If you instead have a static list of addresses that you want to look up, you should use the Geocoding web service, which is better suited for that particular task. You can find it at

`http://code.google.com/apis/maps/documentation/geocoding/index.html`.

The Geocoder Object

All the functionality for doing geocoding lookups is found in the Geocoder object. It doesn't take any arguments upon initialization and has only one method: gecode(). This makes it one of the smallest objects in the Google Maps API. To initialize the Geocoder object, simply call its constructor:

```
var geocoder = new google.maps.Geocoder();
```

Building an Address Lookup Web Page

In the following sections, I will take you through the steps of building a web page with which you can look up the location of addresses. The web page will consist of a simple form and a map. The form will contain a text input for entering an address and a button for submitting the form. The map will place a marker where the address is located and add an InfoWindow, which will contain information about the address and its coordinates. Figure 10-1 shows how the finished web page will look.

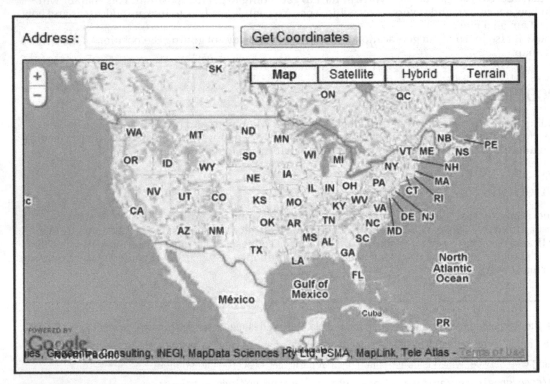

Figure 10-1. A web page for address lookups

Adding the HTML

Let's start by adding the HTML for this web page. It will look almost identical to the HTML you've used in the other examples throughout the book with an additional HTML form (Listing 10-1).

Listing 10-1. The HTML for Example 10-1

```
<!DOCTYPE html PUBLIC "-//W3C//DTD XHTML 1.0 Strict//EN"
  "http://www.w3.org/TR/xhtml1/DTD/xhtml1-strict.dtd">

<html xmlns="http://www.w3.org/1999/xhtml" lang="en">
  <head>
    <meta http-equiv="Content-Type" content="text/html; charset=utf-8" />
    <title>Geocoding- Google Maps API 3</title>
    <link rel="stylesheet" href="css/style.css" type="text/css" media="all" />
    <script type="text/javascript"
        src="http://maps.google.com/maps/api/js?sensor=false&language=en"></script>
    <script type="text/javascript" src="js/10-1.js"></script>
</head>
<body>

  <form id="addressForm">
    <div>
      <label for="address">Address:</label>
      <input type="text" name="address" id="address" />
      <input type="submit" id="addressButton" value="Get Coordinates" />
    </div>
  </form>

  <div id="map"></div>

</body>
</html>
```

The form has the id="addressForm". You're going to use this ID to catch the submit event from the JavaScript. Other than that, it's a form with a text input with a label and a submit button.

The CSS

You're going to do some light styling to the web page (Listing 10-2). First you'll set the font of the page. Then you'll give the form a bottom margin of 10 pixels to leave some whitespace between it and the map. Last, you'll add the dimensions of the map container and add a black 1-pixel border to it. This code will be located in the file style.css.

Listing 10-2. The CSS for Example 10-1

```
body {
  font-family: Verdana, Geneva, Arial, Helvetica, sans-serif;
  font-size: small;
}
form {
```

```
  margin-bottom: 10px;
}
#map {
  width: 500px;
  height: 300px;
  border: 1px solid black;
}
```

The Starting JavaScript

With the HTML and CSS in place, you get to the interesting part, the JavaScript code (Listing 10-3). You start by laying a foundation. This code will create a regular map centered over the United States.

Listing 10-3. The Starting JavaScript for Example 10-1

```
(function() {

  // Defining some global variables
  var map, geocoder, marker, infowindow;

  window.onload = function() {

    // Creating a new map
    var options = {
      zoom: 3,
      center: new google.maps.LatLng(37.09, -95.71),
      mapTypeId: google.maps.MapTypeId.ROADMAP
    };

    map = new google.maps.Map(document.getElementById('map'), options);

    // Code for catching the form submit event goes here

  }

  // Function stub
  function getCoordinates() {

  }
})();
```

Notice that you define some variables at the top of the code. They are defined there since you need to have access to them from a function that you will create later.

Now that you have the foundation laid out, it's time to start building the functionality for finding the position of an address.

Setting Up the Event Handler

The first thing you will do is to set up the event handler for the form. You do this by catching the form's submit event. On submit, you take the address from the text input and use it as a parameter for the function getCoordinates() that you're going to create in a minute.

This code will go just after the code that creates the map, right where there's a comment that says, "Code for catching the form submit event goes here":

```
// Getting a reference to the HTML form
var form = document.getElementById('addressForm');

// Catching the forms submit event
form.onsubmit = function() {

  // Getting the address from the text input
  var address = document.getElementById('address').value;

  // Making the Geocoder call
  getCoordinates(address);

  // Preventing the form from doing a page submit
  return false;

}
```

With that in place, you have the form set up. When you enter something into the text input and click the submit button, the getCoordinate() function will be invoked. The next step is to create the functionality for that function.

Looking Up an Address

You will put this functionality in the function getCoordinates(). It will take one argument, and that is the address. It will then use the Geocoder object to look up the position of the address. You already have the stub for this function set up. It's located almost at the end of the code, right under the comment "Function stub":

```
function getCoordinates(address) {

  // Check to see if we already have a geocoded object. If not we create one
  if(!geocoder) {
    geocoder = new google.maps.Geocoder();
  }

}
```

Doing this, you now have a Geocoder object that you can use to make lookups. The Geocoder object has only one method: geocode(). It takes two arguments. The first argument is a GeocoderRequest object, and the second one is a callback function. The GeocoderRequest object is an object literal with five properties. For now we're going to stick with only the most important one, the address property. This property takes a string containing the address you want to look up. So if, for example, you want to look up where Regent Street 4 in London is located, you just define that as its value.

```
var geocoderRequest = {
  address: 'Regent Street 4, London'
};
```

In our case, since you want to do lookups based on user input, you can't have the value for the address property hard-coded. Instead, you want to pass the address argument in your function as the value for the property:

```
function getCoordinates(address) {

  // Check to see if we already have a geocoded object. If not we create one
  if(!geocoder) {
    geocoder = new google.maps.Geocoder();
  }

  // Creating a GeocoderRequest object
  var geocoderRequest = {
    address: address
  }

}
```

The second argument of geocode() is a callback function that takes care of its response. The geocode() method return two values that need to be passed to the callback function: results and status.

```
function getCoordinates(address) {

  // Check to see if we already have a geocoded object. If not we create one
  if(!geocoder) {
    geocoder = new google.maps.Geocoder();
  }

  // Creating a GeocoderRequest object
  var geocoderRequest = {
    address: address
  }

  // Making the Geocode request
  geocoder.geocode(geocoderRequest, function(results, status) {

    // Code that will handle the response

  });

}
```

Taking Care of the Response

The geocode method passes two values along with its response, results and status. First let's take a look at status.

You can use the status code to see how the request went. It will basically tell you whether the request was successful. All the statuses are of the type google.maps.GeocoderStatus. One status is, for example, OK, and it will look like this: google.maps.GeocoderStatus.OK.

Here's a list of all the possible status codes:

- **OK**
  This code indicates that everything went all right and that a result is returned.

- **ZERO_RESULTS**
  If you get this status code, the request went all right but didn't return any results.
  Maybe the address you looked for doesn't exist.

- **OVER_QUERY_LIMIT**
  This status indicates that you've used up your quota. Remember that there's a
  limit of 2,500 requests a day.

- **REQUEST_DENIED**
  This indicates exactly what it says. The request was denied for some reason. The
  most common reason for this is that the sensor parameter is missing.

- **INVALID_REQUEST**
  This status indicates that something was wrong with your request. Maybe you
  didn't define an address (or latLng).

When you take care of the response, you should always check the status code to see that the request
was successful before doing anything with it. If something went wrong, you should also provide the
users with some feedback of this.

For now you will only check to see that the request was successful, so you extend the callback
function with a check of that:

```
function getCoordinates(address) {

  // Check to see if we already have a geocoded object. If not we create one
  if(!geocoder) {
    geocoder = new google.maps.Geocoder();
  }

  // Creating a GeocoderRequest object
  var geocoderRequest = {
    address: address
  }

  // Making the Geocode request
  geocoder.geocode(geocoderRequest, function(results, status) {

    // Check if status is OK before proceeding
    if (status == google.maps.GeocoderStatus.OK) {

      // Do something with the response

    }

  });

}
```

Interpreting the Result

Now that you've checked the status of the request to make sure that it was successful, you can start
looking at the results parameter. It contains the actual geocoding information. It's a JSON object that
can contain more than one result for an address. After all, there can be addresses with the same name
at different locations. Therefore, the results come as an array. This array contains a number of fields:

- **types**
  This is an array that contains what type of location the returned result is. It could, for example, be a country or a locality, which indicates that it's a city or town.

- **formatted_address**
  This is a string that contains the address in a readable format. If you, for example, search for *Boston*, this will return "Boston, MA, USA." As you can see, it actually contains several facts about the address. In this case, it's the name of the city, the name of the state, and the name of the country.

- **address_components**
  This is an array containing the different facts about the location. Each of the parts listed in formatted_address is an object in this array with a long_name a short_name and the types.

- **geometry**
  This field is an object with several properties. The most interesting one is location, which contains the position of the address as a LatLng object. It also has other properties such as viewport, bounds, and location_type.

You are now going to use the returned JSON object to create a marker and put it at the correct position in the map.

Even if the Gecoder returns more than one result, you're going to trust that it returns the most relevant one first. So, instead of showing them all on the map, you're going to just show the first one. The first thing you're going to do is center the map on the returned location. You do this by using the map object's setCenter() method and pass the returned location as its value. You're also going to check whether you already have a marker; if you don't, you're going to create one and then position it at the returned location. Note that I've shortened the code for brevity.

```
function getCoordinates(address) {

[…]

// Making the Geocode request
geocoder.geocode(geocoderRequest, function(results, status) {

  // Check if status is OK before proceeding
  if (status == google.maps.GeocoderStatus.OK) {

    // Center the map on the returned location
    map.setCenter(results[0].geometry.location);

    // Check to see if we've already got a Marker object
    if (!marker) {

      // Creating a new marker and adding it to the map
      marker = new google.maps.Marker({
        map: map
      });

    }
```

```
  // Setting the position of the marker to the returned location
  marker.setPosition(results[0].geometry.location);

  }
 });

}
```

Adding an InfoWindow

The next step is to create an InfoWindow, which will contain a description of the address and its coordinates. You start by checking whether you already have an InfoWindow object; if you don't, you create one. You then create the content for the InfoWindow and add it using its setContent() method. Finally, you open the InfoWindow.

```
function getCoordinates(address) {

  [...]

  // Making the Geocode request
  geocoder.geocode(geocoderRequest, function(results, status) {

    // Check if status is OK before proceeding
    if (status == google.maps.GeocoderStatus.OK) {

      // Center the map on the returned location
      map.setCenter(results[0].geometry.location);

      // Check to see if we've already got a Marker object
      if (!marker) {

        // Creating a new marker and adding it to the map
        marker = new google.maps.Marker({
          map: map
        });

      }

      // Setting the position of the marker to the returned location
      marker.setPosition(results[0].geometry.location);

      // Check to see if we've already got an InfoWindow object
      if (!infowindow) {
        // Creating a new InfoWindow
        infowindow = new google.maps.InfoWindow();
      }

      // Creating the content of the InfoWindow to the address
      // and the returned position
      var content = '<strong>' + results[0].formatted_address + '</strong><br />';
      content += 'Lat: ' + results[0].geometry.location.lat() + '<br />';
      content += 'Lng: ' + results[0].geometry.location.lng();
```

```
    // Adding the content to the InfoWindow
    infowindow.setContent(content);

    // Opening the InfoWindow
    infowindow.open(map, marker);

  }

});

}
```

Now you have a working example. If you try it and look for an address, it will put a marker on the map at its location, accompanied by an InfoWindow that indicates the name of the place and its coordinates (Figure 10-2).

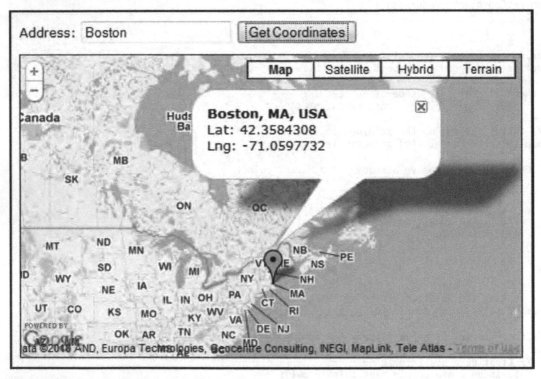

Figure 10-2. The result you get when searching for Boston

The Complete JavaScript Code for This Example

Listing 10-4 shows the complete JavaScript code for this example.

Listing 10-4. The Complete JavaScript Code for Example 10-1

```
(function() {

 // Defining some global variables
 var map, geocoder, marker, infowindow;

 window.onload = function() {

   // Creating a new map
   var options = {
     zoom: 3,
     center: new google.maps.LatLng(37.09, -95.71),
     mapTypeId: google.maps.MapTypeId.ROADMAP
   };

   map = new google.maps.Map(document.getElementById('map'), options);

   // Getting a reference to the HTML form
   var form = document.getElementById('addressForm');

   // Catching the forms submit event
   form.onsubmit = function() {
     // Getting the address from the text input
     var address = document.getElementById('address').value;

     // Making the Geocoder call
     getCoordinates(address);

     // Preventing the form from doing a page submit
     return false;

   }

 }

 // Create a function the will return the coordinates for the address
 function getCoordinates(address) {
   // Check to see if we already have a geocoded object. If not we create one
   if(!geocoder) {
     geocoder = new google.maps.Geocoder();
   }

   // Creating a GeocoderRequest object
   var geocoderRequest = {
     address: address
   }

   // Making the Geocode request
```

```
geocoder.geocode(geocoderRequest, function(results, status) {

    // Check if status is OK before proceeding
    if (status == google.maps.GeocoderStatus.OK) {

        // Center the map on the returned location
        map.setCenter(results[0].geometry.location);

        // Check to see if we've already got a Marker object
        if (!marker) {
            // Creating a new marker and adding it to the map
            marker = new google.maps.Marker({
                map: map
            });
        }

        // Setting the position of the marker to the returned location
        marker.setPosition(results[0].geometry.location);

        // Check to see if we've already got an InfoWindow object
        if (!infowindow) {
            // Creating a new InfoWindow
            infowindow = new google.maps.InfoWindow();
        }

        // Creating the content of the InfoWindow to the address
        // and the returned position
        var content = '<strong>' + results[0].formatted_address + '</strong><br />';
        content += 'Lat: ' + results[0].geometry.location.lat() + '<br />';
        content += 'Lng: ' + results[0].geometry.location.lng();

        // Adding the content to the InfoWindow
        infowindow.setContent(content);

        // Opening the InfoWindow
        infowindow.open(map, marker);

    }

});

}

})();
```

Extending the Example

You can do several things to improve this example. First, you should include better error handling so when something goes wrong, you can let the user know what happened. Second, you could take care of all the results instead of just the first one in the results array. This is done by looping through the results array and adding each location as a marker to the map.

Reverse Geocoding

Reverse geocoding is the exact opposite of geocoding. Instead of looking up a position from an address, you look up an address from a position.

The nice thing about reverse geocoding is that it's done the same way as geocoding. The only difference is that instead of providing the service with the property address, you provide it with the property latLng.

Building a Reverse Geocoding Map

You're going to build a map that, when you click in it, returns the address information for the location being clicked. The information will be shown in an InfoWindow (Figure 10-3).

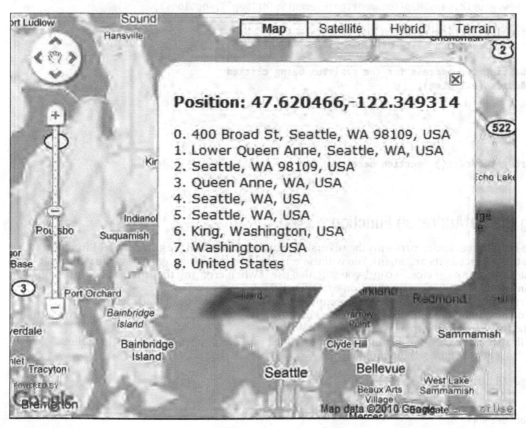

Figure 10-3. *The address returned for the location of the Space Needle in Seattle*

You will start by creating a map and adding an event listener to it that will listen for clicks in it (Listing 10-5). When the map is being clicked, the position for the point in the map where the click occurred will be passed to a function called getAddress(). This function doesn't yet exist, but you will create it in a moment.

Listing 10-5. Starting Code for Example 10-2

```
(function() {
  var map, geocoder, infoWindow;

  window.onload = function() {

    // Creating a new map
    var options = {
      zoom: 3,
      center: new google.maps.LatLng(37.09, -95.71),
      mapTypeId: google.maps.MapTypeId.ROADMAP
    };

    map = new google.maps.Map(document.getElementById('map'), options);

    // Attaching a click event to the map
    google.maps.event.addListener(map, 'click', function(e) {

      // Getting the address for the position being clicked
      getAddress(e.latLng);

    });

  }

  // Insert getAddress() function here

})();
```

Creating the getAddress() Function

Now to the code that actually performs the reverse geocoding. You need the getAddress() function to accept a latLng object as its argument. You will use this position for two things. First, you will use it as input to the Geocoding service. Second, you will also use it when creating the InfoWindow since you want the InfoWindow to point at the position that was clicked.

The first thing you will do inside the function is to check whether you already have a Geocoder object. If you already have one (that is, a request has already been made), you reuse it. Otherwise (that is, this is the first click in the map), you create a new one.

You will insert the code for the function almost at the end of the starting code, right at the comment: "Insert getAddress() function here":

```
function getAddress(latLng) {

  // Check to see if a geocoder object already exists
  if (!geocoder) {
    geocoder = new google.maps.Geocoder();
  }

}
```

Now that you've made sure that you have a Geocoder object, you use it to make your request. But before doing that, you will create a GeocoderRequest object with the input parameters for the call. It's the same object that you used in the previous example with one big difference. Instead of inputting an address to its address property, you use its latLng property and provide your latLng parameter as its value.

The call to the Geocoder service will look exactly the same as in the previous example. You will use its geocode() method to make your call, inputting the GeocoderRequest object and an anonymous function that will take care of the response.

```
function getAddress(latLng) {

  // Check to see if a geocoder object already exists
  if (!geocoder) {
    geocoder = new google.maps.Geocoder();
  }

  // Creating a GeocoderRequest object
  var geocoderRequest = {
    latLng: latLng
  }

  geocoder.geocode(geocoderRequest, function(results, status) {

    // Code that will take care of the returned result

  });

}
```

Now that the call to the geocoder is made, you need to handle the response. First you will make sure that you have an InfoWindow object to display the result in. If you don't have one, you create it. Then you set the position of the InfoWindow to the same as the latLng parameter to make sure that it'll point at the right spot.

```
function getAddress(latLng) {

  [...]

  geocoder.geocode(geocoderRequest, function(results, status) {

    // If the infoWindow hasn't yet been created we create it
    if (!infoWindow) {
      infoWindow = new google.maps.InfoWindow();
    }

    // Setting the position for the InfoWindow
    infoWindow.setPosition(latLng);

  });

}
```

With the InfoWindow set up, you will start creating the content to fill it with. You do this by defining a variable called content. The heading in the InfoWindow will be the LatLng for the clicked position. You know that you have this information, so you add it right away to content.

As for the result of the Geocoder request, you're not so sure that you get something back, so you need to check the status variable for this. If the status is OK, you will proceed to add all the returned addresses to it. If it's not OK, you will instead add a message that no address was returned. The most common case when you don't get an address back is that the Geocoder service simply couldn't find an address. It will then return ZERO_RESULTS. If, for example, you click in the middle of the ocean, this will be the case (Figure 10-4).

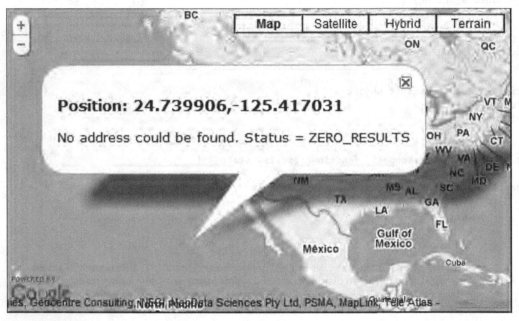

Figure 10-4. *If you click in the middle of the ocean, you won't get an address back.*

In the case where the call was successful, you probably have several addresses to display. They are the same address but expressed in different levels of detail. They typically go from very specific to more general, where the most specific one is probably the street address, and the most general one is the country that the address is found in. These values are all found in the results parameter, which actually is an array. You will loop through this array and use its formatted_address property to add to the content variable.

The last thing you will do is to add the content to the InfoWindow by using its setContent() method and open it using its open() method:

```
function getAddress(latLng) {

  [...]

  geocoder.geocode(geocoderRequest, function(results, status) {

    // If the infoWindow hasn't yet been created we create it
```

```
  if (!infoWindow) {
    infoWindow = new google.maps.InfoWindow();
  }

  // Setting the position for the InfoWindow
  infoWindow.setPosition(latLng);

  // Creating content for the InfoWindow
  var content = '<h3>Position: ' + latLng.toUrlValue() + '</h3>';

  // Check to see if the request went allright
  if (status == google.maps.GeocoderStatus.OK) {

    // Looping through the results
    for (var i = 0; i < results.length; i++) {
      if (results[0].formatted_address) {
        content += i + '. ' + results[i].formatted_address + '<br />';
      }
    }

  } else {
    content += '<p>No address could be found. Status = ' + status + '</p>';
  }

  // Adding the content to the InfoWindow
  infoWindow.setContent(content);

  // Opening the InfoWindow
  infoWindow.open(map);

  });

}
```

That's it; you now have a reverse geocoding map that will display the address of the location being clicked.

The Complete Code for This Example

Listing 10-6 shows the complete JavaScript code for this example.

Listing 10-6. The Complete JavaScript Code for Example 10-2

```
(function() {
  var map, geocoder, infoWindow;

  window.onload = function() {

    // Creating a new map
      var options = {
        zoom: 3,
        center: new google.maps.LatLng(37.09, -95.71),
        mapTypeId: google.maps.MapTypeId.ROADMAP
```

```
    };
    map = new google.maps.Map(document.getElementById('map'), options);

    // Attaching a click event to the map
    google.maps.event.addListener(map, 'click', function(e) {

  // Getting the address for the position being clicked
  getAddress(e.latLng);

    });

}

function getAddress(latLng) {

  // Check to see if a geocoder object already exists
  if (!geocoder) {
    geocoder = new google.maps.Geocoder();
  }

  // Creating a GeocoderRequest object
  var geocoderRequest = {
    latLng: latLng
  }

  geocoder.geocode(geocoderRequest, function(results, status) {

    // If the infoWindow hasn't yet been created we create it
    if (!infoWindow) {
      infoWindow = new google.maps.InfoWindow();
    }

    // Setting the position for the InfoWindow
    infoWindow.setPosition(latLng);

    // Creating content for the InfoWindow
    var content = '<h3>Position: ' + latLng.toUrlValue() + '</h3>';

    // Check to see if the request went allright
    if (status == google.maps.GeocoderStatus.OK) {

      // Looping through the result
      for (var i = 0; i < results.length; i++) {
        if (results[0].formatted_address) {
          content += i + '. ' + results[i].formatted_address + '<br />';

        }
      }

    } else {
      content += '<p>No address could be found. Status = ' + status + '</p>';
    }

    // Adding the content to the InfoWindow
```

```
        infoWindow.setContent(content);

        // Opening the InfoWindow
        infoWindow.open(map);

    });

  }

})();
```

Finding the Location of the User

As more people are using advanced mobile devices such as the iPhone and Android phones, location-aware applications are getting more and more common. There are several ways of finding the location of the user. The best and most accurate one is if the device using the application has a GPS, but even if it doesn't, there are ways of locating it, although not with the same precision.

Desktop browsers normally don't have access to a GPS, but the computer is connected to a network and has an IP address, which can reveal the approximate location of the user.

IP-Based Geocoding

One way of finding the location of the user is through IP-based geocoding. So far in the book, you've been loading the Google Maps API by simply referring to it in a <script> element. There is another way of loading it, and that's through google.load, which is part of the Google AJAX API. If you use it to load the Maps API, you get the additional benefit of the location of the user.

To use the Google AJAX API, you need to load it into the page using a <script> element and then utilize its google.load() method to load additional APIs. You include the Google AJAX API like this in the <head> section of the web page:

```
<script type="text/javascript" src="http://www.google.com/jsapi"></script>
```

Once the Google AJAX API is loaded, its load() method is available, and you can use to load additional APIs from your JavaScript code. Here's how to load v3 of the Google Maps API:

```
google.load('maps', 3, {'other_params': 'sensor=false'});
```

The parameters passed are the name of the API (maps), the version of the API (3), and an option object containing additional settings. In this case, you want to add the sensor parameter to the query string of the URL to the API, and this is done with the other_params property.

■ **Note** Just like with the old Google Maps API v2, it's possible to use an API key when inserting the Google AJAX API. This is, however, optional. The reason you might want to use it is that it enables Google to contact you if it detects a problem that involves your application. The API key is free and can be obtained at http://code.google.com//apis/ajaxsearch/signup.html.

Getting the Position

The interesting part of using google.load is that you now have access to an approximate location of the user. This information is found in google.loader.ClientLocation. Note that the location determined from IP is not very accurate, so the greatest level of detail is the metro level, which is a city or a town. Sometimes the location is not even available at all, so you need to take this into account when building your map by providing a fallback.

The ClientLocation object has several properties that are of interest:

- **latitude**
  Returns a number representing the latitude for the location

- **longitude**
  Returns a number representing the longitude for the location

- **address.city**
  Returns the name of the city associated with the location

- **address.country**
  Returns the name of the country associated with the location

- **address.country_code**
  Specifies the ISO 3166-1 country code associated with the location, for example US for the United States, JP for Japan, and SE for Sweden

- **address.region**
  Returns the country-specific region name associated with the location

---

■ **Note** To learn more about the Google AJAX APIs, check out the documentation at http://code.google.com/apis/ajax/documentation/.

Creating a Location-Aware Map

You will now build a map that will try to determine the location of the user, put a marker on that location, and add an InfoWindow, which will contain the name of the location. If you're not able to determine the location of the user, you will default to center the map on (0, 0).

Creating the HTML

You start by creating the HTML file for this example (Listing 10-7). What makes this HTML file different from the other examples in the book is that instead of adding the Google Maps API directly using a <script> element in the head section of the page, you add the Google AJAX API.

Listing 10-7. The HTML Code for Example 10-3

```
<!DOCTYPE html PUBLIC "-//W3C//DTD XHTML 1.0 Strict//EN"
    "http://www.w3.org/TR/xhtml1/DTD/xhtml1-strict.dtd">

<html xmlns="http://www.w3.org/1999/xhtml" lang="en">
```

```
<head>
  <meta http-equiv="Content-Type" content="text/html; charset=utf-8" />
  <title>Chapter 10 - Example 10-3</title>
  <link rel="stylesheet" href="css/style.css" type="text/css" media="all" />
  <script type="text/javascript"
      src="http://www.google.com/jsapi"></script>
  <script type="text/javascript" src="js/10-3.js"></script>
</head>
<body>
  <div id="map"></div>
</body>
</html>
```

As you can see in the previous HTML code, you also add a reference to an external JavaScript file called 10-3.js. That's where you will write your code.

Creating the JavaScript Code

You start the code by loading the Google Maps API. Then you create a handler for the window.onload event (Listing 10-8).

Listing 10-8. The Starting JavaScript Code for Example 10-3

```
(function() {

  // Loading the Google Maps API
  google.load('maps', 3, {
    'other_params': 'sensor=false&language=en'
  });

  window.onload = function() {

    // The rest of the code will go here

  }

})();
```

Now you're ready to try to get the position of the user by using the google.loader.ClientLocation object. You will first check to see that you really have a location before proceeding. As a fallback, you provide a default location at (0, 0). You will also create the content for the InfoWindow, which will consist of the name of the city and country of the location.

```
window.onload = function() {

  // Getting the position
  if (google.loader.ClientLocation.latitude && google.loader.ClientLocation.longitude) {

    // Defining the position
    var latLng = new google.maps.LatLng(google.loader.ClientLocation.latitude,
                  google.loader.ClientLocation.longitude);
```

```
    // Creating the content for the InfoWindow
    var location = 'You are located in '
    location += google.loader.ClientLocation.address.city + ', ';
    location += google.loader.ClientLocation.address.country;

  } else {

    // Providing default values as a fallback
    var latLng = new google.maps.LatLng(0, 0);
    var location = 'Your location is unknown';

  }

}
```

Having done that, you have all the information you need to create the map and add a marker and an InfoWindow to it. You will use the latLng for both the map and the marker.

```
window.onload = function() {

  // Getting the position
  [...]

  // Creating a map
  var options = {
    zoom: 2,
    center: latLng,
    mapTypeId: google.maps.MapTypeId.ROADMAP
  };

  map = new google.maps.Map(document.getElementById('map'), options);

  // Adding a marker to the map
  var marker = new google.maps.Marker({
    position: latLng,
    map: map
  });

  // Creating a InfoWindow
  var infoWindow = new google.maps.InfoWindow({
    content: location
  });

  // Adding the InfoWindow to the map
  infoWindow.open(map, marker);

}
```

Now if you use your map, it will try to determine your location. In my case, the location is Stockholm, Sweden, which is a bit weird since I'm actually sitting in Växjö (Figure 10-5). IP-based geolocating is unfortunately not an exact science. A lot of times it gets it right, but then again, sometimes it doesn't. But hey, at least it got the country right!

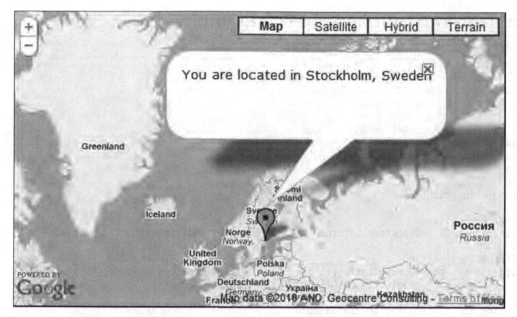

Figure 10-5. My location is determined to be Stockholm, Sweden.

If the map is entirely unable to detect your location, it will default to position (0, 0) and let you know that your location is unknown (Figure 10-6).

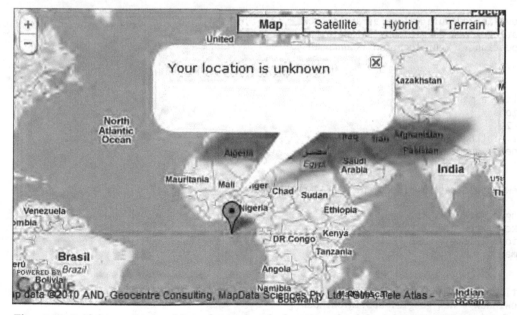

Figure 10-6. If the map is unable to determine the location, the default location is being used as a fallback.

The Complete JavaScript Code for This Example

Listing 10-9 shows complete JavaScript code for this example.

Listing 10-9. The Complete JavaScript Code for Example 10-3

```
(function() {

  // Loading the Google Maps API
  google.load('maps', 3, {
    'other_params': 'sensor=false&language=en'
  });

  window.onload = function() {

    // Getting the position
    if (google.loader.ClientLocation.latitude && google.loader.ClientLocation.longitude) {

      // Defining the position
      var latLng = new google.maps.LatLng(google.loader.ClientLocation.latitude,
                         google.loader.ClientLocation.longitude);

      // Creating the content for the InfoWindow
      var location = 'You are located in '
      location += google.loader.ClientLocation.address.city + ', ';
      location += google.loader.ClientLocation.address.country;

    } else {

      // Providing default values as a fallback
      var latLng = new google.maps.LatLng(0, 0);
      var location = 'Your location is unknown';

    }

    // Creating a map
    var options = {
      zoom: 2,
      center: latLng,
      mapTypeId: google.maps.MapTypeId.ROADMAP
    };

    map = new google.maps.Map(document.getElementById('map'), options);

    // Adding a marker to the map
    var marker = new google.maps.Marker({
      position: latLng,
      map: map
    });

    // Creating a InfoWindow
    var infoWindow = new google.maps.InfoWindow({
```

```
      content: location
    });

    // Adding the InfoWindow to the map
    infoWindow.open(map, marker);

  }

})();
```

Getting Better Accuracy

As you noticed with IP-based geolocation, it's not very accurate and can actually be completely wrong about the user's whereabouts, as the case was for me. Fortunately, better options for getting the location of the user are starting to emerge. Several browsers are already supporting the Geolocation API, which is an emerging W3C standard for finding the location of a device.

Right now, Firefox 3.5+, Chrome 5.0+, iPhone 3.0+, and Android 2.0+ support this standard. This means that you can use it to get a more accurate position.

■ **Tip** The Geolocation API specification is found at www.w3.org/TR/geolocation-API/.

Different Levels of Accuracy

There are several levels of accuracy when trying to determine the user's location. You've already looked at the least accurate one, IP-based. Mobile devices such as the iPhone and Android phones have a few other methods. The first and fastest one is to calculate the position by triangulating the relative distance to different cellular towers. This method, depending on the number of nearby cell towers, gives you accuracy from a few hundred meters to a kilometer. The second and most accurate method is by using GPS. It takes a bit longer to find the location but can provide an accuracy of a few meters.

Privacy Concerns

Does this sound a bit scary to you, that a remote web server is able to know your location? Don't worry; sharing your location is always something that you have to give your consent for—well, except for IP-based geolocating, as you've already looked at, but it gives such a rough estimate of where you are, so it's not really a concern.

A browser will always ask for your permission to use your location. Exactly how it's implemented is different in different browsers. In Firefox, for example, an info bar will appear at the top of the page asking whether you want to share your location (Figure 10-7).

Figure 10-7. An info bar at the top of the page is how Firefox asks your permission to use your location.

Different Implementations

If the browser doesn't support the Geolocation API, there are two more options. First there's Google Gears, which is an open source browser plug-in. If the browser doesn't support the Geolocation API, Google Gears will provide a similar API. Some mobile devices also have their own proprietary Geolocation APIs. Some of these devices are Blackberry, Nokia, and Palm.

Unfortunately, all these APIs are implemented differently, which means that if you would like to use them, you have to provide different solutions for each API.

Fortunately, someone has already done this for you. geo.js is an open source JavaScript library that will do all the hard work for you and provide you with a unified API.

■ **Tip** You'll find geo.js at http://code.google.com/p/geo-location-javascript/.

Building a More Accurate Map

In the following section, you will use geo.js to build a web page that will detect the location of the user and show it on a map. This location will be a lot more accurate than the one that you built in the previous example. What it will do is to first load a map that is zoomed out to show the whole world. Once the location of the user is detected, it will use that location to add a marker and an InfoWindow to the map.

Creating the HTML

You will need to add three JavaScript libraries to the web page in order for this to work (Listing 10-10). The first one is the Google Maps API. You will go back to adding it with a <script> element. The second one is a script called gears_init.js. It will initialize Google Gears if it's installed. The third script is geo.js, which contains the unified API that you're going to use. Lastly, you will of course also add a reference to an external JavaScript file where you will add your own code; in this case, it's called 10-4.js.

Listing 10-10. The HTML Code for Example 10-4

```
<!DOCTYPE html PUBLIC "-//W3C//DTD XHTML 1.0 Strict//EN"
  "http://www.w3.org/TR/xhtml1/DTD/xhtml1-strict.dtd">

<html xmlns="http://www.w3.org/1999/xhtml" lang="en">
  <head>
    <meta http-equiv="Content-Type" content="text/html; charset=utf-8" />
    <title>Chapter 10 - Example 10-4</title>
    <link rel="stylesheet" href="css/style.css" type="text/css" media="all" />
    <script type="text/javascript"
        src="http://maps.google.com/maps/api/js?sensor=false"></script>
    <script type="text/javascript"
        src="http://code.google.com/apis/gears/gears_init.js"></script>
    <script type="text/javascript" src="js/geo.js"></script>
    <script type="text/javascript" src="js/10-4.js"></script>
  </head>
```

```
<body>
  <div id="map"></div>
</body>
</html>
```

The Starting JavaScript

You'll start with a script (Listing 10-11) that creates a map on page load (Figure 10-8) that will display the entire world. Note that you define the variable map at the top so that you'll have access to it in functions that you will create later.

Listing 10-11. The Starting JavaScript Code for Example 10-4

```
(function() {

  var map;

  window.onload = function() {

    // Creating a map
    var options = {
      zoom: 1,
      center: new google.maps.LatLng(31.35, 3.51),
      mapTypeId: google.maps.MapTypeId.ROADMAP
    };

    map = new google.maps.Map(document.getElementById('map'), options);

    // Call to geo.js goes here

  }

  // Function stubs
  function handleError() {

  }

  function setPosition() {

  }
})();
```

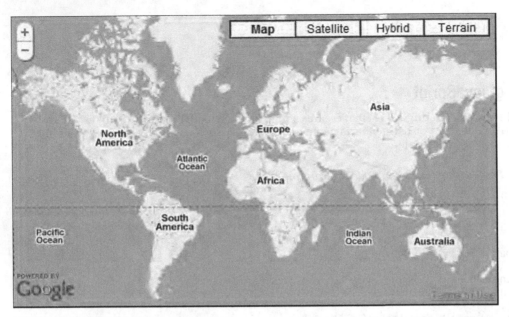

Figure 10-8. The inital map

Now, the next step is to try to determine the location of the user. All the methods of geo.js reside in the geo_position_js object. First you need to initialize the geo_position_js object. This is done with its method init(). It'll return true if the initialization went well and geofunctionality is available. Because of this, you can make the call to that method inside an if statement. If it returns true, you proceed; otherwise, you throw an alert with an error message. Put this code right below the creation of the map where a comment says "Call to geo.js goes here":

```
// Checking if geo positioning is available
if (geo_position_js.init()) {

  // Try to determine the location of the device

} else {

  alert('Geo functionality is not available');

}
```

If the initialization went well, you use the getCurrentPosition() method to determine the location of the device. This method takes three arguments. The first one is a callback function that will be invoked if the API was able to determine the location. The second argument is a callback function that will be invoked if an error was thrown, and the last argument is a settings object.

You're going to use just one setting, and that is enableHighAccuracy. By setting it to true, the detection might be slower, but you're going to get as accurate a position as possible.

```
// Checking if geo positioning is available
if (geo_position_js.init()) {
```

```
  // Creating a settings object
  var settings = {
    enableHighAccuracy: true
  };

  // Trying to determine the location of the device
  geo_position_js.getCurrentPosition(setPosition, handleError, settings);

} else {

  alert('Geo functionality is not available');

}
```

Now you need to create the two callback functions, setPosition() and handleError(). You already have stubs for these set up, and now it's time to fill them with functionality. The latter function, handleError(), is the easiest one. All it will do is to catch the error being thrown and show it in an alert. The object being passed to it contains a message property with the error message. You'll find the stub for this function almost at the end of the code, right below the comment "Function stubs":

```
function handleError(error) {
  alert('Error = ' + error.message);
}
```

The setPosition() method does a bit more. It will use the position being passed to it to create a marker and an InfoWindow. The object that's being passed to it contains the property coords, which contains the latitude and the longitude that you need to create a LatLng object. The function stub for this is found right after the handleError() function.

```
function setPosition(position) {

  // Creating a LatLng from the position info
  var latLng = new google.maps.LatLng(position.coords.latitude, position.coords.longitude);

  // Adding a marker to the map
  var marker = new google.maps.Marker({
    position: latLng,
    map: map
  });

  // Creating an InfoWindow
  var infoWindow = new google.maps.InfoWindow({
    content: 'You are here!'
  });

  // Adding the InfoWindow to the map
  infoWindow.open(map, marker);

  // Zooming in on the map
  map.setZoom(6);

}
```

That's it. You should now have a working example. If you run the web page, it will first show you a page with a map on it. If the browser has support for geolocation, it will then ask you whether you want to share your location (Figure 10-9).

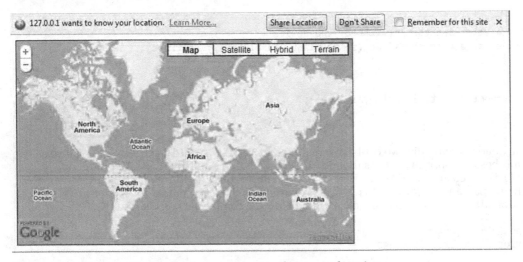

Figure 10-9. Firefox will ask whether you want to share your location.

If you allow the browser to share your location, your script will try to grab your current location and then put a marker and an InfoWindow there (Figure 10-10). Note that it can take a while for the API to get your location, so be patient.

Figure 10-10. The map puts a marker at your current location.

This time, the script managed to get a more correct location for me, proving that this technique is a lot more reliable and accurate than just using the IP address.

Extending the Example

You could do several things to enhance this example. First, you should add a check to make sure that the map is loaded before trying to put a marker on it. You should also have better error handling. Since geolocating is still a very immature technique, there's a high probability that the browser won't support it, even if you're using geo.js. There's also a big risk that the user won't allow you to use their current location. In both of these cases, you should provide fallbacks and don't have the code relying on being able to detect the location.

■ **Tip** To learn more about how to determine the user's location, read the excellent article "You Are Here (and So Is Everybody Else)" on http://diveintohtml5.org/geolocation.html.

The Complete JavaScript Code for This Example

Listing 10-12 shows the complete JavaScript code for this example.

Listing 10-12. The Complete JavaScript Code for Example 10-4

```
(function() {

  var map;

  window.onload = function() {

    // Creating a map
    var options = {
      zoom: 1,
      center: new google.maps.LatLng(31.35, 3.51),
      mapTypeId: google.maps.MapTypeId.ROADMAP
    };

    map = new google.maps.Map(document.getElementById('map'), options);

      // Checking if geo positioning is available
      if (geo_position_js.init()) {

        // Creating a settings object
        var settings = {
          enableHighAccuracy: true
        };

        // Trying to determine the location of the user
        geo_position_js.getCurrentPosition(setPosition, handleError, settings);
```

```
        } else {

            alert('Geo functionality is not available');

        }

    };

    function handleError(error) {
      alert('Error = ' + error.message);
    }

    function setPosition(position) {

        // Creating a LatLng from the position info
        var latLng = new google.maps.LatLng(position.coords.latitude,
                        position.coords.longitude);

        // Adding a marker to the map
        var marker = new google.maps.Marker({
          position: latLng,
          map: map
        });

        // Creating an InfoWindow
        var infoWindow = new google.maps.InfoWindow({
          content: 'You are here!'
        });

        // Adding the InfoWindow to the map
        infoWindow.open(map, marker);

        // Zooming in on the map
        map.setZoom(6);

    }

})();
```

Summary

In this chapter, you learned how to do address lookups using the Geocoder service. This is very useful for finding the right addresses and the right locations for addresses. You also looked at different ways of determining the location of the user. This is something increasingly important because we're moving toward a context-driven mobile web.

This is also the end of the last chapter of the book. I hope that you've enjoyed the book and found it useful. I also hope that you're now able to build your own mapping solutions with the Google Maps API. And remember anything is possible; only your own imagination sets the limit.

■ ■ ■

API Reference

Use this appendix to look up specific classes, objects, methods, and properties that are available in the API. Note, however, that this is not a complete reference; it contains only the classes and objects that are covered in this book. The API also changes over time, mostly with new additions, but sometimes with changed functionality. The complete and most up-to-date API reference is therefore always found at http://code.google.com/apis/maps/documentation/javascript/reference.html.

How to Read the Reference

The way the constructors and methods are described is as follows:

Map(mapDiv:Node, opts?:MapOptions)

First you see the name of the method and then within the parentheses is its arguments. The arguments are described as follows:

variableName:variableType

Before the colon is a descriptive variable name, and after the colon is the type of the variable. If there's a question mark after the variable name, it means that it's an optional argument.

Data Types

For both methods and properties, the data type is described. These data types can be either primitive, like string, number, and boolean, or custom like MouseEvent and StreetviewPanorama. The primitive ones are self-explained, and the custom ones refer to classes and objects within the Maps API. The notation for describing arrays and MVCArrays look a bit different, though. The type for the mapTypeIds property of the MapTypeControlOptions object, for example, looks like this:

Array.<MapTypeId>

What this means is that the type is an array that contains MapTypeId objects. MVCArrays are a special kind of array, so the notation for them looks the same. Here's what the overlayMapTypes property of the Map object looks like:

MVCArray.<MapType>

In this case, it means that the value for this property is an MVCArray that contains MapType objects.

The Namespace

All the classes of the Google Maps API reside in the namespace google.maps. That means whatever class or method you want to call always starts with google.maps. Here's, for example, how to call the constructor for the Marker class:

```
new google.maps.Marker();
```

So, whenever you need to use a class or object, make sure to always insert the namespace name in front of it.

The Reference

Use the following sections as reference.

Map Class

This class contains all the method and properties for creating a map. It extends MVCObject (described later).

Constructor

Table A-1 shows the constructor of the Map class.

Table A-1. Constructor of the Map Class

Constructor	Description
Map(mapDiv:Node, opts?:MapOptions)	This is the constructor for the entire Map object. It creates a new map inside mapDiv, which is typically a reference to a <div> in the HTML. This is of type MapOptions.

Methods

Table A-2 shows the methods of the Map object.

Table A-2. The Methods of the Map Object

Method	Return Value	Description
fitBounds(bounds:LatLngBounds)	None	Adjusts the map so that it fits inside the bounds being passed to it.
getBounds()	LatLngBounds	Returns the bounds of the map. If the map hasn't been initialized, it returns null.
getCenter()	LatLng	Returns the coordinates for the center of the map as a LatLng.
getDiv()	Node	Returns a reference to the <div> containing the map.
getMapTypeId()	MapTypeId	Gets the current MapTypeId.
getProjection()	Projection	Returns the current projection. Returns null if the map is not set.
getStreetView()	StreetViewPanorama	Gets the default StreetViewPanorama that is bound to the map. It may be either the default panorama or a panorama that's been set with the setStreetView() method or the streetView property.
getZoom()	Number	Gets the current zoom level.
panBy(x:number, y:number)	None	Pans the map in the direction indicated by the numbers in pixels. The transition will be animated.
panTo(latLng:LatLng)	None	Pans the map to set its center at the given LatLng. The transition will be animated if the distance is less than the width and height of the map.
panToBounds (latLngBounds:LatLngBounds)	None	Pans the map to contain the given LatLngBounds. If the changes are smaller than the width and height of the map, it will be animated.

Method	Return Value	Description
setCenter(latLng:LatLng)	None	Sets the center of the map.
setMapTypeId(mapTypeId:MapTypeId)	None	Sets the current mapTypeId
setOptions(options:MapOptions)	None	Sets the options of the map according to the properties being set in the MapOptions object.
setStreetView(panorama:streetView Panorama)	None	Changes the default StreetViewPanorama to a custom one that can be outside the map. By passing null to this method, the default StreetViewPanorama is again bound to the map.
setZoom(zoom:number)	None	Sets the current zoom level.

Properties

Table A-3 gives the properties of the Map object.

Table A-3. The Properties of the Map Object

Property	Type	Description
controls	Array.<MVCArray.<Node>>	Additional controls to attach to the map. To add a control to the map, add the control's <div> to the MVCArray corresponding to the ControlPosition where it should be rendered.
mapTypes	MapTypeRegistry	A registry of MapType instances by string ID.
overlayMapTypes	MVCArray.<MapType>	Contains more map types that will be used as overlays.

Events

Table A-4 gives the events of the Map object.

Table A-4. The Events of the Map Object

Event	Argument	Description
bounds_changed	None	Is fired when bounds of the viewport is changed.
center_changed	None	Is fired when the center of the map changes.
click	MouseEvent	Is fired when the user clicks the map. Note that it will not fire when the user clicks a marker or on an InfoWindow.
dblclick	MouseEvent	Is fired when the user double-clicks the map. Note that this will also trigger the click event, which will fire right before the dblclick event fires.
drag	None	Is fired over and over again as when the user is dragging the map.
dragend	None	Is fired when the user stops dragging the map.
dragstart	None	Is fired when the user starts dragging the map.
idle	None	Is fired when the map becomes idle after panning and zooming.
maptypeid_changed	None	Is fired when the mapTypeId property has changed.
mousemove	MouseEvent	Is fired over and over again as the user moves the mouse pointer over the map.
mouseout	MouseEvent	Is fired when the mouse pointer leaves the map container.
mouseover	MouseEvent	Is fired when the mouse pointer enters the map.
projection_changed	None	Is fired when the projection is changed.
resize	None	Is fired when the map <div> changes size. It should be triggered manually with this: `google.maps.event.trigger(map, 'resize')`
rightclick	MouseEvent	Is fired when the user right-clicks the map.
tilesloaded	None	Is fired when the visible map tiles have loaded.
zoom_changed	None	Is fired when the zoom property of the map is changed.

MapOptions Object

The following sections relate to the MapOptions object.

Properties

Table A-5 gives the properties of the MapOptions object. They are ordered with the required properties first and then the optional properties in alphabetic order.

Table A-5. *The Properties of the MapOptions Object*

Property	Type	Description
center	LatLng	Determines the initial center of the map. Required.
mapTypeId	MapTypeId	Determines the initial map type. Required.
zoom	number	Determines the initial zoom level of the map. Required.
backgroundColor	string	Sets the color being used for the background of the <div> containing the map. It can be set only when the map is initialized.
disableDefaultUI	boolean	Enables or disables the default UI, which is the navigation control and the map type chooser.
disableDoubleClickZoom	boolean	Enables or disables zoom-in by double-clicking the map. The default value is false.
draggable	boolean	Sets the map to be draggable or not. The default value is true.
draggableCursor	string	The name of a standard cursor or the URL to an image that will be used as a cursor indicating that an object is draggable.
draggingCursor	string	The name of a standard cursor or the URL to an image that will be used as a cursor when an object is being dragged.
keyboardShortcuts	boolean	Enables or disables keyboard shortcuts. The default value is true.

Property	Type	Description
mapTypeControl	boolean	Enables or disable the mapTypeControl. The default value is true.
mapTypeControlOptions	MapTypeControlOptions	The initial display options for the map type control.
navigationControl	boolean	Enables or disables the navigation control. The default value is true.
navigationControlOptions	NavigationControlOptions	Sets the options for the navigation control.
noClear	boolean	Prevents the map <div> to be cleared when the map loads. The default value is false.
scaleControl	boolean	Enables or disables the scale control.
scaleControlOptions	ScaleControlOptions	Sets the options for the scale control.
scrollwheel	boolean	Disables or enables scroll wheel zooming. The default value is true.
streetView	StreetViewPanorama	The StreetViewPanorama to be used by Street view. The map container will be used by default.
streetViewControl	boolean	Enables or disables the Street view control, aka the pegman.

MapTypeId Class

This class contains the default map types.

Constants

Table A-6 gives the constants in the MapTypeId class.

Table A-6. Constants in the MapTypeId Class

Constant	Description
HYBRID	This map type shows major streets on satellite images.
ROADMAP	This is the default map type. It shows a street map.

Constant	Description
SATELLITE	This map type shows satellite images.
TERRAIN	This map type shows terrain and vegetation.

MapTypeControlOptions Object

These are the options available for rendering the map type control.

Properties

Table A-7 gives the properties of the MapTypeControlOptions object.

Table A-7. The Properties of the MapOptions Object

Property	Type	Description
mapTypeIds	Array.<MapTypeId>|Array.<string>	An array containing the map types that will be available in the control
position	ControlPosition	Specifies the position for the control. The default position is TOP_RIGHT
style	MapTypeControlStyle	Determines what style the control will have

MapTypeControlStyle Class

The following sections related to the MapTypeControlStyle class.

Constants

Table A-8 gives the constants in the MapTypeControlStyle class.

Table A-8. Constants in the MapTypeControlStyle class

Constant	Description
DEFAULT	Displays the default MapTypeControl. Exactly what this is varies depending on the map size and other factors.
DROPDOWN_MENU	Displays a compact drop-down menu.
HORIZONTAL_BAR	Displays the standard horizontal map control.

NavigationControlOptions Object

The NavigationControlOptions object contains the options for displaying the navigation control.

Properties

Table A-9 gives the properties of the NavigationControlOptions object.

Table A-9. The Properties of the NavigationControlOptions Object

Property	Type	Description
position	ControlPosition	Specifies the position for the control. The default position is TOP_LEFT.
style	NavigationControlStyle	Determines what style the control will have.

NavigationControlStyle Class

The NavigationControlStyle class contains the constants for the different types of navigation controls.

Constants

Table A-10 gives the constants for the NavigationControlStyle class.

Table A-10. The Constants for the NavigationControlStyle Class

Constant	Description
ANDROID	A zoom control similar to the ones used by the native Google Maps application on Android.
DEFAULT	Displays the default control. Exactly what this is varies depending on the map size and other factors.
SMALL	The small control that only lets you zoom the map.
ZOOM_PAN	The large control that lets you both zoom and pan.

ScaleControlOptions Object

The ScaleControlOptions object contains options for displaying the scale control.

Properties

Table A-11 gives the properties of the ScaleControlOptions object.

Table A-11. The Properties of the ScaleControlOptions Object

Property	Type	Description
position	ControlPosition	Specifies the position for the control. The default position is BOTTOM_LEFT.
style	ScaleControlStyle	Determines what style the control will have.

ScaleControlStyle Class

The ScaleControlStyle class contains constants for the scale control. Well, it actually has one constant.

Constants

Table A-12 gives the constants for the ScaleControlStyle class.

Table A-12. The Constants for the ScaleControlStyle Class

Constant	Description
DEFAULT	The default control

ControlPosition Class

This class contains the different positions possible for a control.

Constants

Table A-13 gives the constants for the ControlPosition class (see also Figure A-1).

Table A-13. The Constants for the ControlPosition *Class*

Constant	Description
BOTTOM	The center of the bottom
BOTTOM_LEFT	The bottom left. They will be positioned to the right of the Google logo.
BOTTOM_RIGHT	The bottom left. They will be positioned to the left of the copyrights.
LEFT	They will be positioned to the left, under the controls positioned to the top left.
RIGHT	They will be positioned to the right, under the controls positioned to the top right.
TOP	The center of the top.
TOP_LEFT	The top left.
TOP_RIGHT	The top right.

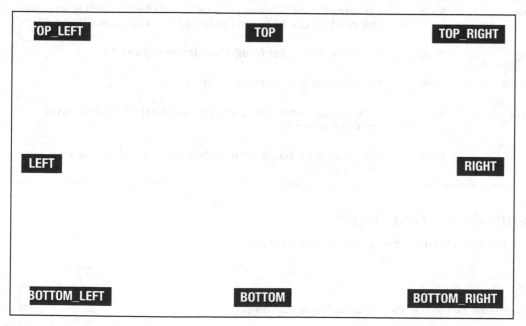

Figure A-1. The possible positions for a control

MapPanes Object

All the DOM elements in which the overlays are rendered reside in this object. They are listed in the order of their z-index, where the first one will appear at the top and the last one will appear at the bottom of the stack.

Properties

Table A-14 gives the properties of the MapPanes object.

Table A-14. The Properties of the MapPanes Object

Property	Type	Description
floatPane	Node	Contains the InfoWindows. It's at the top of the stack. (Pane 6.)
overlayMouseTarget	Node	Contains transparent element whose sole purpose is to receive the DOM mouse events for the markers. It sits above the floatShadow making the markers clickable. (Pane 5.)
floatShadow	Node	Contains the InfoWindows shadow. It is above the overlayImage so that markers can be in the shadow of the InfoWindows. (Pane 4.)
overlayImage	Node	Contains the marker foreground images. (Pane 3.)
overlayShadow	Node	Contains the marker shadows. (Pane 2.)
overlayLayer	Node	Contains polylines, polygons, ground overlays, and tile layer overlays. (Pane 1.)
mapPane	Node	The pane at the bottom of the stack. It sits just above the map tiles. (Pane 0.)

MapCanvasProjection Object

The following sections relate to the MapCanvasProjection object.

Methods

Table A-15 give the methods of the MapCanvasProjection object.

Table A-15. The Methods of the MapCanvasProjection Object

Method	Return Value	Description
fromContainerPixelToLatLng (pixel:Point)	LatLng	Converts a pixel coordinate to a geographical coordinate in the map container
fromDivPixelToLatLng(pixel:Point)	LatLng	Converts a pixel coordinate to a geographical coordinate in the <div> that holds the draggable map
fromLatLngToContainerPixel (latLng:LatLng)	Point	Calculates the pixel coordinate in the map container from a geographical coordinate
fromLatLngToDivPixel (latLng:LatLng)	Point	Calculates the pixel coordinate in the DOM element that holds the draggable map from a geographical coordinate
getWorldWidth()	number	The width of the world in pixels in the current zoom level

Marker Class

This class is used to create markers. It extends MVCObject.

Constructor

Table A-16 gives the constructor of the Marker class.

Table A-16. The Constructor of the Marker Class

Constructor	Description
Marker(opts?:MarkerOptions)	Creates a new marker. Passing the MarkerOption is optional, but if you do pass it with its map and position properties defined, the marker is instantly added to the map.

Methods

Table A-17 gives the methods of the Marker class.

Table A-17. The Methods of the Marker Class

Method	Return Value	Description
getClickable()	boolean	Returns true if the marker is clickable and false if it's not.
getCursor()	string	Returns the current cursor that's being used when the user holds the mouse pointer over the marker.
getDraggable()	boolean	Returns true if the marker is draggable and false if it's not.
getFlat()	boolean	Returns true if the marker shadow is disabled (using the flat property) and false if it's not.
getIcon()	string|Marker Image	Returns the icon of the marker.
getMap()	Map|StreetView Panorama	Returns a reference to the map or panorama that the marker is attached to.
getPosition()	LatLng	Returns the position of the marker.
getShadow()	string|Marker Image	Returns the shadow of the marker.
getShape()	MarkerShape	Returns the shape of the marker.
getTitle()	string	Returns the title of the marker.
getVisible()	boolean	Returns true if the marker is visible and false if it's not.
getZIndex()	number	Returns the zIndex of the marker.
setClickable(flag:boolean)	None	Sets the marker to be clickable or not.
setCursor(cursor:string)	None	Sets the cursor that will be used when the user holds the mouse pointer over the marker.
setDraggable(flag:boolean)	None	Sets the marker to be draggable or not.
setFlat(flag:boolean)	None	Sets the marker to be able to have a shadow or not.

Method	Return Value	Description
setIcon(icon:string|MarkerImage)	None	Sets the icon of the marker.
setMap(map:Map|StreetViewPanorama)	None	Add the marker to the specified map or panorama. To remove the marker, set map to null.
setOptions(options:MarkerOptions)	None	Changes the features of the marker to the properties set in the passed MarkerOptions object.
setPosition(latlng:LatLng)	None	Sets the position of the marker.
setShadow(shadow:string|MarkerImage)	None	Sets the shadow of the marker icon.
setShape(shape:MarkerShape)	None	Sets the shape of the marker.
setTitle(title:string)	None	Sets the title of the marker. It will be displayed as a tooltip when the user holds the mouse cursor over it.
setVisible(visible:boolean)	None	Sets the visibility of the marker.
setZIndex(zIndex:number)	None	Sets the order of the marker in the stack of markers.

Events

Table A-18 gives the events of the Marker class.

Table A-18. The Events of the Marker Class

Event	Argument	Description
click	Event	Fires when the marker is clicked
clickable_changed	None	Fires when the clickable property is changed
cursor_changed	None	Fires when the cursor property is changed
dblclick	Event	Fires when the marker is double-clicked
drag	MouseEvent	Fires over and over again while the marker is being dragged
dragend	MouseEvent	Fires when the marker stops being dragged

Event	Argument	Description
draggable_changed	None	Fires when the draggable property is changed
dragstart	MouseEvent	Fires when the user starts dragging the marker
flat_changed	None	Fires when the flat property is changed
icon_changed	None	Fires when the icon property is changed
mousedown	Event	Fires when the user presses the left mouse button on the marker
mouseout	Event	Fires when the mouse cursor leaves the marker
mouseover	Event	Fires when the mouse cursors enters over the marker
mouseup	Event	Fires when the user releases the left mouse button on the marker
position_changed	None	Fires when the position property is changed
rightclick	Event	Fires when the user right-clicks the marker
shadow_changed	None	Fires when the shadow property is changed
shape_changed	None	Fires when the shape property is changed
title_changed	None	Fires when the title property is changed
visible_changed	None	Fires when the visible property is changed
zindex_changed	None	Fires when the zIndex property is changed

MarkerOptions Object

The following sections relate to the MarkerOptions object.

Properties

Table A-19 gives the properties of the MarkerOptions object.

Table A-19. The Properties of the MarkerOptions Object

Property	Type	Description
clickable	boolean	Enables and disables if the marker should respond to mouse and touch events. The default value is true.
cursor	string	The name of a standard cursor or the URL to an image that will be used as a cursor when the user holds the mouse over the marker.
draggable	boolean	Enable or disables the marker to be draggable. The default value is false.
flat	boolean	Enables or disable the marker shadow. If set to true, the shadow will be disabled, and vice versa. The default value is false.
icon	string|MarkerImage	The marker icon.
map	Map|StreetViewPanorama	The map on which the marker will appear.
position	LatLng	The position of the marker.
shadow	string|MarkerImage	The marker's shadow.
shape	MarkerShape	The clickable area of the marker.
title	string	The title of the marker. It will be displayed as a tooltip when the user holds the mouse over it.
visible	boolean	Shows or hides the marker. The default value is true.
zIndex	number	The order of the marker in the stack of markers.

MarkerImage Class

The following sections relate to the MarkerImage class.

Constructor

Table A-20 gives the constructor of the MarkerImage class.

Table A-20. The Constructor of the MarkerImage Class

Constructor	Description
MarkerImage(url:string, size?:Size, origin?:Point, anchor?:Point, scaledSize?:Size)	Creates an image that can be used either as the icon or as the shadow for a marker. url defines the image to use, size defines the size of the image, and origin is used to select which part of the image will be used if you are using sprites. anchor sets the point of the marker that will point at its position in the map. scaledSize is used to scale the image. Note that once the MarkerImage is created, it can't be changed.

MarkerShape Object

This object defines what part of the marker to use. It works like an HTML image map, which means that you can define the shape as a circle, a poly, or a rectangle.

Properties

Table A-21 gives the properties of the MarkerShape object.

Table A-21. The Properties of the MarkerShape Object

Property	Type	Description
type	string	What type of shape to use. The available shapes are circle, poly, and rectangle.
coord	Array.<number>	Depending of what type you've chosen, this property works a little bit different. It basically works the same way as the <area> element in HTML.
		If the type is set to circle, coord will consist of [x, y, r] where x and y represent the center of the circle and r represents its radius.
		If the type is set to poly, coord will consist of [x1,y1,x2,y2,x3,y3... and so on] where each coordinate pair represents a point in the polygon.
		For rectangle, coord will look like [x1, y1, x2, y2] where x1, y1 represents the upper-left corner of the rectangle and x2,y2 represents the lower-right corner.

Polyline Class

Polylines are a series of points connected with lines. They are, for example, very useful for marking roads. This class extends MVCObject.

Constructor

Table A-22 gives the constructor of the Polyline class.

Table A-22. The Constructor of the Polyline Class

Constructor	Description
Polyline(opts?:PolylineOptions)	Creates a polyline. The passed PolylineOptions object defines how the polyline will appear. If you provide the polyline with a PolylineOptions object with the property LatLng and map specified, it will instantly be added to the map.

Methods

Table A-23 gives the methods of the Polyline class.

Table A-23. The Methods of the Polyline Class

Method	Return Value	Description
getMap()	Map	Returns a reference to the map that the polyline is attached to.
getPath()	MVCArray.<LatLng>	Returns the first path.
setMap(map:Map)	None	Adds the polyline to a map. To remove the polyline, pass null to it.
setOptions(options:Polyline Options)	None	Sets the options of the polyline.
setPath(path:MVCArray.<LatLng>| Array.<LatLng>)	None	Sets the first path.

Events

Table A-24 gives the events of the Polyline class.

Table A-24. *The Events of the Polyline class*

Event	Argument	Description
click	MouseEvent	Fires when the polyline is being clicked
dblclick	MouseEvent	Fires when the polyline is being double-clicked
mousedown	MouseEvent	Fires when the user press down the left mouse key on the polyline
mousemove	MouseEvent	Fires when the DOM mouse move event is triggered on the polyline
mouseout	MouseEvent	Fires when the mouse leaves the area over the polyline
mouseover	MouseEvent	Fires when the mouse enters the area over the polyline
mouseup	MouseEvent	Fires when the user releases the left mouse key over the polyline
rightclick	MouseEvent	Fires when the user right-clicks the polyline

PolylineOptions Object

The following sections relate to the PolylineOptions object.

Properties

Table A-25 gives the properties of the PolylineOptions object.

Table A-25. *The Properties of the PolylineOptions Object*

Property	Type	Description
clickable	boolean	Enables or disables if the polyline will be clickable. The default value is true.
geodesic	boolean	Enables or disables geodesic rendering of the polyline.
map	Map	The map that the polyline will be added to.
path	MVCArray.<LatLng> | Array.<LatLng>	The coordinates that make up the points in the polyline. It can be either an MVCArray of LatLngs or a regular array of LatLngs. The benefit of using an MVCArray is that if you add or remove LatLngs in it, the polyline will immediately be updated with the changes.

Property	Type	Description
strokeColor	string	The color of the polyline. The value used is as string in hex format, so the color red will be #ff0000. The default value is #000000, which is the color black.
strokeOpacity	number	This property is a number that defines the opacity of the line. 1.0 means that it's 100 percent opaque, and 0 means that it's 0 percent opaque, in other words, completely transparent. Anything in between such as 0.5 will render a semi-transparent line. The default value is 1.0.
strokeWeight	number	This property is a number and defines the width of the line in pixels. To create a 5-pixel-wide line, pass it the value 5. The default value is 3.
zIndex	number	The order in which the polyline will appear in the stack of polylines.

Polygon Class

A polygon is very similar to a polyline. The difference is that it's always closed and has a filled region. This class extends MVCObject.

Constructor

Table A-26 gives the constructor of the Polygon class.

Table A-26. The Constructor of the Polygon Class

Constructor	Description
Polygon(opts?:PolygonOptions)	Creates a polygon. The passed PolygonOptions object defines how the polygon will appear. If you provide the polygon with a PolygonOptions object with the property LatLng and map specified, it will instantly be added to the map.

Methods

Table A-27 gives the methods of the Polygon class.

Table A-27. The Methods of the Polygon Class

Method	Return Value	Description
getMap()	Map	Returns a reference to the map the polygon is attached to.
getPath()	MVCArray.<LatLng>	Returns the first path.
getPaths()	MVCArray.<MVCArray.<LatLng>>	Returns all the paths for the polygon.
setMap(map:Map)	None	Adds the polygon to a map. To remove the polygon from a map, pass null as the value.
setOptions(options:PolygonOptions)	None	Sets the features of the polyline by passing a PolygonOptions object.
setPath(path:MVCArray.<LatLng>|Array.<LatLng>)	None	Sets the first path of the polygon.
setPaths(paths:MVCArray.<MVCArray.<LatLng>>|MVCArray.<LatLng>|Array.<Array.<LatLng>>|Array.<LatLng>)	None	Sets all the paths for the polygon.

Events

Table A-28 gives the events of the Polygon class.

Table A-28. The Events of the Polygon Class

Event	Argument	Description
click	MouseEvent	Fires when the polygon is being clicked
dblclick	MouseEvent	Fires when the polygon is being double-clicked
mousedown	MouseEvent	Fires when the user press down the left mouse key on the polygon
mousemove	MouseEvent	Fires when the DOM mouse move event is triggered on the polygon
mouseout	MouseEvent	Fires when the mouse leaves the area over the polygon
mouseover	MouseEvent	Fires when the mouse enters the area over the polygon

Event	Argument	Description
mouseup	MouseEvent	Fires when the user releases the left mouse key over the polygon
rightclick	MouseEvent	Fires when the user right-clicks the polygon

PolygonOptions Object

The following sections relate to the PolygonOptions object.

Properties

Table A-29 gives the properties of the PolygonOptions object.

Table A-29. The Properties of the PolygonOptions Object

Property	Type	Description
clickable	boolean	Enables or disables if the polygon will be clickable. The default value is true.
fillColor	string	The color of the "inside" of the polygon. The value used is as string in hex format, so the color red will be #ff0000. The default value is #000000, which is the color black.
fillOpacity	number	The opacity of the "inside" fill. This is a decimal number between 0 and 1. The value 0.5 will make the fill 50 percent opaque.
geodesic	boolean	Enables or disables geodesic rendering of the polygon.
map	Map	The map that the polygon will be added to.
paths	MVCArray .<MVCArray.<LatLng>>| MVCArray.<LatLng>| Array.<Array.<LatLng> Array.<LatLng>	The coordinates that make up the points in the polygon. It can be either an MVCArray of LatLngs or a regular array of LatLngs. The benefit of using an MVCArray is that if you add or remove LatLngs in it, the polygon will immediately be updated with the changes.
strokeColor	string	The color of the border of the polygon. The value used is as string in hex format, so the color red will be #ff0000. The default value is #000000, which is the color black.

Property	Type	Description
strokeOpacity	number	This property is a decimal number that defines the opacity of the border as a number between 0 and 1. The value 0.5 will make the border 50 percent opaque. The default value is 1.
strokeWeight	number	This property is a number and defines the width of the border in pixels. The default value is 3.
zIndex	number	The order in which the polygon will appear in the stack of polygons.

InfoWindow Class

This is a kind of overlay that looks like a speech balloon. It's perfect for displaying information about a location. It extends MVCObject.

Constructor

Table A-30 gives the constructor of the InfoWindow class.

Table A-30. The Constructor of the InfoWindow Class

Constructor	Description
InfoWindow(opts?:InfoWindowOptions)	Creates a new InfoWindow object.

Methods

Table A-31 gives the methods of the InfoWindow class.

Table A-31. The Methods of the InfoWindow Class

Method	Return Value	Description
close()	None	Closes the InfoWindow.
getContent()	string|Node	Returns the content of the InfoWindow.
getPosition()	LatLng	Returns the position of the InfoWindow.
getZIndex()	number	Returns the z-index of the InfoWindow.

Method	Return Value	Description
`open(map:Map|StreetViewPanorama, anchor?:MVCObject)`	None	Opens a `InfoWindow` on the passed map or panorama. If an `MVCObject` such as an marker is passed as an anchor, the tip of the `InfoWindow` will point at it.
`setContent(content:string|Node)`	None	Sets the content of the `InfoWindow`.
`setOptions(options:InfoWindow Options)`	None	Sets the options of the `InfoWindow`.
`setPosition(position:LatLng)`	None	Sets the position of the `InfoWindow`.
`setZIndex(zIndex:number)`	None	Sets the z-index of the `InfoWindow`.

Events

Table A-32 lists the events of the `InfoWindow` class.

Table A-32. The Events of the InfoWindow Class

Event	Argument	Description
`closeclick`	None	Fires when the close button in the `InfoWindow` is clicked.
`content_changed`	None	Fires when the content of the `InfoWindow` is changed.
`domready`	None	Fires when the `<div>` that contains the `InfoWindow` is added to the DOM.
`position_changed`	None	Fires when the position of the `InfoWindow` is changed.
`zindex_changed`	None	Fires when the z-index of the `InfoWindow` is changed.

InfoWindowOptions Object

The following sections relate to the `InfoWindowOptions` object.

Properties

Table A-33 gives the properties of the `InfoWindowOptions` object.

Table A-33. The Properties of the InfoWindowOptions Object

Property	Type	Description
content	string|Node	The content that will be displayed in the InfoWindow. It can be either plain HTML or a reference to a DOM node.
disableAutoPan	boolean	Disables the autopan behavior of the InfoWindow. Normally when it opens, the map will be panned to fit the InfoWindow. The default value is false.
maxWidth	number	The maximum width of the InfoWindow. It's considered only if defined before the InfoWindow is opened.
pixelOffset	Size	Defines the offset from the tip of the InfoWindow and the point it's pointing at.
position	LatLng	The position at which the tip of the InfoWindow should point.
zIndex	number	The order in the stack of InfoWindows where the InfoWindow will appear.

Geocoder Class

This is a service with which you can look up the geographic coordinates of an address known as *geocoding*. It can also return addresses from a geographical coordinate, a process known as reverse *geocoding*.

Constructor

Table A-34 gives the constructor of the Geocoder class.

Table A-34. The Constructor of the Geocoder Class

Constructor	Description
Geocoder()	Creates a Geocoder object that you can use to perform geocode requests

Methods

Table A-35 gives the methods of the Geocoder class.

Table A-35. The Methods of the Geocoder Class

Method	Return Value	Description
geocode(request:GeocoderRequest, callback:function(Array.<GeocoderResult>, GeocoderStatus)))	None	Performs a geocode request based on the information in the GeocoderRequest object being passed to it

GeocoderRequest Object

This object contains the information needed to perform a geocoder request. If you define the address, property positions will be returned, and if you define the location property, addresses will be returned.

Properties

Table A-36 gives the properties of the GeocoderRequest object.

Table A-36. The Properties of the GeocoderRequest Object

Property	Type	Description
address	string	The address to look up. Optional.
bounds	LatLngBounds	The LatLngBounds within the search shall be performed. Optional.
language	string	The preferred language that the result will be returned in.
location	LatLng	The LatLng to look up. Optional.
region	string	The country in which the search shall be performed. The value must be in country code format. Optional.

GeocoderStatus Class

This class contains the possible statuses that will be returned when performing a geocoder request.

Constants

Table A-37 gives the constants in the GeocoderStatus class.

Table A-37. Constants in the GeocoderStatus Class

Constant	Description
ERROR	The Geocoder object couldn't contact the Google servers.
INVALID_REQUEST	The GeocoderRequest was not valid.
OK	The request succeeded.
OVER_QUERY_LIMIT	The request limit has been reached.
REQUEST_DENIED	The web page is not allowed to use the Geocoder object.
UNKNOWN_ERROR	A server error occurred.
ZERO_RESULTS	No result could be found for the request.

GeocoderResult Object

When performing a successful geocoder request, a result in JSON format is returned. The result can contain several result objects.

Properties

Table A-38 gives the properties of the GeocoderResult object.

Table A-38. The Properties of the GeocoderResult Object

Property	Type	Description
address_components	Array.<GeocoderAddressComponent>	An array containing the different facts about the location.
geometry	GeocoderGeometry	An object with several properties. The most interesting one is location, which contains the position of the address as a LatLng object. It also has other properties such as viewport, bounds, and location_type.
types	Array.<string>	An array that contains what type of location the returned result is. It could, for example, be a country or a locality, which indicates that it's a city or town.

GeocoderAddressComponent Object

This object contains information about the address of the result returned from a geocoder request.

Table A-39 gives the properties of the GeocoderAddressComponent object.

Table A-39. The Properties of the GeocoderAddressComponent Object

Property	Type	Description
long_name	string	The full address.
short_name	string	The address in a shorter format.
types	Array.<string>	Contains what type of location the returned result is. It could, for example, be a country or a locality that indicates that it's a city or town.

GeocoderGeometry Object

This object contains information about the location of the result returned from a geocoder request.

Properties

Table A-40 gives the properties of the GeocoderGeometry object.

Table A-40. The Properties of the GeocoderGeometry Object

Property	Type	Description
bounds	LatLngBounds	The bounds of the result
location	LatLng	The position of the result
location_type	GeocoderLocationType	The type of location
viewport	LatLngBounds	A recommended bounds for the viewport for displaying the returned result

GeocoderLocationType Class

This class contains the different types of locations that can be returned from a geocode request.

Constants

Table A-41 gives the constants in the GeocoderLocationType class.

Table A-41. Constants in the GeocoderLocationType Class

Constant	Description
APPROXIMATE	An approximate location
GEOMETRIC_CENTER	A center of a result such as a line or a polygon
RANGE_INTERPOLATED	An approximated location between two precise points
ROOFTOP	A precise geocode

MapsEventListener Object

This class does not have any methods and has no constructor. Its instance is returned from addListener() and addDomListener() and is passed back to removeListener().

event Namespace

The following sections relate to the event namespace.

Static Methods

Table A-42 gives the static methods of the event namespace.

Table A-42. The Static Methods of the event Namespace

Static Method	Return Value	Description
addDomListener(instance:Object, eventName:string, handler:Function)	MapsEventListener	Provides a cross-browser event handler registration.
addDomListenerOnce(instance:Object, eventName:string, handler:Function)	MapsEventListener	Provides a cross-browser event handler registration that is automatically removed once it has been triggered.

Static Method	Return Value	Description
addListener(instance:Object, eventName:string, handler:Function)	MapsEventListener	Adds an event listener to a certain object and a certain event.
addListenerOnce(instance:Object, eventName:string, handler:Function)	MapsEventListener	Adds an event listener to a certain object and a certain event. Removes itself once it's been triggered.
clearInstanceListeners(instance:Object)	None	Removes all event listeners that are bound to an object.
clearListeners(instance:Object, eventName:string)	None	Removes all event listeners of a certain type that are bound to an object.
removeListener(listener:MapsEventListener)	None	Removes a specific event listener.
trigger(instance:Object, eventName:string, var_args:*)	None	Triggers an event on a particular object. All the arguments passed after the eventName are passed as arguments to the event listener.

MouseEvent Object

The MouseEvent object is returned from almost all mouse events on almost all the different objects. The Marker object is the exception. It returns a MouseEvent object only on some of its mouse events.

Properties

Table A-43 gives the properties of the MouseEvent object.

Table A-43. The Properties of the MouseEvent Object

Property	Type	Description
latLng	LatLng	The position of the mouse pointer at the time of the event

273

LatLng Class

This class represents a geographical location consisting of a latitude and a longitude.

Constructor

Table A-44 shows the constructor of the LatLng class.

Table A-44. The Constructor of the LatLng Class

Constructor	Description
LatLng(lat:number, lng:number, noWrap?:boolean)	Creates a LatLng object. The order of latitude and longitude is always latitude first and longitude second. If noWrap is set to true, it will take the passed coordinates as is; otherwise, it will force the latitude to lie between -90 and +90 degrees and longitude between -180 and +180 degrees.

Methods

Table A-45 gives the methods of the LatLng class.

Table A-45. The Methods of the LatLng Class

Method	Return Value	Description
equals(other:LatLng)	boolean	Compares a LatLng with another LatLng. If they are equal, true is returned.
lat()	number	Returns the latitude.
lng()	number	Returns the longitude.
toString()	string	Returns a string representation of the object.
toUrlValue(precision?:number)	string	Returns a string with the latitude and longitude rounded to six decimals.

LatLngBounds Class

This represents a rectangle in geographical coordinates.

Constructor

Table A-46 gives the constructor of the LatLngBounds class.

Table A-46. *The Constructor of the LatLngBounds Class*

Constructor	Description
LatLngBounds(sw?:LatLng, ne?:LatLng)	Creates a LatLngBounds object that is a rectangle with the inputted points as its southwest and northeast corners.

Methods

Table A-47 gives the methods of the LatLngBounds class.

Table A-47. *The Methods of the LatLngBounds Class*

Method	Return Value	Description
contains(latLng:LatLng)	boolean	Checks whether a LatLng is within the bounds. If it does, it returns true.
equals(other:LatLngBounds)	boolean	Compares the bounds with another bounds. Returns true if they are approximately equal.
extend(point:LatLng)	LatLngBounds	Extends the bounds to include the inputted LatLng.
getCenter()	LatLng	Returns the center of the bounds.
getNorthEast()	LatLng	Returns the northeast corner of the bounds.
getSouthWest()	LatLng	Returns the southwest corner of the bounds.
intersects(other:LatLngBounds)	boolean	Checks whether another bounds shares any points with this bounds.
isEmpty()	boolean	Returns true if the bounds is empty.
toSpan()	LatLng	Converts the bounds to a latitude/longitude span.

Method	Return Value	Description
toString()	string	Converts the bounds to a string.
toUrlValue(precision?:number)	string	Returns the bounds as a string in the format "lat_lo,lng_lo,lat_hi,lnghi" where "lo" is the southwest corner and "hi" is the northeast corner of the bounds.
union(other:LatLngBounds)	LatLngBounds	Extends the bounds with the passed bounds.

Point Class

This represents a point on a two-dimensional plane expressed in pixels.

Constructor

Table A-48 gives the constructor of the Point class.

Table A-48. The Constructor of the Point Class

Constructor	Description
Point(x:number, y:number)	Creates a new point from the given numbers. The numbers represent pixels.

Methods

Table A-49 gives the methods of the Point class.

Table A-49. The Methods of the Point Class

Method	Return Value	Description
equals(other:Point)	Boolean	Compares this point with another point. Returns true if they are the same.
toString()	string	Converts the point to a string.

Properties

Table A-50 gives the properties of the Point class.

Table A-50. The Properties of the Point Class

Property	Type	Description
x	number	The X coordinate
y	number	The Y coordinate

Size Class

This represents a two-dimensional size. Width is the distance on the x-axis, and height is the distance on the y-axis.

Table A-51 gives the constructor of the Size class.

Table A-51. The Constructor of the Size Class

Constructor	Description
Size(width:number, height:number, widthUnit?:string, heightUnit?:string)	Creates a new Size from the passed width, height, and units. The default unit is pixels.

Methods

Table A-52 gives the methods of the Size class.

Table A-52. The Methods of the Size Class

Method	Return Value	Description
equals(other:Size)	boolean	Compares this size with another size. Returns true if they are the same.
toString()	string	Converts the size to a string.

Properties

Table A-53 gives the properties of the Size class.

Table A-53. The Properties of the Size Class

Property	Type	Description
height	number	The height in pixels
width	number	The width in pixels

MVCObject Class

Table A-54 gives the constructor of the MVCObject class.

Table A-54. The Constructor of the MVCObject Class

Constructor	Description
MVCObject()	The base class implementing KVO

Methods

Table A-55 gives the methods of the MVCObject class.

Table A-55. The Methods of the MVCObject Class

Method	Return Value	Description
bindTo(key:string, target:MVCObject, targetKey?:string, noNotify?:boolean)	None	Binds a view to a model.
changed(key:string)	None	Generic handler for state changes. Override this in derived classes to handle arbitrary state changes.
get(key:string)	*	Gets a value.
notify(key:string)	None	Notify all observers of a change on this property. This notifies both objects that are bound to the object's property as well as the object that it is bound to.
set(key:string, value:*)	None	Sets a value.
setValues(values:Object|undefined)	None	Sets a collection of key-value pairs.
unbind(key:string)	None	Removes a binding. Unbinding will set the unbound property to the current value. The object will not be notified, because the value has not changed.
unbindAll()	None	Removes all bindings.

MVCArray Class

This is a mutable MVCArray. This class extends MVCObject. See Table A-56 for the constructor.

Table A-56. The Constructor of the MVCArray Class

Constructor	Description
MVCArray(array?:Array)	Creates a new MVC array

Methods

Table A-57 gives the methods of the MVCArray class.

Table A-57. The Methods of the MVCArray Class

Method	ReturnV	Description
forEach(callback:function(*, number))	None	Iterates over each element, calling the provided callback. The callback is called for each element, like so: callback(element, index).
getAt(i:number)	*	Gets an element at the specified index.
getLength()	number	Returns the number of elements in this array.
insertAt(i:number, elem:*)	None	Inserts an element at the specified index.
pop()	*	Removes the last element of the array and returns that element.
push(elem:*)	number	Adds one element to the end of the array and returns the new length of the array.
removeAt(i:number)	*	Removes an element from the specified index.
setAt(i:number, elem:*)	None	Sets an element at the specified index.

Index

■H